GCSE/KEY STAGE 4

REVISE GUIDES

INFORMATION SYSTEMS
AND INFORMATION TECHNOLOGY

Roger Crawford

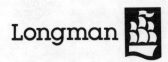

Longman

LONGMAN REVISE GUIDES

SERIES EDITORS:
Geoff Black and Stuart Wall

TITLES AVAILABLE:
Biology*
Business Studies*
Chemistry*
Economics*
English*
English Literature*
French
Geography
German
Information Systems and Information Technology*
Mathematics*
Mathematics: Higher Level*
Music
Physics*
Psychology
Religious Studies*
Science*
Sociology
Spanish
Technology*
World History

* new editions for Key Stage 4

Addison Wesley Longman Limited,
Edinburgh Gate, Harlow,
Essex CM20 2JE, England
and Associated Companies throughout the world.

© Longman Group Limited 1994

First Published 1994
Fourth impression 1996

ISBN 0 582 24494 3

British Library Cataloguing-in-Publication Data

A catalogue record for this book is
available from the British Library

Set by 19QQ in 10/12pt Century Old Style
Produced by Longman Singapore Publishers Pte Ltd
Printed in Singapore

CONTENTS

AUTHOR'S PREFACE

Throughout this book the emphasis is on understanding how Information Technology and Information Systems are used. The chapters are arranged in a fairly logical order but it is not necessary to study them in the sequence they appear. Each chapter is self-contained and can be studied independently of the other chapters. There is a glossary of jargon in Chapter 4 that should help explain unfamiliar technical words.

In writing this book I have valued the help and advice given to me both directly and indirectly. I especially thank Stuart Wall and Geoff Black for their editorial advice and assistance. I am grateful to colleagues at Rhodesway Upper School and at Queensbury School for their help and assistance while I was employed at each school. I am also grateful for the help and assistance given to me by the School of Education at the University of Huddersfield where I am now employed as a Senior Lecturer in Information Technology in Education. My wife, Jennie, has patiently tolerated the long hours I have spent at the wordprocessor. Without the support of colleagues, friends and family this book would not have been written.

Roger Crawford

ACKNOWLEDGEMENTS

The following commercial and industrial companies have kindly given their permission to use material they have provided for illustrations or refer to their products.

Apple Computers UK Ltd.
Amstrad Plc
Barclays Bank Plc
Computer Associates Plc
The Data Consultancy
IBM UK Ltd.
TSB Plc
Valiant Technology Ltd.

The following GCSE examination boards have given permission for questions from their sample papers to be used at the end of each chapter. The answers given are the author's, except for Midland Examination Group questions, where answers were provided. The questions may not indicate the format and content of future examination papers.

C & Gj10

MEG
NDTEF
NEAB
RSA
SEG
ULEAC
WJEC

CHAPTER 1

THE EXAMINATIONS AND ASSESSED COURSEWORK

AIMS

ASSESSMENT OBJECTIVES

THE 5 STRANDS OF IT

DIFFERENT WAYS OF STUDYING IT & IS

THE ASSESSMENT

THE SYLLABUSES:-
 C & G
 MEG
 NDTEF
 NEAB
 RSA
 SEG
 ULEAC
 WJEC

LEVEL DESCRIPTIONS FOR COURSEWORK

GETTING STARTED

You can use this chapter *selectively* by turning to *your own* exam board and syllabus rather than reading through all the syllabuses presented. There are several examination boards in England and Wales offering syllabuses for **National Curriculum Information Technology** (IT) and **GCSE Information Systems** (IS). These syllabuses are based on the part of the National Curriculum (NC) Technology orders that cover IT. **GCSE Technology** syllabuses also contain a substantial proportion of IT. There are also GCSE syllabuses in IT combined with another subject, for example, Art.

A syllabus states exactly what topics should be studied. Each syllabus is different but they are all very similar. They are based on the aims and assessment objectives for IT and IS described in the National Criteria for Technology.

Assessment is the process of finding out what a student can do and awarding a NC level or GCSE grade in recognition of the standard of performance attained. This is done using a combination of **written exams** and **coursework**. The level or grade awarded will be in the range from A* to G with A* as the highest level or grade awarded.

Every assessment scheme includes written exams and coursework. Written exams may be based on a case study or a theme; coursework consists of one or more **tasks.**

Level descriptions help teachers and examiners decide what GCSE grade or NC level should be awarded. You might find them useful in assessing your own progress.

ESSENTIAL PRINCIPLES

There are several examination boards in England and Wales for the General Certificate of Secondary Education (GCSE). These are City & Guilds (C & G) of London Institute, Midland Examining Group (MEG), the National Design & Technology Education Foundation (NDTEF), the Northern Examinations and Assessment Board (NEAB), the Royal Society of Arts (RSA), the Southern Examining Group (SEG), the University of London Examinations and Assessment Council (ULEAC) and the Welsh Joint Education Committee or Cyd-bwyllgor Addysg Cymru (WJEC).

These exam boards all publish syllabuses in **Information Technology** (IT) and **Information Systems** (IS). These syllabuses are based on the parts of the National Curriculum (NC) Technology orders that cover Information Technology. The **Technology GCSE** syllabus also contains a substantial proportion of Information Technology. There are also GCSE syllabuses in IT combined with another subject, for example, Art.

> **1** > AIMS

A course in **Information Technology** (IT) or **Information Systems** (IS) should be a worthwhile experience in itself. It should encourage you to develop your interest in Information Technology and help you to become more confident and expert in using IT.

Your study of IT or IS should put the use of Information Technology in context. You will be expected to gather, store, process and present information in a range of contexts. The contexts used will include the home, school, recreation, the community, business and industry. You will view IT from the standpoints of the designer, maker, manager and client.

You should gain some idea of how Information Technology works and understand it's capabilities and limitations. You will use IT as a tool for making and designing and as an element of made artefacts, structures and systems. You will have the opportunity to design, implement and document information systems and develop an understanding of their wider applications and effects. You will evaluate the suitability of software and hardware as elements of a particular information system.

> **2** > ASSESSMENT OBJECTIVES

> 66 HMSO's address is P.O. Box 276, London SW8 5DT 99

The **assessment objectives** of syllabuses in IT or IS must cover the relevant Attainment Targets, Statements of Attainment and Programmes of Study of NC Technology. These are described in detail in the NC Technology orders, available from HMSO.

A syllabus in IT must cover the NC Technology Attainment Target called 'IT Capability'. You will be expected to demonstrate your ability to work with IT to:

- ■ Select, communicate and handle information.
- ■ Analyse situations and design and develop models.
- ■ Measure and control physical variables and movement.

You should make reasoned judgements about the effects of IT and the benefits and drawbacks of particular applications.

A syllabus in IS will make demands on your skills and knowledge beyond those required for IT.

You should demonstrate your knowledge and understanding of information systems and show your ability to:

- ■ Describe how information systems are used.
- ■ Describe how to design, implement, test and write the documentation for an information system.
- ■ Evaluate the suitability of the hardware and software for use in a particular information system.
- ■ Describe the methods used to gather, store, process and present information.

You should identify a range of needs and opportunities and analyse, design and evaluate an appropriate information system. You should be able to:

- ■ Decide if an information system should be used.
- ■ Decide what inputs are needed to give the desired outcomes.

■ Design the inputs, outputs, information storage requirements and feedback for an information system.

■ Design a suitable user interface for interaction with the information system.

You should implement a working information system. You should be able to:

■ Break down what has to be done into a series of smaller tasks.

■ Choose the appropriate hardware and software to use.

■ Test and evaluate the information system you have built.

■ Refine your information system in response to your testing and evaluation of it.

3 > THE FIVE STRANDS OF IT

Your work should demonstrate that you can use a broad range of IT. You will be expected to show competency within the five *strands* of IT. These are:

■ Communicating Information

■ Handling Information

■ Modelling

■ Measurement and Control

■ Applications and Effects

These strands are described in detail in the Non-Statutory Guidance for IT which is available from HMSO.

Software needed to deliver IT

This is some of the **software** you will need to be able to understand and use:

■ wordprocessor	■ spreadsheet
■ graphics	■ programming languages
■ desk top publishing	■ simple modelling or simulation software
■ database	■ data logging and control software

At least one piece of software must be programmable to some extent, for example, using a macro facility.

The software should allow the import and export of files to/from other software. Alternatively, this could be achieved using an integrated software package.

Information Systems syllabuses will require you to use the software to design and build an information system.

4 > THE DIFFERENT WAYS OF STUDYING INFORMATION TECHNOLOGY AND INFORMATION SYSTEMS

Each examination group has a *range of syllabuses* that cover NC Technology. Information Technology is a part of NC Technology. Technology can be studied as a GCSE in itself or it can be split into two parts:

■ Design and Technology (ATs 1 to 4)

■ Information Technology (AT 5)

Information Technology can be studied on courses leading to the award of a NC level in IT only. There is no GCSE syllabus in IT only. IT can also be studied as part of a GCSE course in **Information Systems** or combined with another subject, for example, Art. Technology, including Information Technology, in the National Curriculum, is described in the NC Technology orders. The 'National Criteria for GCSE Technology' contains information about all of GCSE Technology, NC Information Technology and GCSE Information Systems. These publications are available from HMSO.

These are the different ways in which IT and IS can be studied and assessed:

1. National Curriculum Information Technology (NC IT)

A) You will do a number of cross-curricula activities in IT leading to a certificate in IT. These activities take place in various NC subjects. There is no allocated teaching time for IT. The certificate shows the NC level in IT you have been awarded.

B) You will do a taught course in IT leading to a certificate in IT. This takes 5% of teaching time in school. The certificate shows the NC level in IT you have been awarded.

2. GCSE Information Systems

A) GCSE Information Systems (GCSE IS)

You will do a taught course in Information Systems combined with either 1.A. or 1.B. above. This takes either 5% or 10% of teaching time in school, respectively. The GCSE certificate may show the NC level in IT you have been awarded and/or the GCSE grade. The NC IT level and the GCSE grade are not necessarily the same.

B) GCSE Information Systems: Business (GCSE IS:B)

You will do a taught course in Information Systems: Business combined with either 1.A. or 1.B. above. This takes either 5% or 10% of teaching time in school, respectively. The GCSE certificate may show the NC level in IT you have been awarded and/or the GCSE grade. The NC IT level and the GCSE grade are not necessarily the same.

3. GCSE Technology (GCSE Tech.)

You will do a taught course in GCSE Technology which includes IT. This takes 10% of teaching time in school. The GCSE certificate may show the NC level in Technology you have been awarded and/or the GCSE grade. The NC level and the GCSE grade are not necessarily the same. IT is 25% of the final award for GCSE Technology.

4. GCSE Information Technology and a combined subject (GCSE IT+)

Typical GCSE IT+ courses are:

IT and Art
IT and Business
IT and Catering
IT and Fashion
IT and Music

You will do a taught course in the combined subject and either 1.A. or 1.B. above. This takes either 5% or 10% of teaching time in school, respectively. The GCSE certificate may show the NC level in IT you have been awarded and/or the GCSE grade. The NC IT level and the GCSE grade are not necessarily the same.

5 > THE ASSESSMENT

The **assessment** is based on coursework and written papers. The emphasis of assessment is always on what you can do. You will be given marks for what you *can* do rather than having marks deducted for what you cannot do.

Coursework consists of one or more IT or IS tasks. A task may be focused on the development and demonstration of a narrow range of IT skills or it may involve analysing, designing and making a working information system to solve a practical problem.

Written exams are externally marked, that is, they are not marked by teachers who work at the school where the exams are done. Coursework is not externally marked. It is marked by the teachers who work at the school where it is done.

Resource Tasks and Capability Tasks in coursework

Some syllabuses refer to Resource Tasks and Capability Tasks.

A **Resource Task** has a sharp focus on learning and applying a narrow range of knowledge, understanding, techniques and skills. A Resource Task may also be be called a Coursework Task or an IT Task.

A **Capability Task** involves the whole process of Technology, for example, it could include designing, making and evaluating an information system. A Capability Task may also be called a Systems Task.

The use of different terminology may be confusing, however, the underlying definitions are the same.

Spelling, Punctuation and Grammar

You should be aware that 5% of the marks in all the written papers of a scheme of assessment are for **Spelling**, **Punctuation** and **Grammar** (SPG).

The performance criteria for SPG are:

Threshold	You are reasonably accurate and make use of a limited range of specialist terms.
Intermediate	You are usually accurate and make use of a good range of specialist terms.
High	You are almost always accurate and use a range of grammatical constructions. You use a wide range of specialist terms adeptly and with precision.

More information about the assessment of spelling, punctuation and grammar can be found in the 'Mandatory code of practice for the GCSE' published by SCAA and available from HMSO.

THE SYLLABUSES

CITY AND GUILDS OF LONDON INSTITUTE – C & G

1. NC INFORMATION TECHNOLOGY

Award:
You are awarded one of levels 4–10 for NC IT.

Coverage of syllabus:
National Curriculum Technology, IT Capability.

Learning context:
The five strands of IT.

Tiers of entry:
You are entered for one of 3 tiers.
Everyone may do the same coursework but the written paper taken is determined by your tier of entry.

Tier	NC Level available
P (Foundation)	4–6
Q (Intermediate)	6–8
R (Higher)	8–10

Assessment
You will do :
    Coursework
    Written paper

Coursework (60%)
The coursework consists of three or more pieces of work, in total covering all the strands of IT. The subject matter may be taken from any curriculum area.

Written paper (40%)
The written paper you will take is determined by your tier of entry. There is a different written paper for each tier. Each paper is 90 mins long.

2.A. GCSE INFORMATION SYSTEMS

Award:
You are awarded one of levels 4–10 for NC IT and/or one of levels 4–10 on GCSE Information Systems.

Coverage of syllabus:
National Curriculum Technology, IT Capability and additional material relating to Information Systems.

Learning context:
The five strands of IT and three additional IS strands.
The IS strands are:
    Business Applications and Systems Analysis
    Design and Development
    Hardware and Software Subsystems

Tiers of entry:
You are entered for one of 3 tiers.
Everyone may do the same coursework but the written papers taken are determined by your tier of entry.

Tier	NC Level available	GCSE IS level available
P(Foundation)	4–6	4–6
Q(Intermediate)	6–8	6–8
R(Higher)	8–10	8–10

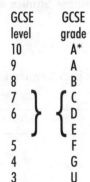
❝ Although the syllabuses published by the GCSE boards refer to the *levels* to be awarded, these have since been changed to *grades*. You can convert levels to grades using the following table:

GCSE level	GCSE grade
10	A*
9	A
8	B
7	C
6	D
	E
5	F
4	G
3	U

❞

Assessment
You will do:

Coursework	– as for IT
	– an extended practical assignment
	– a case study
Written papers	– paper A
	– paper B

Coursework (60%)

The course work consists of three or more pieces of work covering all the strands of IT. You will also do an extended practical assignment and a case study. In the extended practical assignment you will develop an information system; in the case study you will investigate an existing information system.

Written papers (40%)

The written papers taken are determined by your tier of entry. In each tier you are expected to take two papers called paper A and paper B. These papers are different for each tier.

Paper A – 20% – 1.5 hours
Paper A is the same as the written paper for IT.

Paper B – 20% – 1.5 hours
Paper B will assess the additional material relating to Information Systems.

There are *two* syllabuses in each of IT, IS and Technology. These are called Syllabus A and Syllabus B. We first look at Syllabus A for IT, IS and Technology; we then look at Syllabus B for each of these.

1. NC INFORMATION TECHNOLOGY – SYLLABUS A

Award:
You are awarded one of levels 4–10 for NC IT.

Coverage of syllabus:
National Curriculum Technology, IT Capability.

Learning context:
The five strands of IT.
Parts of Syllabus A could be taught in a Business context at the same time as parts of the MEG Business Studies syllabus. However, this is not in itself a Business Studies syllabus.

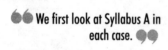
We first look at Syllabus A in each case.

Tiers of entry:
You are entered for one of 3 tiers.
Everyone may do the same coursework but the written paper taken is determined by your tier of entry.

Tier	NC Level available
Basic	4–6
Standard	5–8
Higher	7–10

Assessment
You will do :
Coursework
Written paper

Coursework (60%)

The coursework may consist of up to three pieces of work, in total covering all the strands of IT except Applications and Effects. The subject matter may be taken from any curriculum area.

Written paper (40%)

The written paper you will take is determined by your tier of entry. All the questions targeted at a particular level are grouped in a section within the paper.

Tier	Length	Paper number
Basic	40 mins	1
Standard	60 mins	2
Higher	80 mins	3

In each paper, 20% is for Applications and Effects and 20% is for the remaining strands of IT.

2.A. GCSE INFORMATION SYSTEMS – SYLLABUS A

Award:

You are awarded one of levels 4–10 for NC IT and/or one of levels 4–10 on GCSE Information Systems.

Coverage of syllabus:

National Curriculum Technology, IT Capability and additional material relating to Information Systems.

Learning context:

The five strands of IT. Parts of Syllabus A could be taught in a Business context at the same time as parts of the MEG Business Studies syllabus. However, this is not in itself a Business Studies syllabus.

Tiers of entry:

You are entered for one of 3 tiers.

Everyone may do the same coursework but the written papers taken are determined by your tier of entry.

Tier	GCSE IS level available
Basic	4–6
Standard	5–8
Higher	7–10

Assessment

You will do:

    Coursework
    Written paper

Coursework (40%)

The coursework may consist of up to three pieces of work, in total covering all the strands of IT except Applications and Effects. The subject matter may be taken from any curriculum area

Written paper (60%)

The written paper you will take is determined by your tier of entry. These papers are different for each tier.

Tier	Length	Paper number
Basic	1.5 hours	1
Standard	2 hours	2
Higher	2.5 hours	3

Each paper has two parts:

Part A

        This part assesses IT Capability.

Part B

This part will assess IT Capability and the additional material relating to Information Systems.

3. GCSE TECHNOLOGY – SYLLABUS A

Award:
You are awarded one of levels 4–10 for NC IT and/or one of levels 4–10 on GCSE Technology.

Coverage of syllabus:
National Curriculum Technology, all Attainment Targets including IT Capability.

Learning context:
Technology as described in the NC orders.

Tiers of entry:
You are entered for one of 3 tiers.
Everyone may do the same coursework but the written papers taken are determined by your tier of entry.

Tier	GCSE level available
Basic	4–6
Standard	5–8
Higher	7–10

Assessment
You will do:

    Coursework   – project 1
                  – project 2

    Written paper

IT is 25% of the total assessment: there is 15% IT in the coursework and 10% IT in the written paper.

Coursework (60%)
Project 1 (30%)
You will cover all the aspects of Technology in an integrated project. You will cover all the strands of IT except Applications and Effects. The subject matter may be taken from any curriculum area.

Project 2 (30%)
You will cover all the aspects of Technology in an integrated project. You will focus on one of:

    Modelling
    Measurement and Control
    Communicating Information and Handling Information.

The subject matter may be taken from any curriculum area.

Written paper (40%)
The written papers taken are determined by your tier of entry. These papers are different for each tier.

Tier	Length	Paper number
Basic	1.5 hours	1
Standard	2 hours	2
Higher	2.5 hours	3

Each paper consists of two sections:

Section A   20%   core content and IT.

Section B   20%   additional material relating to the optional content, eg. food.

We now look at Syllabus B in each case

1. NC INFORMATION TECHNOLOGY – SYLLABUS B

This syllabus is one of a suite of syllabuses under the general heading 'Technology 21'. These syllabuses are 'looking forward to the 21st Century'.

Award:
You are awarded one of levels 4–10 for NC IT.
Coverage of syllabus: National Curriculum Technology, IT Capability.

Learning context:
The five strands of IT.

Tiers of entry:
You are entered for one of 3 tiers.
The coursework and the written paper taken are determined by your tier of entry.

Tier	NC Level available
Basic	4–7
Standard	6–9
Higher	7–10

Assessment
You will do :
    Coursework
    Written paper

Coursework (60%)
The coursework you will do is determined by your tier of entry. The coursework is different for each tier.
You will do at least three Resource Tasks or one Capability Task, in total covering all the strands of IT except Applications and Effects. The coursework will be set by MEG or approved centres.
The subject matter may be chosen from five contexts with five 'interest' settings.

Written paper (40%)
The written paper you will take is determined by your tier of entry. This paper will be the same as Section A of the written paper for GCSE IS Syllabus B.

Tier	Length
Basic	75 mins
Standard	75 mins
Higher	75 mins

2.A.　GCSE INFORMATION SYSTEMS – SYLLABUS B

This syllabus is one of a suite of syllabuses under the general heading 'Technology 21'. These syllabuses are 'looking forward to the 21st Century'.

Award:
You are awarded any of levels 4–10 for NC IT and/or one of levels 4–10 on GCSE Information Systems.

Coverage of syllabus:
National Curriculum Technology, IT Capability and additional material relating to Information Systems.

Learning context:
The five strands of IT.

Tiers of entry:
You are entered for one of 3 tiers.
The coursework and the written paper taken are determined by your tier of entry.

Tier	GCSE IS level available
Basic	4–7
Standard	6–9
Higher	7–10

Assessment

You will do:

Coursework	– Capability Task
	– Resource Tasks
Written paper	

Coursework (60%)

The coursework you will do is determined by your tier of entry. The coursework is different for each tier.

Capability Task (40%)

You will do one Capability task covering all the strands of IT except Applications and Effects.

The coursework will be set by MEG or approved centres.

The subject matter may be chosen from five contexts with five 'interest' settings.

Resource Task (20%)

You will do one or more Resource Tasks, in total covering all the strands of IT except Applications and Effects.

The coursework will be set by MEG or approved centres.

The subject matter may be chosen from five contexts with five 'interest' settings.

Written papers (40%)

The written paper you will take is determined by your tier of entry. These papers are different for each tier.

Tier	Length
Basic	2.5 hours
Standard	2.5 hours
Higher	2.5 hours

Each paper has two sections:

Section A – 20%

This section assesses IT Capability. It is the same as the paper for NC IT Syllabus B

Section B – 20%

This section will assess, in the main, the additional material relating to Information Systems.

3. GCSE TECHNOLOGY – SYLLABUS B

This syllabus is one of a suite of syllabuses under the general heading 'Technology 21'. These syllabuses are 'looking forward to the 21st Century'.

Award:

You are awarded one of levels 4–10 for NC IT and/or one of levels 4–10 on GCSE Technology.

Coverage of syllabus:

National Curriculum Technology, all Attainment Targets including IT Capability.

Learning context:

Technology as described in the NC orders.

Tiers of entry:

You are entered for one of 3 tiers.

The coursework and the written papers taken are determined by your tier of entry.

Tier	GCSE level available
Basic	4–7
Standard	6–9
Higher	7–10

Assessment

You will do:

> Coursework   Capability Task
>
>   Resource Tasks
>
> Written paper

Coursework (60%)

The coursework you will do is determined by your tier of entry. The coursework is different for each tier.

Capability Task (40%)

You will do one Capability Task. You must cover the IT strand Measurement and Control.

The coursework will be set by MEG or approved centres.

The subject matter may be chosen from five contexts with five 'interest' settings.

Resource Task (20%)

You will do one or more Resource Tasks. These will include the use of IT.

The coursework will be set by MEG or approved centres.

The subject matter may be chosen from five contexts with five 'interest' settings.

Written papers (40%)

The written papers taken are determined by your tier of entry. These papers are different for each tier.

Tier	Length (each paper)
Basic	2.5 hours
Standard	2.5 hours
Higher	2.5 hours

Each paper consists of two sections:

> Section A   20%   core content and IT.
>
> Section B   20%   additional material relating to the optional content, eg. food, and including IT.

8 > **NATIONAL DESIGN AND TECHNOLOGY EDUCATION FOUNDATION (NDTEF)**

1. NC INFORMATION TECHNOLOGY

Award:

You are awarded one of levels 1–10 for NC IT.

Coverage of syllabus:

National Curriculum Technology, IT Capability.

Learning context:

The five strands of IT.

Tiers of entry:

You are entered for one of 3 tiers.

Everyone may do the same coursework but the written paper taken is determined by your tier of entry.

	NC Level available
(Foundation)	1–4
(Intermediate)	3–6
	5–8
(Higher)	7–10

Assessment

You will do :

    Coursework

    Written paper

Coursework (60%)

You will submit between three and six pieces of work, showing how you have applied IT in a variety of cross-curricula contexts. You should cover all the strands of IT. You are encouraged to do coursework that can be assessed for IT and submitted for assessment in other GCSE subjects, for example, English.

Written paper (40%)

The written paper taken is determined by your tier of entry. There is a different written paper for each tier of entry each of 1 hour.

2.A. GCSE INFORMATION SYSTEMS

Award:

You are awarded one of levels 1–10 for NC IT and/or one of levels 4–10 on GCSE Information Systems.

Coverage of syllabus:

National Curriculum Technology, IT Capability and additional material relating to Information Systems.

Learning context:

The five strands of IT and an additional strand, 'Designing, Implementing and Refining a System'.

Tiers of entry:

You are entered for one of 3 tiers.

Everyone may do the same coursework but the written papers taken are determined by your tier of entry.

	NC Level available	GCSE level available
(Foundation)	1–4	
	3–6	3–6
(Intermediate)	5–8	5–8
(Higher)	7–10	7–10

Assessment

You will do:

    Coursework

    Written papers   paper 1

                    paper 2

Coursework (60%)

You will submit between three and six pieces of work, showing how you have applied IT in a variety of cross-curricula contexts. You should cover all the strands of IT and the additional IS strand. You are encouraged to do coursework that can be assessed for IT/IS and submitted for assessment in other GCSE subjects, for example, English.

Written papers (40%)

The written papers taken are determined by your tier of entry. In each tier you are expected to take two papers called paper 1 and paper 2. These papers are different for each tier.

Paper 1 – 20% – 1 hour – NC IT

Paper 1 is the same as the written paper for IT.

Paper 2 – 20% – 1 hour – IS

Paper 2 will assess, in the main, the additional material relating to Information Systems. It refers to a research topic given out in advance. You have to identify, design and develop an information system.

2.B. GCSE INFORMATION SYSTEMS: BUSINESS

Award:
You are awarded one of levels 1–10 for NC IT and/or one of levels 4–10 on GCSE Information Systems.

Coverage of syllabus:
National Curriculum Technology, IT Capability and additional material relating to Information Systems: Business.

Learning context:
The five strands of IT and an additional strand, 'Designing, Implementing and Refining a System' set in the context of business.

Tiers of entry:
You are entered for one of 3 tiers.
Everyone may do the same coursework but the written papers taken are determined by your tier of entry.

	NC Level available	GCSE level available
	1–4	
(Foundation)	3–6	3–6
(Intermediate)	5–8	5–8
(Higher)	7–10	7–10

Assessment
You will do:

    Coursework

    Written papers   paper 1
                                paper 2

Coursework (60%)
You will submit four or more pieces of work, showing how you have applied IT in a variety of business contexts. You should cover all the strands of IT and the additional IS strand.

Written papers (40%)
The written papers taken are determined by your tier of entry. In each tier you are expected to take two papers called paper 1 and paper 2. These papers are different for each tier.

Paper 1 – 20% – 1 hour – NC IT

Paper 1 is the same as the written paper for IT.

Paper 2 – 20% – 1 hour – IS

Paper 2 will assess, in the main, the additional material relating to Information Systems: Business. It refers to a research topic given out in advance. You have to identify, design and develop an information system.

3. GCSE TECHNOLOGY

Award:
You are awarded one of levels 1–10 on NC Technology and/or one of levels 4–10 on GCSE Technology.

Coverage of syllabus:
National Curriculum Technology, all Attainment Targets including IT Capability.

Learning context:
Technology as described in the NC orders. You study an extension area which is one of food, textiles or graphics.

Tiers of entry:
You are entered for one of 3 tiers.
Everyone may do the same coursework but the written papers taken are determined by your tier of entry.

	NC Level available	GCSE level available
(Foundation)	1–4 3–6	3–6
(Intermediate)	5–8	5–8
(Higher)	7–10	7–10

Assessment
You will do:

Coursework 60%
Written papers 40% paper 1
paper 2

IT is 25% of the total assessment.

Coursework (60%)
One of the two extended tasks must use computer control, robotics or a related system.

Extended task 1
You will submit a portfolio of your work. The portfolio may consist of several pieces of work. You should demonstrate your capabilities in NC Technology across ATs 1 to 5, using IT wherever possible. You should use wood, metal and plastics.

Extended task 2
You will submit a portfolio of your work. The portfolio may consist of several pieces of work. You should demonstrate your capabilities in NC Technology across ATs 1 to 5, using IT wherever possible. You should use food, textiles and graphics.

Written papers (40%)
The written papers taken are determined by your tier of entry. In each tier you are expected to take two papers called paper 1 and paper 2. These papers are different for each tier. Each paper is 1.5 hours long.
Paper 1 – includes IT control systems and construction materials.
Paper 2 – includes questions on the chosen extension area.

4. GCSE INFORMATION TECHNOLOGY AND A COMBINED SUBJECT

You can take these GCSE IT+ combinations:

IT and Art
IT and Business
IT and Music

The IT is covered as for NC IT.

> 9
> **NORTHERN EXAMINATIONS AND ASSESSMENT BOARD – (NEAB) AND THE WELSH JOINT EDUCATION COMMITTEE – (WJEC)**

1. NC INFORMATION TECHNOLOGY

Award:
You are awarded one of levels 4–10 for NC IT.

Coverage of syllabus:
National Curriculum Technology, IT Capability.

Learning context:
The five strands of IT.

Tiers of entry:
You are entered for one of 3 tiers.
Everyone may do the same coursework but the written paper taken is determined by your tier of entry.

Tier	NC Level available
P (Foundation)	4–6
Q (Intermediate)	5–8
R (Higher)	7–10

Assessment
You will do:
    Coursework
    Written paper

Coursework (60%)
You submit a portfolio of your work. The portfolio may consist of several pieces of work, in total covering all the strands of IT except Applications and Effects. The subject matter may be taken from any curriculum area.

Written paper (40%)
The written paper taken is determined by your tier of entry.

Tier	Length	Coverage
P (Foundation)	1 hour	All strands at levels 4 to 6
Q (Intermediate)	1.5 hours	All strands at levels 5 to 8 except Communicating Information at level 8
R (Higher)	2 hours	As for level Q plus Applications and Effects at levels 9 and 10 and some questions from the other strands at levels 9 and 10.

The papers are the same as Paper 1 for the IS papers.

2.A. GCSE INFORMATION SYSTEMS

Award:
You are awarded one of levels 4–10 for NC IT and/or one of levels 4–10 on GCSE Information Systems.

Coverage of syllabus:
National Curriculum Technology, IT Capability and additional material relating to Information Systems.

Learning context:
The five strands of IT.

Tiers of entry:
You are entered for one of 3 tiers.
Everyone may do the same coursework but the written papers taken are determined by your tier of entry.

Tier	NC Level available	GCSE IS level available
P (Foundation)	4–6	4–6
Q (Intermediate)	5–8	5–8
R (Higher)	7–10	7–10

Assessment
You will do:

Coursework	portfolio
	project
Written papers	paper 1
	paper 2

Coursework (60%)
Portfolio – 30%
You will submit a portfolio of your work. The portfolio may consist of several pieces of work, in total covering all the strands of IT except Applications and Effects. The subject matter may be taken from any curriculum area.

Project – 30%
You will write a report on the solution to a problem. The solution must consist of an information system. The subject matter may be taken from any curriculum area.

Written papers (40%)
The written papers taken are determined by your tier of entry. In each tier you are expected to take two papers called paper 1 and paper 2. These papers are different for each tier.

Tier	Length (each paper)	Coverage
P (Foundation)	1 hour	All strands at levels 4 to 6
Q (Intermediate)	1.5 hours	All strands at levels 5 to 8 except Communicating Information at level 8
R (Higher)	2 hours	As for level Q plus Applications and Effects at levels 9 and 10 and some questions from the other strands at levels 9 and 10.

Paper 1 – 20%

Paper 1 is the same as the written paper for IT.

Paper 2 – 20%

Paper 2 will assess, in the main, the additional material relating to Information Systems.

3. GCSE TECHNOLOGY

Award:
You are awarded one of levels 4–10 on NC Technology and/or one of levels 4–10 on GCSE Technology.

Coverage of syllabus:
National Curriculum Technology, all Attainment Targets including IT Capability.

Learning context:
Technology as described in the NC orders.

Tiers of entry:
You are entered for one of 3 tiers.
Everyone may do the same coursework but the written papers taken are determined by your tier of entry.

Tier	NC Level available	GCSE level available
P (Foundation)	4–6	4–6
Q (Intermediate)	5–8	5–8
R (Higher)	7–10	7–10

Assessment
You will do:

Coursework	60%	portfolio	20%	(5% IT)
		project	40%	(10% IT)
Written papers	40%	paper 1	–	(no IT)
		paper 2	–	(10% IT)

IT is 25% of the total assessment.

Coursework (60%)

Portfolio – 20%

You will submit a portfolio of your work. The portfolio may consist of several pieces of work.

The IT strands that must be covered are:

> Handling Information
> Measurement and Control
> Modelling

The subject matter may be taken from any curriculum area.

Project – 40%

This is an extended Design and Technology task including the use of control technology, robotics and IT. It should involve the application of IT to Design and Technology activities. The IT strand covered is Communicating Information.

The subject matter may be taken from any curriculum area.

Written papers – 40%

The written papers taken are determined by your tier of entry. In each tier you are expected to take two papers called paper 1 and paper 2. These papers are different for each tier.

Tier	Length (each paper)
P (Foundation)	1.5 hours
Q (Intermediate)	2 hours
R (Higher)	2 hours

Paper 1

> Section A   Design concepts and skills
> Section B   Materials, tools, processes and skills related to construction materials

Paper 2

> Control systems, IT and one other construction material

4. GCSE INFORMATION TECHNOLOGY AND A COMBINED SUBJECT

You can take these GCSE IT+ combinations:

> IT and Art
> IT and Business Studies
> IT and Catering
> IT and Fashion
> IT and Music

The IT is covered as for NC IT.

1. NC INFORMATION TECHNOLOGY

Award:

You are awarded one of levels 4–10 for NC IT.

Coverage of syllabus:

National Curriculum Technology, IT Capability.

Learning context:

The five strands of IT.

Tiers of entry:

You are entered for one of 3 tiers.

Everyone may do the same coursework but the written paper taken is determined by your tier of entry.

Tier	NC Level available
Foundation	4–6
Intermediate	6–8
Higher	8–10

Assessment
You will do:

Coursework   Practical Tasks
               System Task
  Written paper

Coursework (60%)
Practical Tasks
You will submit up to 4 IT tasks. In total the tasks should cover all the IT strands except Applications and Effects.
The subject matter may be taken from any curriculum area.
The tasks will be set by your school.

System Task
The type of System Task you will do depends on your tier of entry. You do not need to do a System Task if you are aiming for a level 4; if you are aiming for levels 5 to 7, you will evaluate the use of IT in a Practical Task; if you are aiming for levels 8 to 10, you will develop a system for use by others. Your System Task could be an extension of one of your Practical Tasks or it could be a completely separate task.

Written paper (40%)
The written paper taken is determined by your tier of entry. These papers are different for each tier.

Tier	Length
Foundation	45 mins
Intermediate	60 mins
Higher	90 mins

2.A. GCSE INFORMATION SYSTEMS

Award:
You are awarded one of levels 4–10 for NC IT and/or one of levels 4–10 on GCSE Information Systems.

Coverage of syllabus:
National Curriculum Technology, IT Capability and additional material relating to Information Systems.

Learning context:
The five strands of IT.

Tiers of entry:
You are entered for one of 3 tiers.
Everyone may do the same coursework but the written papers taken are determined by your tier of entry.

Tier	NC Level available	GCSE IS level available
Foundation	4-6	4-6
Intermediate	6–8	6–8
Higher	8–10	8–10

Assessment

You will do:

Coursework   Practical Tasks
                              System Task
                              Case Studies

    Written paper

Coursework (60%)

Practical Tasks

You will submit up to 4 IT tasks. In total the tasks should cover all the IT strands except Applications and Effects.

The subject matter may be taken from any curriculum area.

The tasks will be set by your school.

System Task

The type of System Task you will do depends on your tier of entry. You do not need to do a System Task if you are aiming for a level 4; if you are aiming for levels 5 to 7, you will evaluate the use of IT in a Practical Task; if you are aiming for levels 8 to 10, you will develop a system for use by others. Your System Task could be an extension of one of your Practical Tasks or or it could be a development of one of the Case Studies or it could be a completely separate task.

Case Studies

You will do two Case Studies, at least one from the context of 'Business and Industry'. The second may be located in the context of the home, the school, recreation or the community.

Written paper (40%)

The written paper taken is determined by your tier of entry. These papers are different for each tier.

Tier	Length
Foundation	1 hour
Intermediate	1 hour and 15 mins
Higher	1 hour and 45 mins

4. GCSE INFORMATION TECHNOLOGY AND A COMBINED SUBJECT

You can take these GCSE IT+ combinations:
    IT and Computer Art
    IT and Music Technology
The IT is covered as for NC IT.

For the coursework and examinations in 1995 and 1996 you will be expected to be familiar with the Technology Theme of 'transport'. The theme of transport will cover:
    transport media
    transport infrastructure
    transport and organisation
    transport and the individual
Questions on the technology theme will be included in all written papers.

11   **SOUTHERN EXAMINING GROUP – (SEG)**

1. NC INFORMATION TECHNOLOGY

Award:

You are awarded one of levels 4–10 for NC IT.

Coverage of syllabus:

National Curriculum Technology, IT Capability.

Learning context:

The five strands of IT.

Tiers of entry:

You are entered for one of 3 tiers.

Everyone may do the same coursework but the written paper taken is determined by your tier of entry.

Tier	NC Level available
Foundation	4–6
Intermediate	5–8
Higher	7–10

Assessment
You will do :
> Coursework
> Written paper

Coursework (60%)
You will submit at least 1 and at most 4 IT tasks. The complete set of tasks should take you between 12 and 20 hours. Your report on each task will be about two printed A4 pages plus printouts of evidence, for example, printed spreadsheets. In total the tasks should cover all the IT strands.

The subject matter may be taken from any curriculum area.

Written paper - 1 hour (40%)
All questions are compulsory. Questions are set in a context, in particular, in the context of the Technology theme.

2.A. GCSE INFORMATION SYSTEMS

Award:
You are awarded one of levels 4–10 for NC IT and/or one of levels 4–10 on GCSE Information Systems.

Coverage of syllabus:
National Curriculum Technology, IT Capability and additional material relating to Information Systems.

Learning context:
The five strands of IT.

Tiers of entry:
You are entered for one of 3 tiers.
Everyone may do the same coursework but the written papers taken are determined by your tier of entry.

Tier	NC Level available	GCSE IS level available
Foundation	4–6	4–6
Intermediate	5–8	5–8
Higher	7–10	7–10

Assessment
You will do:
> Coursework
> Written paper

Coursework (60%)
IT tasks – 30%
You will submit at least 1 and at most 4 IT tasks. The complete set of tasks should take you between 12 and 20 hours. Your report on each task will be about two printed A4 pages plus printouts of evidence, for example, printouts of spreadsheets. In total the tasks should cover all the IT strands.

The subject matter may be taken from any curriculum area.

The IT tasks will be less demanding and more sharply focused than the Information Systems tasks. You may use the IT tasks to develop your IT skills and understanding.

IS tasks – 30%
You will submit at least 1 and at most 2 IS tasks. The complete set of tasks should take you between 16 and 24 hours. Your report on each task will be about six printed A4 pages plus printouts of evidence and other supplementary materials, for example, printouts of spreadsheets and graphs.

The subject matter may be taken from any curriculum area.

The IS tasks will be more demanding than the IT tasks. They will involve using an information system to solve a substantial problem.

Written paper – 1 and a half hours (40%)

All questions are compulsory. Questions are set in a context, in particular, in the context of the Technology Theme. Questions will be designed so that half of the total mark for the paper can be used to determine your level for IT Capability. The other half of the paper will test your knowledge and understanding of information systems.

3. GCSE TECHNOLOGY

Award:
You are awarded one of levels 4–10 on NC Technology and/or one of levels 4–10 on GCSE Technology.

Coverage of syllabus:
National Curriculum Technology, all Attainment Targets, including IT Capability.

Learning context:
Technology as described in the NC orders.

Tiers of entry:
You are entered for one of 3 tiers.

Everyone may do the same coursework but the written papers taken are determined by your tier of entry.

Tier	NC Level available	GCSE level available
Foundation	4–6	4–6
Intermediate	5–8	5–8
Higher	7–10	7–10

Assessment
You will do:

      Coursework 60%   (15% IT)

      Written paper 40%   (10% IT)

IT is 25% of the total assessment.

Coursework (60%)
You will submit at least 1 and at most 2 tasks. The complete set of tasks should take you about 40 hours. In total the tasks should cover all the Technology Attainment Targets, including IT Capability.

Written paper – 2 hours (40%)

Each paper has three sections:

Section 1:   compulsory questions

Section 2:   optional questions

Section 3:   compulsory questions on IT

4. GCSE INFORMATION TECHNOLOGY – A COMBINED SUBJECT

You can take this GCSE + IT combination:
    IT and Business Studies

The IT is covered as for NC IT.

1. NC INFORMATION TECHNOLOGY

Award:
You are awarded one of levels 4–10 for NC IT.

Coverage of syllabus:
National Curriculum Technology, IT Capability.

Learning context:
The five strands of IT.

Tiers of entry:
You are entered for one of 3 tiers.
Everyone may do the same paper 1 (coursework) but the paper 2 (written) taken is determined by your tier of entry.

Tier	NC Level available
NC-1 (Foundation)	4–6
NC-2 (Intermediate)	5–8
NC-3 (Higher)	7–10

Assessment
You will do 2 papers:
    Coursework – paper 1
    Written paper – paper 2

Coursework – Paper 1 (60%)
You will solve three problems using each of:
    a database
    a spreadsheet
    data logging and control software

The subject matter is taken from the NC core subjects.
All five strands of IT should be covered.

Written paper – Paper 2 – 1 and a half hours (40%)
The questions are related to a design problem. A detailed specification of the design problem is given to schools at the start of year 11. All questions are compulsory.
This paper is the same as Section A: Systems Design for the IS papers.

2.A. GCSE INFORMATION SYSTEMS (IS)

Award:
You are awarded one of levels 4–10 for NC IT and/or one of levels 4–10 on GCSE Information Systems.

Coverage of syllabus:
National Curriculum Technology, IT Capability and additional material relating to Information Systems.

Learning context:
The five strands of IT.

Tiers of entry:
You are entered for one of 3 tiers.
Everyone may do the same paper 1 (coursework) but the paper 2 (written) taken is determined by your tier of entry.

Tier	NC Level available	GCSE IS level available
GCSE-F (Foundation)	4–6	4–6
GCSE-I (Intermediate)	5–8	5–8
GCSE-H (Higher)	7–10	7–10

Assessment
You will do 2 papers:
Coursework – paper 1
Written paper – paper 2

Coursework – paper 1 (50%)
You will solve five problems in total.
You will solve three of the problems using each of:
a database
a spreadsheet
data logging and control
You will solve a further two problems of your choice.
The subject matter is taken from the NC subjects (not necessarily core).
All five strands of IT should be covered.
There should be evidence of group work.

Written paper – Paper 2 – 2 and a half hours (50%)
All questions are compulsory.

Section A: Systems Design – 25%
The questions are related to a design problem. A detailed specification of the design problem is given to schools at the start of year 11.

Section B: Structured questions – 25%
This paper covers additional material relating to Information Systems.

2.B. GCSE INFORMATION SYSTEMS: BUSINESS

Award:
You are awarded one of levels 4–10 for NC IT and/or one of levels 4–10 on GCSE Information Systems: Business.

Coverage of syllabus:
National Curriculum Technology, IT Capability and additional material relating to Business Methods.

Learning context:
The five strands of IT set in the context of business.

Tiers of entry:
You are entered for one of 3 tiers.
Everyone may do the same paper 1 (coursework) but the paper 2 (written) taken is determined by your tier of entry.

Tier	NC Level available	GCSE IS level available
GCSE-F (Foundation)	4–6	4–6
GCSE-I (Intermediate)	5–8	5–8
GCSE-H (Higher)	7–10	7–10

Assessment
You will do 2 papers:
Coursework – paper 1
Written paper – paper 2

Coursework – paper 1 (50%)
Section A: Business assignment – 25%

Section B: IT portfolio – 25%

You will solve three problems using each of:
a database
a spreadsheet
data logging and control

The subject matter is problem solving within a business.
All five strands of IT should be covered.

Written paper – Paper 2 – 2 and a half hours (50%)
All questions are compulsory.

Section A: Systems Design – 25%
The questions are related to a design problem. A detailed specification of the design problem is given to schools at the start of year 11.

Section B: Business Methods – 25%
This paper covers additional material relating to Business Methods. This includes the use of wordprocessing, graphics and Desk Top Publishing software within a business context.

3. GCSE TECHNOLOGY

Award:
You are awarded one of levels 4–10 on NC Technology and/or one of levels 4–10 on GCSE Technology.

Coverage of syllabus:
National Curriculum Technology, all Attainment Targets, including IT Capability.

Learning context:
Technology as described in the NC orders.

Tiers of entry:
You are entered for one of 3 tiers.
Everyone may do the same papers 1 and 2 (coursework) but the paper 3 (written) taken is determined by your tier of entry.

Tier	NC Level available	GCSE level available
GCSE-F (Foundation)	4–6	4–6
GCSE-I (Intermediate)	5–8	5–8
GCSE-H (Higher)	7–10	7–10

Assessment
You will do 2 papers for NC assessment:

| Coursework | Paper 1 | Extended task 1 | 60% |
| Written paper | Paper 3 | Section A | 40% |

You will do 3 papers for GCSE assessment:

Coursework	Paper 1	Extended task 1	22.5%
Coursework	Paper 2	Extended task 2	22.5%
Written paper	Paper 3		
		Section A	30%
		Section B	25%

IT is 25% of the total assessment.

Coursework – Paper 1 – Extended task 1 This task should demonstrate your capabilities in NC Technology. It should include the application of IT to Design and Technology activities. You should use at least two construction materials chosen from wood, metal, plastics and clay.

Coursework – Paper 2 – Extended task 2
This task should demonstrate your capabilities in NC Technology. It should include the application of IT to Design and Technology activities. You should use at least one material chosen from food, textiles and graphics.

Written paper – Paper 3 – 2 and a half hours

All questions are compulsory.
Section A: The questions are related to the Technology core syllabus.
Section B: This paper covers extension work necessary for the award of GCSE Technology.

13

LEVEL DESCRIPTIONS FOR COURSEWORK

Level descriptions help teachers decide what GCSE grade or NC level should be awarded. These could help you in assessing your own progress and achievements.

AT LEVEL 5 (GRADE F):

- You can use all the features of a wordprocessor, including mail merge.

- You can use graphics software. You can scan images, edit them and import/export them from/to other software.

- You can create and use a database.

- You can use a spreadsheet for financial applications and simple modelling.

- You can use data logging and control software with control interfaces and devices such as robots.

- You can list some aspects of an information systems problem and identify one way of tackling it. Your design will not be complete.

- You have an incomplete understanding of the inputs, outputs and processing performed by an information system.

- You can partially test and evaluate an information system.

- You can partially document an information system.

AT LEVEL 9 (GRADE A):

- You can design and build an information system for others to use.

- You can identify different ways of tackling an information systems problem and justify your solution.

- You have a thorough knowledge of the inputs, outputs and processing performed by an information system.

- You can thoroughly test an information system.

- You can fully document an information system. Your documentation is complete, clear and easy to use.

- You can suggest refinements that would improve the operation of an information system.

- You have a good knowledge of the technical aspects of IT and IS.

- You can evaluate the usefulness of software.

- You can use complex modelling software effectively.

- You know when IT should be used.

IMPROVING YOUR PERFORMANCE IN EXAMS AND COURSEWORK

COURSEWORK

WRITTEN EXAMINATIONS

EXAM TECHNIQUES

GETTING STARTED

Your eventual grade in GCSE Information Systems and your level in NC Information Technology is based on the assessed **coursework** and the written **examinations**. This could be an under-estimate of your real ability. Your performance can be improved by better preparation, planning and presentation.

The coursework should be started as soon as possible. Work steadily and plan ahead to meet deadlines. Present your coursework in an attractive manner, illustrating it with pictures, flowcharts or diagrams.

Preparation for the written examinations starts on the first day of the course. Do all the work you are asked to and improve your background knowledge by closely observing any information systems you may use, for example, an on-line library catalogue. Prior to the exams revise all your work, condense and learn it. Make sure you are alert on the day of the exams. Take with you all the equipment you will need. Arrive for the exam on time. During the exam, use your time effectively, write neatly and express yourself clearly. If you finish early, check your work. Never leave before the end of the exam.

ESSENTIAL PRINCIPLES

Why is GCSE **Information Systems** or NC **Information Technology** important to you? If you know you need a good grade, you will work harder and may do better. Many students study Information Technology because they believe it will be a useful preparation for work. Some students particularly want to work with computers as part of an information system. If money is of interest to you look at the adverts for jobs in Information Technology and computing. You will find they are well paid! Convince yourself it is important to succeed. Always do your best work. If you have a clear idea of why you are studying Information Systems or Information Technology you may find it easier to put in the effort required to do well in the coursework and exams. If you are well motivated you are already on the road to success.

1 ▷ COURSEWORK

Coursework is an important part of GCSE assessment. It is often 60% of the total marks available. Coursework usually takes the form of a project or task involving some practical aspect of Information Technology. You will be asked to use Information Technology sensibly to solve a problem. This includes designing and setting up a simple information system and documenting your solution. This may involve learning to use a wordprocessor, a database, a spreadsheet, Desk Top Publishing software, graphics software, data logging and control software, simple simulation or modelling software or some other software package. You should test and evaluate the information system you set up.

Coursework is an excellent opportunity to show what you can do if you have plenty of time. You will have to meet deadlines in handing in coursework but you should still have enough time to work carefully and produce your best work. Don't leave things to the last minute. Start your coursework as soon as you know what is required of you. However, there is no need to do everything in the first lesson! Find out when the deadline is and plan ahead. It is possible that your teacher is planning lessons that will help you with your coursework. At some stage you will study the different aspects of information system design, such as systems analysis and design, data files and documentation. All these topics and others may be helpful to you. Don't rush your project. Don't leave it too late. Plan ahead and work steadily.

For your coursework assessment you will have to prepare one or more project reports describing the practical work you have done. The evidence that you have done what you describe in your project will be written work, drawings, printed material and possibly photographs. The assessment of your project will be based on the documentation you prepare and hand in. To improve your marks it is important to communicate clearly what you have done. Write neatly or use a wordprocessor. Express yourself clearly. Too much detail is much better than too little. Use diagrams, flowcharts, pictures, printed output, etc. to illustrate your work. A cheerful, topical front cover will make your project look more attractive. Show the examiner clearly what you have done and emphasise your achievements.

While you are doing your coursework you have access to a wide range of resources. You can refer to any material you need to help you. You can ask other people for advice and discuss your progress with them. You may be expected to work cooperatively with other students. However, you must make sure that you do your project. You will be asked to sign a form by the examination board certifying that your coursework is all your own work. If you find exams difficult and they make you nervous then coursework may be your best chance to demonstrate your skills. You must not neglect your coursework and expect to pass only on the results of the examinations. Every candidate who wishes to succeed must take coursework very seriously indeed.

2 ▷ WRITTEN EXAMINATIONS

To do well in an exam you need to pay careful attention to preparing yourself for it. You will need knowledge of the subject. You will do better if you are alert and in good health. If you follow some simple techniques in the exam you may improve your marks.

Knowledge

The purpose of exams is to test your **knowledge and understanding** of a subject. If you do not know your subject well then you cannot expect to do well in an exam. Preparation for the exam begins on the first day of the course. Try not to miss lessons. If you do, catch up with the work quickly. Keep all the notes you write and the work you do. Do all your homework to your best standard. Learn your work as you progress. If you have any spare time go back over the course and revise the work. Make sure you understand all the work you do. Use the library to look up topics you are unsure of. Reading another book about the same topic can often make things clearer. Improve your notes in the light of any new insights. If you have problems, ask your teacher. You can extend your background knowledge by a variety of other activities. Talk to a friend who is also doing the course and see if you can improve your knowledge of the subject by discussing topics which interest you. Read computer magazines. Go into local shops that sell computers and ask the sales staff about the computers they are selling and what they can be used for. Go on trips to computer exhibitions. Get to know someone who works with Information Technology and talk to them about their job. Try and arrange a visit to an office or factory where information systems are used. If you have access to a microcomputer this can be helpful.

When you are preparing for the exams this is the time to make sure you have learnt all that is required. A useful technique for learning a large volume of material is to repeatedly **revise, condense and learn**. Read through your notes and all the work you have done and, as you revise your knowledge, take a brief note of all the topics studied. These brief notes should cover all the important points in enough detail to refresh your memory of them at a later date. Try and learn these brief notes. If there is still too much material to learn then condense these brief notes yet again. Your objective is to end up with condensed notes covering two or three A4 sheets which summarise the course. These can be learnt and revised frequently. You can carry them with you and revise on the bus, in the queue for the cinema, waiting for a friend or taking the dog for a walk!

Practice for the exam by doing questions from previous exam papers. Work through these carefully making sure that you understand the answers to all the questions. It is likely that similar questions will appear on the written papers that you will take. Try to complete a paper under exam conditions in the time that was allowed for it. This will give you some idea of what you need to do to improve your performance. When you take your GCSE Information Systems exam or your NC Information Technology exam you will probably be taking other subjects which are also important to you. You will find that you are short of time. You will need to plan ahead and use your time effectively.

Alertness

However much you know, if you are not *alert* you will not do your best work. You will perform better if you are wide awake, healthy and relaxed. Make sure you get plenty of sleep in the days before the exam. You may think it is necessary to stay up late revising but if you make yourself too tired you will not learn very much. If you need to do a lot of revision start it a long time before the exam. Go to bed reasonably early and you will be more alert and cope with the exam much better. This is particularly important the night before the exam. Don't go to a disco, party or any activity that might involve staying up late. You will regret it the following day when you are too tired to cope.

You are also likely to perform better if you are fit and healthy. A bad cold, hay fever, headaches, broken bones, sprained ankles and other maladies can distract you from your work in the exam. The best remedy is to avoid situations that could make you ill. Perhaps the days before your exam are not the time to go horse riding, skiing, sky diving, etc. Avoid accidents. If you have unavoidable medical problems, your doctor may be able to help. Lastly, make sure you go to the toilet just before the exam. You could waste five or ten minutes of valuable exam time if you have to go to the toilet during the exam!

Many people find that exams make them nervous. They get so nervous they make silly mistakes and are unable to do their best. Most people are affected by exam nerves to some extent. Being too nervous will probably have a bad effect on your work. On-the-other-hand some people are so relaxed they do sloppy, careless work.

Being too relaxed is as inappropriate as being too nervous. Make sure you are keen to do well but keep calm.

You can waste months of careful preparation by lack of consideration for your own needs. Look after yourself! You are likely to do your best work if you are alert. Alertness depends on good health, plenty of sleep and a calm determination to do well.

3 > EXAM TECHNIQUES

Exam techniques are not magic! Using them will not make up for lack of thorough preparation or ignorance. In an exam you try to communicate your knowledge to the examiner who will mark your work. Exam techniques are common sense methods to help you communicate what you know effectively.

Before you arrive at the exam, make sure you have any equipment you will need in the exam. You will require at least a pencil, a pencil sharpener, a rubber, a ruler and at least two pens, in case one runs out. A calculator might be useful. This equipment is essential for accurate, written communication. If you have to borrow a pen, for example, it may not suit you or it may not work properly and consequently you may work at a slower pace. It is possible that equipment may not be available to borrow and you will have to manage without it. Make sure you are well prepared so that you can get down to work quickly and are not interrupted.

The first task to do in any exam is to find out what questions you are expected to answer. Doing extra questions will not earn extra marks but if you leave questions out you will lose marks.

Next, work out how much time you can spend on each question. It is often useful to work out how much time you can devote to each mark. This is the number of **minutes per mark**. You can use this to work out how long can be spent on questions that may not be worth the same amount of marks. For example, in a two hour paper you have 120 minutes to earn perhaps 100 marks. This is 1.2 minutes per mark. You can spend 2.4 minutes on a question worth 2 marks and 6 minutes on a question worth 5 marks. Having worked out the time you can spend on a question, stick to it. This is very important. The first part of each question is usually the easiest to answer and the first few marks on any question are the easiest to obtain. After the first half of a question, marks become increasingly difficult to obtain. Try to answer all the questions. You cannot be given marks for questions you haven't answered. Higher marks will almost certainly be given for correct answers to part of all the required questions than for complete answers to only a few questions.

Always arrive on time for an exam. Never leave an exam before the end. Spend all the time allowed to you to do the exam answering questions or checking your answers. Make sure that what you can do is correct and make a determined attempt at the more difficult questions. Marks are given for correct answers but you will not have marks deducted if you are wrong.

Make sure you read the question thoroughly. Many candidates lose marks because they read the question in a hurry and do not fully grasp what it means. They then answer the question they think they have read. This means their answer may be inappropriate to the actual question. You will only be awarded marks for a correct answer to the actual question set. Read questions slowly and carefully.

The examiner who marks your written paper will be looking for opportunities to give you marks. If it is impossible to read your answers because your writing is illegible you will probably lose marks. Write neatly. Set out your work clearly. Give examples and draw diagrams to illustrate your answers. Communicate clearly and in full.

THE IMPORTANCE OF THE TOPIC AREAS

CONTENT OF THE GCSE SYLLABUSES

ADDRESSES OF GCSE EXAMINATION BOARDS

GETTING STARTED

Syllabuses are important because they outline in detail what is to be studied. The syllabus can be used as a checklist to make sure you have studied or revised all those topics you will be asked questions about in the written exams. You can buy a syllabus by writing to one of the addresses given in this chapter.

This chapter includes a table summarising the topics required by each examination board. This will be a useful guide. For a more detailed breakdown you should consult the syllabus you are studying. All the syllabuses are similar but they are not *identical*.

ESSENTIAL PRINCIPLES

Syllabuses are important because they outline in detail what is to be studied. The syllabus can be used as a checklist to make sure you have studied or revised all those topics you will be asked questions about in the written exams. You can buy a syllabus by writing to one of the addresses given in this chapter.

This chapter includes a table summarising the topics required by each examination board. This will be a useful guide. For a more detailed breakdown you should consult the syllabus you are studying. All the syllabuses are similar but they are not identical.

1 **CONTENT OF THE GCSE SYLLABUSES**

All the syllabuses cover the National Criteria for **Technology** and the NC **Technology** Attainment Target 'IT Capability'. These state what topics should be included in each syllabus. Consequently, there is not a great deal of difference between the different syllabuses. Below is a table summarising the topics required by each of the examination boards. You will need to consult your particular syllabus for a more detailed breakdown.

If you want to be sure that you have covered all the topics for the course you are studying, you should buy a syllabus. Syllabuses can be useful when studying and revising as you can be certain you are learning the right topics. Syllabuses cost around £2 each. It is important to get the syllabus you are studying as each exam board has a different one. Find out which syllabus you are studying then write to the **Publications Department** at the address given under the name of the exam board at the end of this chapter.

EXAM BOARDS / CHAPTER NO. & SYLLABUS TOPIC	ULEAC	MEG	NEAB	SEG	WJEC	RSA	NDTEF	C&G
4. An Introduction to Information Technology and Information Systems								
Information Technology	✓	✓	✓	✓	✓	✓	✓	✓
Information Systems	✓	✓	✓	✓	✓	✓	✓	✓
Hardware	✓	✓	✓	✓	✓	✓	✓	✓
Input and Output	✓	✓	✓	✓	✓	✓	✓	✓
Digital and Analogue	✓	✓	✓	✓	✓	✓	✓	✓
Software	✓	✓	✓	✓	✓	✓	✓	✓
Utility and Applications Programs	✓	✓	✓	✓	✓	✓		
Numbers and Characters	✓	✓	✓	✓	✓	✓	✓	✓
Glossary of terms	✓	✓	✓	✓	✓	✓	✓	✓
5. Data Capture and Input								
Questionnaires and data collection forms	✓	✓	✓	✓	✓	✓	✓	✓
Verification	✓	✓	✓	✓	✓	✓	✓	✓
Mark sensing and OCR	✓	✓	✓	✓	✓	✓	✓	✓
Bar codes and bar code readers	✓	✓	✓	✓	✓	✓	✓	✓
Kimball tags	✓	✓	✓	✓	✓	✓	✓	✓
Magnetic Ink Character Recognition	✓	✓	✓	✓	✓	✓	✓	✓
Magnetic Stripe Cards	✓	✓	✓	✓	✓	✓	✓	✓
Voice recognition	✓	✓	✓	✓	✓	✓	✓	✓
Sound sampling and music	✓	✓	✓	✓	✓	✓	✓	✓

CHAPTER NO. & SYLLABUS TOPIC	U L E A C	M E G	N E A B	S E G	W J E C	R S A	N D T E F	C & G
Joystick	✓	✓	✓	✓	✓	✓	✓	✓
Mouse	✓	✓	✓	✓	✓	✓	✓	✓
Tracker ball	✓	✓	✓	✓	✓	✓	✓	✓
Graphics pad	✓	✓	✓	✓	✓	✓	✓	✓
Pen	✓	✓	✓	✓	✓	✓	✓	✓
Scanners	✓	✓	✓	✓	✓	✓	✓	✓
Video digitisers	✓	✓	✓	✓	✓	✓	✓	✓
Sensors	✓	✓	✓	✓	✓	✓	✓	✓
Validation	✓	✓	✓				✓	✓
Garbage In, Garbage Out	✓	✓	✓	✓	✓	✓	✓	✓
6. The Memory, Files and Backing Storage								
Memory	✓	✓	✓	✓	✓		✓	✓
Files, records and fields	✓	✓	✓	✓	✓	✓	✓	✓
Serial and sequential access	✓		✓				✓	✓
Random or direct access	✓	✓	✓				✓	✓
File operations	✓	✓	✓	✓	✓	✓	✓	✓
Magnetic tapes	✓	✓	✓	✓	✓		✓	✓
Magnetic discs, hard discs and floppy discs	✓	✓	✓	✓	✓	✓	✓	✓
File organisation	✓	✓	✓	✓	✓	✓	✓	✓
CD-ROM, Optical Discs, WORM discs	✓	✓	✓	✓	✓		✓	✓
Security	✓	✓	✓	✓	✓	✓	✓	✓
7. Output								
Monitors	✓	✓	✓	✓	✓	✓	✓	✓
Printers	✓	✓	✓	✓	✓	✓	✓	✓
Buffers and spooling	✓	✓	✓	✓	✓	✓	✓	✓
Computer Output on Microfilm	✓	✓	✓	✓	✓	✓	✓	✓
Graph plotters	✓	✓	✓	✓	✓	✓	✓	✓
Speech Synthesis	✓	✓	✓	✓	✓	✓	✓	✓
Electro-mechanical output	✓	✓	✓	✓	✓	✓	✓	✓
Actuators	✓	✓	✓	✓	✓	✓	✓	✓
8. Operating Systems and Networks								
Operating systems	✓	✓	✓	✓	✓	✓	✓	✓
Graphical User Interfaces	✓	✓	✓	✓	✓	✓	✓	✓
Standalone computers	✓	✓	✓	✓	✓	✓	✓	✓
Multitasking	✓	✓	✓	✓	✓	✓	✓	✓
Networks	✓	✓	✓	✓	✓	✓	✓	✓
Network security	✓	✓	✓	✓	✓	✓	✓	✓
9. Communicating Information								
Audience	✓	✓	✓	✓	✓	✓	✓	✓
Wordprocessing	✓	✓	✓	✓	✓	✓	✓	✓
Graphics	✓	✓	✓	✓	✓	✓	✓	✓
Desk Top Publishing	✓	✓	✓	✓	✓	✓	✓	✓

CHAPTER NO. & SYLLABUS TOPIC	ULEAC	MEG	NEAB	SEG	WJEC	RSA	NDTEF	C&G
E-Mail	✓	✓	✓	✓	✓	✓	✓	✓
Multimedia	✓	✓	✓	✓	✓	✓	✓	✓
Conferencing	✓	✓				✓	✓	✓
10. Handling Information								
Databases	✓	✓	✓	✓	✓	✓	✓	✓
Database information system	✓	✓	✓	✓	✓	✓	✓	✓
Videotex: teletext and viewdata	✓	✓		✓			✓	✓
Expert systems	✓	✓		✓			✓	
11. Spreadsheets and Modelling								
Spreadsheets	✓	✓	✓	✓	✓	✓	✓	✓
Spreadsheet information system	✓	✓	✓	✓	✓	✓	✓	✓
Modelling using spreadsheets	✓	✓	✓	✓	✓	✓	✓	✓
12. Measurement and Control Systems								
AND/OR/NOT logic	✓	✓	✓		✓			
NOR/NAND/XOR logic	✓	✓	✓		✓			
Truth tables	✓	✓	✓		✓			
Control signals and data, logic and feedback	✓	✓	✓	✓	✓	✓	✓	✓
Control Systems	✓	✓	✓	✓	✓	✓	✓	✓
Programming languages	✓	✓	✓	✓	✓	✓	✓	✓
13. Information Systems in action								
Information Systems in action	✓	✓	✓	✓	✓	✓	✓	✓
Batch, Real Time and On-line Interactive processing	✓	✓	✓	✓	✓	✓	✓	✓
The systems life cycle	✓	✓	✓	✓	✓	✓	✓	✓
Systems flowcharts	✓	✓	✓	✓	✓	✓	✓	✓
Documentation	✓	✓	✓	✓	✓	✓	✓	✓
Jobs in Information Systems		✓		✓				
14. The Social Impact of Information Systems								
Privacy	✓	✓	✓	✓	✓	✓	✓	✓
Lifestyle and leisure	✓	✓	✓	✓	✓	✓	✓	✓
The social impact of Information Technology and Information Systems: in the home, school, recreation, the community, business and industry.	✓	✓	✓	✓	✓	✓	✓	✓

2 > **ADDRESSES OF GCSE EXAMINATION BOARDS**

City and Guilds Institute of London (C & G)
46 Britannia St
London WC1X 7RG
(0171 278 2468)

Midland Examining Group (MEG)
Syndicate Buildings
1 Hills Rd
Cambridge CB1 2EU
(01223 553311)

National Design and Technology Education Foundation (NDTEF)
The Old Chapel House
Pound Hill
Alresford
Hants.
(01962 735801)

Northern Examinations and Assessment Board (NEAB)
Devas Street
Manchester
M15 6EX
(0161 953 1180)

Royal Society of Arts (RSA)
RSA Examinations Board
Westwood Way
Coventry CV4 8HS
(01203 470033)

Southern Examining Group (SEG)
Stag Hill House
Guildford GU2 5XJ
(01483 506506)

University of London Examinations and Assessment Council (ULEAC)
Stewart House
32 Russell Square
London WC1B 5DN
(0171 331 4000)

Welsh Joint Education Committee (WJEC)
245 Western Avenue
Cardiff CF5 2YX
(01222 561231)

CHAPTER 4

AN INTRODUCTION TO INFORMATION TECHNOLOGY AND INFORMATION SYSTEMS

INFORMATION TECHNOLOGY

INFORMATION SYSTEMS

HARDWARE

SOFTWARE

DATA

GETTING STARTED

Information Technology is the computers and other equipment used to process information. An **Information System** is constructed using Information Technology. Information Systems provide information about specific applications. For example, an Information System is used to calculate gas bills.

Hardware is the physical machinery that is part of a computer system. Computers and their associated input and output peripherals are hardware.

Most computer hardware is digital. Some input devices, for example, sensors, and some output devices, for example, robots, are analogue. When digital computers input from or output to analogue devices DACs or ADCs must be used to convert from digital to analogue and vice versa.

Software is the programs that control the running of the computer. Applications Packages and Content Free Packages are software. The Operating System is the software that controls the operation of a computer system. Utility programs are used to do tasks that help in the successful use of the computer system, for example, formatting a disc.

Information stored by computers takes the form of Numbers and Characters. Numbers may be binary or hexadecimal. Characters are stored using ASCII.

There is a **Glossary of Terms** at the end of this chapter to help you make use of the jargon associated with Information Technology and computers.

ESSENTIAL PRINCIPLES

Computers process data. The data is not understood by the computer. Computers cannot tell the difference between sensible data or nonsense, unless we tell then how to. The use of computers is often referred to as **data processing**. However, because we are only interested in doing *useful* tasks with computers, we actually use them to process information, that is, data that has some meaning to us. For this reason we often call computers **Information Technology** (IT).

❝ Information is data that has some meaning. ❞

■ **information = data + meaning**

e.g.   230575 is *data*.
If we add *meaning* it could be any of the following:
a date; a telephone number; a serial number; £230,575; etc.
It then becomes *information*.

■ Information Technology is the use of computers and other equipment to store, process and transmit information.

An **Information System** (IS) uses IT to store, process or transmit information. An IS is the organisation of human and other resources, including IT, into a coherent system for the purposeful storage, processing and transmission of information.

Information processing is a **cycle** of input, processing and output (see Fig. 4.1). We input the data we have collected, then process it. When the data has been processed, some data is output. In response to the data output we may wish to respond by inputting further data in reply. This is in turn processed and the cycle continues until we have no further data to input.

The information processing cycle may be based on a computer (see Fig. 4.2). The **Central Processing Unit (CPU)** of the computer does the actual processing of the data. Within the CPU are the **Immediate Access Store (IAS)**, the **Control Unit (CU)** and the **Arithmetic and Logic Unit (ALU)**.

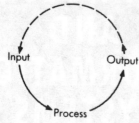

Fig. 4.1 Information processing cycle

■ The **IAS** is the memory of the computer, Programs and data are stored in the IAS while the programs are run and the data is processed. There are two types of memory:

  • **Random Access Memory (RAM)** is the *volatile* or temporary memory in which the programs and data are stored.

  • **Read Only Memory (ROM)** can only be read and is not volatile. It is used to permanently store programs such as the Operating System.

■ A program is a set of instructions that tell a computer what to do. Programs are stored in the memory of the computer and *executed* or *run* in order to process the input data. The input data is also stored in the memory of the computer while it is processed. The processed data is then output. When the computer is switched off the programs and data in the RAM memory of the computer are 'wiped out'. To avoid losing the programs and data when we switch off, the programs and data can be saved on **backing storage**.

■ The **CU** controls the hardware so that it carries out the instructions given in the program being run. It controls the input and output of data and the transfer of data between different parts of the CPU.

■ The **ALU** is a specialised unit within the CPU that does all the arithmetic and logic.

EXAMPLE: CALCULATING A GAS BILL

Suppose we want to use a computer to calculate a gas bill. We will have to do the following:

1 *Switch on* the computer.

2 *Load the program* which will do the calculation into the memory of the computer.

3 *Run* (or *execute*) the program.

4 *Input* the old and the new meter readings in response to requests from the computer.

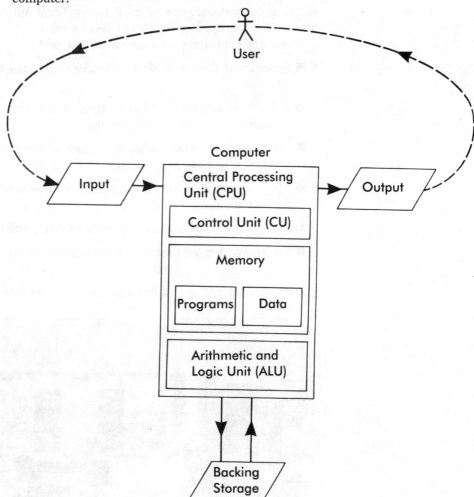

Fig. 4.2 The Information processing cycle based on a computer

Fig. 4.2 The Information processing cycle based on a computer

HARDWARE 3

66 An important distinction between hardware and software. 99

Hardware is the physical machinery that is part of an information system. Hardware is hard! You can touch it and even bump into it and hurt yourself!

MAINFRAMES AND MICROS

Computers are hardware. Computers come in different sizes. Essentially, microcomputers are small computers whilst mainframes are large computers.

A typical microcomputer is small enough to fit on an average-sized desk. Microcomputers are found in homes, offices, schools, etc. They may be 'Personal Computers', 'desk top', 'portable' or 'lap top' computers. In industry the standard microcomputer is the IBM Personal Computer(PC) (see Fig. 4.3).

Fig. 4.3 The IBM PS/2 Personal Computer System. It is a typical example of a powerful desk top computer.

Note the differences between mainframe computers and microcomputers.

Mainframe computers are many and varied. They offer a wide range of facilities and can vary dramatically in size and power. Most of them are very big in size, extremely fast in operation, have very large memories and offer access to a wide range of complex software and hardware. Mainframes are used in large companies and similar organisations, such as major banks, Local Authorities, etc. Typically they are housed in a room measuring 15m by 50m, or more.

Mainframe computers need *special environments*:

■ in particular they need *air conditioning* to dissipate the heat generated when they are in use.

■ *False floors and ceilings* may be used to hide the miles of cable connecting the computer to the various peripherals.

■ The electricity supply is often 'smoothed' to prevent power surges or 'spikes' which may damage the expensive equipment.

■ The computer may have its own *electricity generator* for emergency use in case of a power failure.

■ *Filters* are used to keep the air free from dust particles.

■ *Smoke detectors* are used to help prevent the outbreak of a serious fire.

The IBM Model 3090 is a typical mainframe computer (see Fig. 4.4).

Fig. 4.4 The IBM Model 3090 Mainframe Computer System. (Reproduction courtesy of IBM UK Ltd.)

PERIPHERALS

Peripherals are hardware. They are machines attached to the computer. They are often essential to the successful operation of the computer. They usually have a special purpose.

The following are examples of peripherals:

Input peripherals
keyboard, mouse, joystick, tracker ball, pen
graphics pad, scanner, video digitiser
OCR reader, OMR reader
light pen, laser scanner for bar codes, stripe card reader
Kimball tag reader
MICR reader
sensors

Backing Storage peripherals
magnetic tape drive; using reel to reel and cassette tape
magnetic disc drive; using floppy discs and hard discs
CD-ROM, optical discs

Output peripherals
VDU or monitor, printer
COM recorder
loudspeaker
graph plotter

DIGITAL AND ANALOGUE

Most computers are digital, electronic machines. Their electronic circuitry is constructed using binary logic. **Binary logic** is two-state logic. This means that only two states are possible. These two states are voltage levels of 5V or 0V. 5V is used to represent the digit 1 and 0V is used to represent 0. The memory of the computer is simply a very large number of 1s and 0s that form patterns that are recognised by the computer. The computer is described as being **digital** because everything in its memory is represented using 1s and 0s, i.e. binary digits.

An important distinction between digital and analogue

Data is represented using patterns of 1s and 0s. A 1 or 0 is a **binary digit** or **bit**. Bits are grouped together to form bytes. A byte is the number of bits used to represent one character. It is very common for computers to have 8 bits in a byte. Memory size is measured in bytes.

The *units of memory size*, in bytes, are as follows:

- 1 **Kilobyte** or 1 Kbyte   = 1024 bytes   = 2^{10} bytes
- 1 **Megabyte** or 1 Mbyte   = 1024 K bytes = 2^{20} bytes
- 1 **Gigabyte** or 1 Gbyte   = 1024 M bytes = 2^{30} bytes

ADC's AND DAC's

Most computers and peripherals are digital but some are not. Sensors are analogue devices. For example, a heat sensor produces a small voltage in response to temperature changes. This small voltage is known as an analogue signal. When the analogue signal is input to a digital computer it must be converted from analogue to digital form. This is done using an Analogue to Digital Convertor or ADC.

If a digital computer outputs to an analogue device then a Digital to Analogue Converter or DAC is used. This converts the digital signal from the computer to an analogue form. For example, a motor may need a continuously varying voltage to control its speed. The output from the digital computer to the motor will need to be converted to an analogue voltage using a DAC.

4 SOFTWARE

Software refers to the *programs* that control the running of the computer. Software can be held in the memory of the computer. It can also be recorded on floppy disc. Software is NOT floppy discs. It is the *programs recorded on* the floppy discs.

Software can be obtained in many ways. You can write your own, using a computer language such as BASIC or LOGO. You can buy software. Bought software is referred to as a package. Most packages have a specific purpose or application. You might buy an **applications package** to do the stock keeping in a shop, to calculate the wages for a factory or to do your budgeting at home.

Applications packages

Content free packages are packages which are useful in a *variety* of ways, but used to do *similar* tasks. These packages cover application *areas* rather than specific applications. For example, content free packages are used for Wordprocessing, Databases, Spreadsheets, Graphic Design and Desk Top Publishing.

Content free packages

One of the most important programs that a computer runs is the **operating system**. The operating system is always present when a computer is being used. The operating system makes the hardware available to other software. Applications packages and other user software run on the operating system which, in turn, runs or controls the hardware. The operating system helps the user do a variety of tacks associated with the day-to-day operation of the computer, such as loading and saving programs and data.

The operating system

Utility programs are used to do tasks which relate more to the successful use of

Utility programs

the computer than to any information systems task. For example, some utility programs are part of the Operating System. These would be used to do tasks such as copying or formatting discs. You could buy new utility programs to do the same tasks. You might chose to buy new Utility Programs because they are faster or more versatile than the ones supplied with the Operating System. Utility programs can also do tasks that are often not done by the Operating System, such as recover deleted files from a disc.

5	**DATA: NUMBERS AND CHARACTERS**

Data can be *numbers* or *character strings*. For example, "34 High Road" is a **character string**; 45.6 is a **number**. Note that numbers can be characters as well as numbers (but not both at the same time!). The bit patterns in memory can be interpreted only if we know whether they are meant to be numbers or characters, and if we know the codes and conventions being used.

DENARY OR BASE 10 NUMBERS

While computers use bit patterns to represent numbers, people use **denary**, i.e. **base 10** numbers. Computer number systems are constructed using the same method we use for base 10, so it is useful to analyse our own number system before looking at how the computer represents numbers. By making use of a **place value number system** we can represent any number using only the digits 0, 1, 2, . . ., 9 and no others.

This works as follows:

<table>
<tr><td>❝❝ The denary or base 10 number system ❞❞</td><td>

10^3	10^2	10^1	10^0	: base	Available digits are
1000	100	10	1	: place value	0,1,2,3,4,5,6,7,8,9
2	5	7	4	: denary number	

</td></tr>
</table>

This number is read as two thousand, five hundred and seventy four. We can construct other number systems using this framework.

BINARY OR BASE 2 NUMBERS

We construct binary numbers as follows:

<table>
<tr><td>❝❝ The Binary or base 2 number system ❞❞</td><td>

2^7	2^6	2^5	2^4	2^3	2^2	2^1	2^0	: base	available digits
128	64	32	16	8	4	2	1	: place value	0,1
0	1	0	1	1	1	0	1	: binary number	

</td></tr>
</table>

Binary numbers are constructed using only two digits, 1 and 0, making this system very easy for computers to represent in an electronic two state system. Unfortunately, this system is not so easy for people to use! We must be able to convert binary to denary and vice versa before we can begin to use the same system as the computer.

CONVERTING BINARY TO DENARY

Look again at the binary number 0101 1101 used in the example above. Each bit has a place value depending on its position in the number. These values are expressed in denary. Where there is a 1 in the binary number we add in the place value; where there is a 0 we do not add in the place value. The calculation is as follows:

128	64	32	16	8	4	2	1	: place value
0	1	0	1	1	1	0	1	: binary number

$$\text{denary number} = 64 + 16 + 8 + 4 + 1$$
$$= 93$$

CONVERTING DENARY TO BINARY

To convert 86 in denary to a binary number we use the following algorithm:

Write down the denary number;
REPEAT the following until the place value is less than 1
IF the denary number is bigger than or equal to the place value
THEN
    subtract the place value from the denary number
    put a 1 in the corresponding position
    write down the new denary number
ELSE
    put a 0 in the corresponding position;
IF END;
REPEAT END.

Let's do this for the denary number 86:

number	place value	binary digit
86	128	0
86	64	1
22	32	0
22	16	1
6	8	0
6	4	1
2	2	1
0	1	0

So, denary 86 = binary 0101 0110.

COUNTING IN BINARY

It is useful to be able to count in binary. Fig 4.5 shows the numbers from 1 to 20 in binary. Notice how the patterns of 0s and 1s are repeated in the binary count. Recognising these patterns will help you understand how to count in binary.

denary number	binary number
1	1
2	10
3	11
4	100
5	101
6	110
7	111
8	1000
9	1001
10	1010
11	1011
12	1100
13	1101
14	1110
15	1111
16	10000
17	10001
18	10010
19	10011
20	10100

Fig. 4.5 Counting from 1 to 20 in binary

HEXADECIMAL OR BASE 16

Computers store numbers using the binary number system. Unfortunately, binary numbers are hard for us to remember and when we look at them we do not always get an impression of their relative size. When copying binary numbers it is easy to make mistakes!

For these reasons, other number systems are often used instead of binary. The choice of base number is determined by how easy it is to convert *to* and *from* binary. The most important of these other number bases is **hexadecimal** or **base 16**. This number system is constructed as follows:

The hexadecimal or base 16 number system

16^3	16^2	16^1	16^0	: base
4096	256	16	1	: place value
2	8	A	3	: hexadecimal number

available digits:
0,1,2,3, . . . 9,A,B,C,D,E

In base 16 we should use the single digits 0,1,2,3,4,5,6,7,8,9,10,11,12,13,14,15. However, 10,11,12,13,14,15 expressed in decimal all contain two digits. To avoid this problem we use the digits A,B,C,D,E,F to represent the single digits 10,11,12,13,14,15 respectively.

CONVERTING HEXADECIMAL TO BINARY AND VICE VERSA

Any hexadecimal digit can be represented as four binary bits and four binary bits are always equivalent to a hexadecimal digit. For example:

binary number	:	hexadecimal digit	binary number	:	hexadecimal digit
0000	:	0	1000	:	8
0001	:	1	1001	:	9
0010	:	2	1010	:	A
0011	:	3	1011	:	B
0100	:	4	1100	:	C
0101	:	5	1101	:	D
0110	:	6	1110	:	E
0111	:	7	1111	:	F

To convert *hexadecimal to binary* we change each hexadecimal digit to four binary bits, e.g. A43E = 1010 0100 0011 1110.

To convert *binary to hexadecimal* we divide the bits into groups of four, putting in leading 0s on the left hand side, where necessary, and convert each group to a hexadecimal digit, as follows:

10111 in binary = 0001 0111

= 17 in hexadecimal

If we have to convert *hexadecimal to denary* it is easiest to first convert the hexadecimal to binary and then convert the binary to denary as we did earlier in this chapter.

To convert *denary to hexadecimal*, first convert the denary to binary then convert the binary to hexadecimal.

CHARACTER STRINGS

Character strings are lists of characters, e.g. 'Albert Greenhill' is a character string containing 16 characters including the space.

Characters are represented using codes. These codes are simply bit patterns that we agree to interpret as a particular character. They are arbitrary, although they may be quite well organised. There is no particular reason why a bit pattern should represent one character rather than another. For this reason there are several different codes used to represent characters. They have been developed by different manufacturers of computers and others for their own purposes.

ASCII

●● Part of the ASCII Code ●●

ASCII (American Standard Code for Information Interchange) is the most common code in use for representing characters. Part of this code is shown in the table below:

Character	:	Binary code	Character	:	Binary code
Space	:	010 0000	G	:	100 0111
			H	:	100 1000
0	:	011 0000	I	:	100 1001
1	:	011 0001	J	:	100 1010
2	:	011 0010	K	:	100 1011
3	:	011 0011	L	:	100 1100
4	:	011 0100	M	:	100 1101
5	:	011 0101	N	:	100 1110
6	:	011 0110	O	:	100 1111
7	:	011 0111	P	:	101 0000
8	:	011 1000	Q	:	101 0001
9	:	011 1001	R	:	101 0010
			S	:	101 0011
+	:	010 1011	T	:	101 0100
A	:	100 0001	U	:	101 0101
B	:	100 0010	V	:	101 0110
C	:	100 0011	W	:	101 0111
D	:	100 0100	X	:	101 1000
E	:	100 0101	Y	:	101 1001
F	:	100 0110	Z	:	101 1010

Notice that although ASCII code is in ascending binary number order, the code for the character 3 is not the binary number for three.

CONTROL CHARACTERS

Control characters (or control codes) are not usually displayed or printed. They are not characters that are meaningful to most people as part of a routine communication. When entered at the keyboard or sent to a peripheral they are treated as a signal to begin or end some operation. For example, there is a control code associated with pressing the <ENTER> or <RETURN> key on the keyboard; there are others that tell the printer to turn on and off features such as bold printing and underlining. Control characters are part of the character set and must have different codes from other characters.

THE SIZE OF THE CHARACTER SET

Each different character must have a different binary code associated with it. Hence the number of bits used determines the number of characters it is possible to code. The **character set** is all the characters it is possible to represent using the code. The **size** of the character set is the number of different characters represented. This cannot be more than the maximum number of different codes. The relationship between the number of bits and the maximum size of the character set is shown in the table below:

Number of bits	different codes	maximum size of the character set
1	01	$2 = 2^1$
2	00 01 10 11	$4 = 2^2$
3	000 001 010 011 100 101 110 111	$8 = 2^3$
4	0000 0100 1000 1100 0001 0101 1001 1101 0010 0110 1010 1110 0011 0111 1011 1111	$16 = 2^4$
5	....	$32 = 2^5$
6	....	$64 = 2^6$
7	....	$128 = 2^7$
8	....	$256 = 2^8$
x	....	2^x

Since ASCII is a 7 bit code, the maximum number of possible characters is 128, more than enough for most purposes!

GLOSSARY OF TERMS

Actuator	The device that performs some action required by a control system, e.g. a motor.
Algorithm	A set of rules to solve a problem.
Amend	To change.
Analogue	The representation of data as a range of variable voltages. Only specialist computers represent data in analogue form.
Analogue to Digital Converter	A hardware device to convert analogue voltage to binary digital numbers.
Ancestral system	The ancestral system for file backups consists of the son (the latest version), the father (the previous version) and the grandfather (the version before the previous version).
AND gate	A logic gate that sets the output high if all the inputs are high.
Applications software	Software designed to do a specific job, e.g. payroll.
Arithmetic and Logic Unit (ALU)	The part of the CPU where arithmetic and logical operations are done.
ASCII	The American Standard Code for Information Interchange. This is used to uniquely represent characters.
Assembler	A program that converts a program written in assembly language (the source code) into machine code (the object code).
Assembly language	A low level computer language close to machine code. Each instruction is one machine code instruction.
Backing storage	A means of storing programs and data outside the IAS, e.g. magnetic disc or tape.
Backup	A backup of a file is another copy of it. The ancestral system is often used for backups.
Bar code	A code represented by a series of vertical black and white lines, often used to encode an identity number.
Bar code reader	A hardware device used to read a bar code. This could be a light pen or a laser scanner.
BASIC	Beginners All-purpose Symbolic Instruction Code. A high level language which is suitable for learning to write computer programs.
Batch processing	A method of processing data where the data is gathered into batches before being processed.

Binary	The base 2 number system. Allowable digits are 0 and 1.
BIT	A **BI**nary Digi**T**. This takes the value 1 or 0.
Block	1. A group of records on magnetic tape or disc that is read or written together
	2. A section of the screen display that has been highlighted.
Buffer	A printer buffer is extra memory, usually in the printer itself, which is used to hold output while it is waiting to be printed.
Bug	An error in a computer program.
Byte	A byte is a set of bits used to represent one character. There are normally eight bits to the byte.
Catalogue	A list of all the files on a disc. A catalogue is also known as a directory.
CD-ROM	The use of audio Compact Disc technology for backing storage for computers. CD-ROMs can store text, sound, pictures, music and video. They are used with Multimedia systems.
Ceefax	The teletext service broadcast by the BBC.
Cell	The intersection of a row and a column in a spreadsheet.
Central Processing Unit (CPU)	The main part of the computer, where all the processing takes place. It consists of the CU, the ALU and the memory.
Character	One of the symbols that can be represented by a computer. Characters include A to Z and 0 to 9.
Character code	A code used to represent characters, e.g. ASCII.
Character printer	A printer that prints one character at a time, e.g. a dot matrix printer.
Character set	All the characters that can be represented by a computer.
Character string	A list of characters.
Check digit	An extra digit calculated from the original digits in a number, using a predetermined formula, and attached to the number. It can be re-calculated to check that none of the digits in the number have been altered.
COBOL	**CO**mmon **B**usiness **O**rientated **L**anguage. One of the more popular high level languages used for business and commercial applications.
Compiler	A program used to convert another program written in a high level language to machine code. The compiler will report syntax errors in the high level language.
Computer	A computer is an automatic, information processing machine which inputs, processes and outputs data under the control of a stored program.
Computer Aided Design (CAD)	Using graphics software to help design illustrations, products, etc.
Computer Aided Manufacture (CAM)	Using a computer to control the manufacture of a product. Output from a computer written directly onto microfilm.
Computer Output on Microfilm (COM)	Output in this form is compact and does not deteriorate in storage as rapidly as printout.
Content free software	Software designed to do a range of similar jobs, e.g. spreadsheet.
Control character	Control characters are used to control the setting of peripherals, in particular, printers. They are part of the character set and have an ASCII code but are not usually visible on the monitor screen or printout.
Control Interface box	The hardware that provides the interface between a computer and the control system it is looking after.
Control switch	A switch built of logic gates that is used to switch data lines on and off.
Control system	An information system used to monitor and control environmental conditions.
Control total	A meaningful total calculated from a batch of source documents that is used to check that the batch is complete.
Control Unit (CU)	The part of the CPU that controls the running of programs and the input and output of data.

Corrupt data	Corrupt data is data that has been altered so that it is no longer meaningful.
Create	Set up for the first time.
Cursor	Usually a rectangular block one character in size that appears on a monitor screen at the point at which the next character entered through the keyboard will be displayed. The cursor often flashes on and off to attract attention.
Cursor control keys	The 'arrow' keys used to control the movement of the cursor around the screen.
Daisy wheel printer	A printer that has a daisy wheel print mechanism. Daisy wheel printers give high quality printout.
Data	Numbers or character strings.
Data capture	Data capture is the collection of data prior to input. Data capture can be on-line, e.g. POS terminals for stock keeping, or off-line, e.g. questionnaires.
Data control clerks	The job of a data control clerk is to monitor the flow of data through a computer system.
Data preparation	This is the transfer of data from a source document to a computer readable medium, e.g. disc.
Data preparation clerks	Data preparation clerks work in the data preparation department.
Data processing	Computers input, process and output data. In commerce this is known as data processing.
Database	A database is a collection of structured data (see files, records, fields) and the software to allow the user to easily access the data.
Data logging	The use of sensors, to measure environmental conditions, with a computer to determine when the measurements are made and to record them.
Debug	To look for, find and remove bugs in a computer program.
Delete	Remove. A file is deleted from a disc when it is removed from it.
Denary	The base 10 number system. Available digits are 0 to 9.
Desk Top Publishing (DTP)	Combines graphics and wordprocessing in a format typical of a newspaper
Digital	The representation of data as codes made up of 1's and 0's. These can be stored in the computer as 5v and 0v, respectively.
Direct access	A method of accessing a file where it is possible to store or retrieve data records without the need to read other data records first. Direct access is used with magnetic discs but not with magnetic tape.
Direct data entry	Data entry to the program that processes the data while it is running.
Directory	See catalogue.
Disc	Magnetic discs are a backing storage medium. Microcomputers use floppy discs ($5\frac{1}{4}$" or $3\frac{1}{2}$") or hard discs. Mainframes use disc packs that may be exchangeable or fixed.
Documentation	A written description of what a program does and how it is run. Often containing details of program design, coding and testing.
Dot matrix printer	A printer that has a print head consisting of a matrix of steel pins. Character shapes are made up from a pattern of dots.
Edit	Amend, delete or insert.
Electronic funds transfer (EFT)	A paperless method of transferring money between bank accounts using a communications network.
Electronic Funds Transfer at Point of Sale (EFTPOS)	See Electronic funds transfer and Point of sale.

Electronic mail	A paperless method of sending mail, i.e. letters, etc., from one computer to another using a communications network.
Errors	Logic errors are mistakes in the logic of a program. They are detected by thorough program testing.
	Syntax errors are mistakes in the format of a programming language, e.g. PRONT instead of PRINT. They are detected by the compiler or interpreter.
	Execution errors occur when a program is run, e.g. division by zero.
Execute	To execute a program is to run it.
Expert system	Software that allows users to recognise particular situations and that gives them advice on the appropriate action to take
Feedback	Feedback occurs when a sensor detects a situation that causes the computer to initiate action that alters the data collected by the sensor.
Fibre optics	The use of very thin fibre glass strands to transmit data encoded as light pulses.
Field	A field is an item of data within a record.
File	A file can be stored on backing storage. It may contain programs or data. A data file used with a database, is likely to contain a collection of similar and related records.
File librarian	The person responsible for the library of discs and tapes kept by a computer department.
Filename	The name of a file. This should be unique.
File server	A computer attached to a network whose main function is to enable network stations to access files stored on its hard disc.
Flowchart	A graphical representation of the flow of data through a computer or an algorithm.
Font	A set of consistently shaped characters.
Format	Layout.
Front end processor	A small computer used to control communications between a larger mainframe computer and the terminals and other peripherals connected to it
Gigabyte	1 Gigabyte is 1024 Megabytes or 2^{30} bytes.
Graphics	Pictures or symbols which can be processed by a computer. They can be displayed on the screen, saved on disc, imported into DTP software, etc.
Graphics pad	A peripheral which allows the user to transfer drawings to the computer by drawing on paper resting on the graphics pad.
Graph plotter	An output peripheral that produces detailed pictures and diagrams on paper using a pen.
Graphic design package	A software package that allows the user to draw on the screen, providing a range of design tools, different colours and patterns
Graphic User Interface (GUI)	Another name for a WIMP user interface.
Hacker	An unauthorised user of a computer system who has broken into the system either by guessing a user id and the associated password or by bypassing them.
Hard copy	Printout.
Hardware	The physical components of a computer system.
Hash total	A total calculated from a batch of source documents that is used to check that the batch is complete. The total has no meaning in itself.
Help	Instructions showing how to use software, accessible whilst the software is running.
Hexadecimal	The base 16 number system. Allowable digits are 0 to 9 and A to F.
High level language	A problem orientated programming language, e.g. COBOL, BASIC, Pascal, Logo.

Icon	A picture representing a command or function.
Information	Information is data that is meaningful to us.
Information technology (IT)	The use of computer based technology to store, process and transmit information.
Information system (IS)	The organisation of human and other resources, including IT, into a coherent system for the purposeful storage, processing and transmitting of information.
Input	Data supplied to a computer system.
Insert	To put into. 'To insert a record' means to put a new record into a file.
Integer	Positive and negative whole numbers, e.g. 1, -6, 0, 3, 7.
Interrogate	See search.
Inter block gap	A gap left between two data blocks on a magnetic tape.
Inter sector gap	A gap left between two sectors on a magnetic disc.
Interactive processing	Interactive processing takes place when the user and the computer are in two-way communication.
Interface	The interconnection between two different systems.
Interpreter	An interpreter is a program that converts another program written in a high level language to machine code. It converts one line at a time while the program is run. Syntax errors are reported.
Joystick	A lever used to move a pointer or other image around a monitor screen. A joystick is often used with computer games.
Key field	A field in a record used to identify the record. Used when searching for the record or when sorting the file.
Key-to-disc	A method of data preparation where data is entered at a keyboard and saved on disc.
Key-to-tape	A method of data preparation where data is entered at a keyboard and saved on tape
Kilobyte	1024 or 2^{10} bytes.
Kimball tag	A small punched card that identifies a garment and holds details of its size, colour, price, etc.
Laptop	A portable computer that is small enough and light enough to be carried around. They have a fold-up LCD screen. Portable computers can be powered by battery or mains allowing their use in a variety of locations.
Laser printer	A page printer that works by etching a stencil of the page to be printed in an electrostatic drum.
Laser scanner	A hardware device that inputs bar codes by scanning the pattern of light reflected off a bar code by a laser beam.
Liquid Crystal Display (LCD)	The technology used to provide screen displays on calculators and portable computers.
Light pen	A hardware device that inputs bar codes by scanning the pattern of light reflected off a bar code. It is shaped like a pen.
Line printer	A printer that prints one line at a time.
Load	To retrieve from backing storage.
Local Area Network (LAN)	A network with permanent links between all the hardware connected to the network. Probably located in one building.
Logic circuit	A circuit made up of individual logic gates.
Logic gate	A fundamental logic operation, e.g. AND, OR, NOT, etc.
Logo	From the Greek word 'logos' meaning 'word'. A high level language designed to manipulate words and sentences. Logo is an artificial intelligence language.
Low level language	An assembly language.
Machine code	Program instructions in binary code that can be executed by a computer. All programming languages are converted to machine code, before running, by a compiler, interpreter or assembler.

Magnetic Ink Character Recognition (MICR)	A method of input where characters printed in magnetic ink are read directly into a computer.
Mainframe computer	A large, fast computer, probably having a variety of peripherals, including a high capacity backing store and many terminals.
Mail merge	The merging of a data file and a standard letter
Mark sensing	An input method where pencil marks on paper are detected. Their position on the paper determines their meaning.
Master file	A data file which is used to store most of the data for a particular application. It is updated by the transaction file.
Megabyte	1 Megabyte is 1024 Kilobytes or 2^{20} bytes.
Memory	The part of the CPU that is used to store programs while they are running and data while it is being processed.
Memory address	A number used to identify a storage location in memory.
Memory map	A plan of the computer's memory giving the addresses where programs and data are held.
Menu	A list of tasks which can be carried out by a computer progam. The user selects a task from the menu.
Merge	To combine one or more files into a single file.
Microcomputer	A small computer based on a microprocessor. These are usually relatively cheap, slow and have limited backing storage.
Microfilm	An output medium similar to photographic film.
Microprocessor	A single microchip containing all the elements of the CPU, except the IAS.
Mnemonic	Assembly language operation codes are mnemonics, e.g. LDA represents 'load the accumulator'. LDA is a mnemonic.
Model	A representation of real or imagined system. Computer based models can be constructed using a spreadsheet.
Modem	A **MO**dulator/**DEM**odulator. Used to convert digital data output by a computer to analogue signals that can be transmitted along a telephone line and vice versa.
Monitor	A screen used to display the output from a computer.
Mouse	A hand held input peripheral having buttons on top and a ball underneath. When the mouse is moved over a flat surface, a pointer on the screen moves in a corresponding direction.
Multiaccess	When many users are connected to a single computer
Multimedia	The combination of text, sound, pictures, music and video in database type applications. Often based on CD-ROM backing storage technology.
Multiprogramming	When one computer is running more than one program at the same time, this is multiprogramming. It is likely that some of the programs will be under the control of different users from different terminals attached to a mainframe computer.
Multitasking	When one user, on one computer is apparently running more than one program at the same time,
Network	A network is a system of connecting cables. For example, networks can be used to connect computers; the telephone network connects telephone users.
Network station	A terminal connected to a network.
Non-volatile memory	Non-volatile memory does not lose its contents when the power is switched off. ROM memory is non-volatile.
NAND gate	A logic gate that gives the inverse output to an AND gate.
NOR gate	A logic gate that gives the inverse output to an OR gate.
NOT gate	A logic gate that sets the output high if the input is low and vice versa.
Notebook	A smaller version of a Laptop computer. Usually A4 size.
Object code	A machine code program generated by a compiler or an assembler.

Off-line	Not on-line
On-line	Connected to the computer and in communication with it.
Operating system	The operating system is a program that makes the computer hardware more easily accessible to other programs. An operating system is always present when a computer is used.
Operator	An operator looks after the computer while it is running, changing discs, tapes and printer paper as required.
Optical Character Recognition (OCR)	An input method that can read printed characters. Special fonts are often used.
Optical Mark Recognition (OMR)	An input method that reads marks on a document. The position of the mark is interpreted as data.
OR gate	A logic gate that sets the output high if any of the inputs are high.
Page printer	A printer that prints a page at a time, e.g. a laser printer.
Parity	An automatic hardware check that data that has been transferred or stored has not been corrupted. An extra bit is added to make the number of bits set to 1 odd (odd parity) or even (even parity).
Pascal	A high level language named after Blaise Pascal the French mathematician. Pascal is a structured language.
Password	A code that restricts access to a computer system. Usually associated with the User Id.
Personal digital assistant (PDA)	A pocket sized computer that has similar functions to a filofax. They can often read handwriting.
Pen	An input device used in a similar way to an ordinary pen. You press on a touch sensitive screen. It is often used with a GUI interface on a PDA.
Peripheral	A peripheral is a hardware device that is connected to a computer system but is not part of the computer itself, e.g. a printer.
Pixel	The smallest area of a screen that can be used in building up a picture.
Point Of Sale (POS) terminal	A terminal used to collect data at the point of sale. Often incorporates a laser scanner to read bar codes and a dot matrix printer to print receipts. May be on-line to a supermarket's computer system.
Pointer	An arrow or similar symbol which appears on the monitor screen. The position of the pointer is controlled by a mouse.
Port	A socket built into a computer used to link peripherals to it.
Portable	Portable programs can be run on a variety of different computers.
Printout	The output from a printer.
Procedure	A set of instructions that performs a specific task. A procedure is a part of a computer program but it is not a complete program.
Program	A set of instructions used to control the operation a computer.
Programmer	A computer programmer designs, codes, test and documents programs for a computer.
Programming language	A language that allows a computer user to control the computer. For example: Logo, BASIC, Pascal, COBOL.
Pseudocode	A method of representing an algorithm, using words and sentences, in a structure similar to an actual computer program.
Pull-down menu	A feature of a WIMP user interface where a hidden menu can be revealed, i.e. pulled down, by pointing at it.
Query	See search condition.
Random access	See direct access.
Random Access Memory (RAM)	Read/write memory within the Immediate Access Store. RAM is volatile.
Range check	A check that a data value is within realistic limits.

Read Only Memory (ROM)	Memory within the Immediate Access Store that can only be read. ROM is non-volatile.
Real numbers	For practical purposes, real numbers are all the numbers we can use. Mathematicians sometimes use complex or imaginary numbers as well as real numbers.
Real time processing	The processing of input data that takes place so fast that when more data is input the results of the processing are already available. Real time processing occurs in real time, i.e. as it happens.
Record	A record is a collection of related fields.
Relocatable	A relocatable program can be stored in any part of the computer's memory.
Remote access	Access to a computer using a terminal located a long way from the computer.
Robot	An electro-mechanical device that can be programmed to follow a sequence of commands in order to perform a specified task.
Save	To record on backing storage.
Scanner	A peripheral used to input photographs and pictures into a computer.
Scroll	The display on a monitor screen is said to scroll when it moves off the screen at the top and onto the screen at the bottom, automatically, at the same time.
Search	Look for.
Search condition	A search condition is used to determine which records are selected when searching a database.
Sensor	An input device used to sense environmental conditions.
Sequential access	Similar to serial access but the data records are stored in some order.
Serial access	A method of accessing data records. In order to access a data record in a serial access file, it is necessary to start at the beginning of the file and read all the preceding records. The records are not stored in any particular order.
Software	Computer programs and data.
Software package	A complete set of programs and documentation to enable a particular computer program to be used.
Sort	To put into order. Records in a file are often stored in key field order.
Source code	A program written in a high or low level programming language.
Source document	A document or questionnaire used for data capture. It is a written source of the data input to a computer.
Speech recognition	A method of input to a computer by speaking to it.
Speech synthesis	Sounds generated by a computer that synthesise human speech.
Spooling	A method of queueing output directed to a printer before printing it.
Spreadsheet	Spreadsheets are used to calculate and display financial and other numerical information in rows and columns.
Standalone	A computer that is not connected to any other computer is being used in standalone mode.
Stripe card	A plastic card containing a magnetic stripe which stores data. For example, a credit card.
Subroutine	See procedure.
Systems analysis and design	The in-depth analysis of the software and hardware requirements of an information system and its detailed design.
Systems analyst	A systems analyst is responsible for the progress of an information system throughout the system's life cycle.
Systems life cycle	Information systems go through the cycle of systems investigation; feasibility study; systems analysis and design;

	program design; coding; testing and documentation; implementation maintenance; evaluation.
Syntax	The set of rules which define the way an instruction in a programming language can be written.
Tapes	Magnetic tapes are a backing storage medium. Microcomputers use cassette tapes, tape streamers use tape cartridges and mainframes use reel to reel tape.
Technical documentation	Documentation written for technical specialists, e.g. computer programmers. Technical documentation contains the design of the system, program listings, testing schedules, etc.
Teletext	A form of videotext accessible using a specially adapted television set, eg. Oracle broadcast by ITV and Ceefax by the BBC.
Terminal	A hardware device used to communicate with a computer from a remote site.
Time sharing	A method of meeting the demands of a multiaccess system where many programs are required to be run apparently at the same time. Each program is given access to the CPU for a very short period of time (a time slice) in rotation.
Track	A track is the path on a magnetic tape or disc along which data is stored.
Tracker ball	A ball and buttons with the same function as a mouse. Instead of moving a mouse you turn the ball.
Transaction file	A file used to store recent data captured since the last master file update. The transaction file is used to update the master file.
Truth table	A table showing all the possible inputs to a logic gate or circuit and the corresponding outputs.
Turnaround document	A printout which has data written on it and is then used as a source document.
Turtle	A programmable robot with wheels. A turtle is used to learn how to control the movement of mobile robots on a flat surface. It is often controlled using LOGO or a similar programming language.
Update	To bring a file or program up-to-date.
User documentation	Documentation written for users. User documentation should be user friendly.
User friendly	Easy for users to operate and understand.
User Id	The User Identification number that enables a computer system to recognise a user.
Utility	A program that is used to do a task that is useful only in relation to the organisation of a computer system, e.g. a screen dump.
Validation	A check that data is realistic.
Verification	A check that what is written on a source document is accurately transferred to a computer readable medium.
Videotext	A page based information retrieval system, i.e. teletext and viewdata.
Viewdata	A form of videotext that is accessed by using a microcomputer and a modem via the telephone network to connect to a computer that holds the information required, e.g. Campus 2000 run by British Telecom.
Visual Display Unit (VDU)	A keyboard and screen used as a terminal.
Volatile memory	Volatile memory loses its contents when the power is switched off. RAM memory is volatile.
Wide Area Network (WAN)	A network spread over a wide area, possibly international, making use of both permanent cable connections and temporary connections using the telephone network.
Window	A rectangular subdivision of the screen which enables the user to look at the output from a program. There may be

	more than one window on the screen at the same time.
Windows, Icons, Mouse, Pointers (WIMP)	A user interface that avoids the need to remember complex operating system commands by providing menus and icons that represent the commands. To select a command the user points at it and clicks a button on the mouse.
Wordprocessing	The preparation of letters and other documents using a computer in a manner similar to a typewriter but with additional features.
Wordwrap	A feature of a wordprocessor. When you type beyond the right hand margin, the word automatically carries over to the next line.
WORM (Write once read many) discs	A CD-ROM that can have data written to it by the user once only. The data can then be read many times.
WYSIWYG (What You See Is What You Get)	What is displayed on the screen is what will be printed on the printer. This phrase is particularly used in connection with wordprocessors.
XOR gate	A logic gate that outputs a 1 when exactly one input is a 1. XOR stands for 'exclusive OR'.

EXAMINATION QUESTIONS

Q1. The diagram shows a microcomputer system.

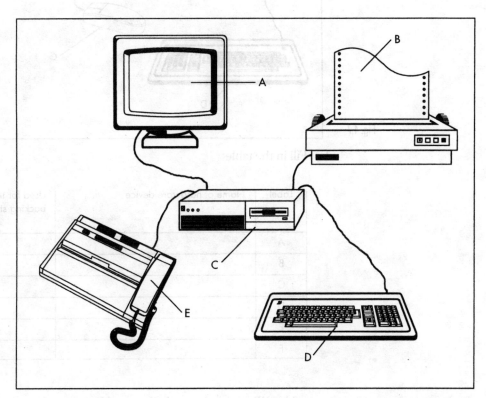

Fig. 4.6

Complete the table below, using words from this list.

Communications   Main Processor   Input   Output   Storage

(A word can be used more than once if necessary)

Label	Description
A	
B	
C	
D	
E	

(SEG, 1993)

Q2.

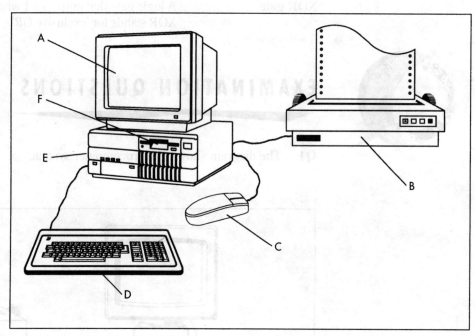

Fig. 4.7

(a) Fill in the table:

Label	Name of hardware device	Used for input, output, backing storage or processing?
A		
B		
C		
D		
E		
F		

(b)   Which hardware device would you use to:

(i)   type a letter

(ii)   draw a picture on the screen

(iii)   save information

(iv)   print a report

(SEG, 1993)

Q3.

MARVELLOUS MAGI-MICRO

Yours for only £300. The new Magi-Micro comes with a

16-bit procesor

processor speed 16MHz

800 X 400 pixel high resolution visual display unit

10 MB hard disk

3.5" floppy disk drive

512K RAM

MS-DOS

A ROM chip containing a boot file

Integrated wordprocessing, spreadsheet, database and graphics
software

and a choice of a quality printer, either an ink jet or daisy wheel printer.

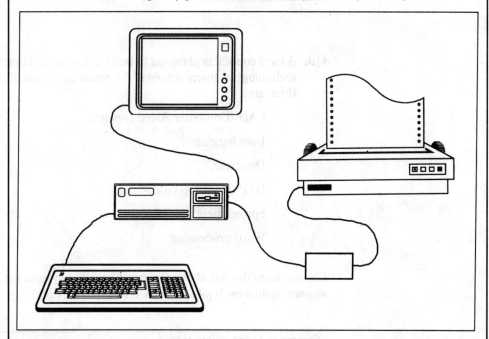

Fig. 4.8

Look at the above advertisement for a microcomputer.

Name the hardware units shown in the Magi-micro.

(City and Guilds 1993)

Q4. (a) Draw and label a diagram of a computer system which will allow you to print
out your work.

(b) Describe TWO things a computer is used for.

(NDTEF, 1993)

Q5. A pelican crossing has input, processing and output. Write the word input,
output or process to describe each of the following:

Bleeper ....

Button ....

Red light ....

(SEG, 19930

Q6. Ring TWO items of software.

OMR form   spreadsheet   weather station   compiler   printed paper   Kimball tag

(MEG, 1993)

Q7. From the list write down *two* items of hardware.

> documentation
> floppy disc
> mouse
> printer
> wordprocessor

(SEG, 1993)

Q8. A letter is stored on a computer disk and needs editing . Show which order you would carry out the following instructions by entering a number between 1 and 4 in each round bracket.

edit and insert corrections   (   )

load the data file   (   )

print a copy   (   )

load and run the software   (   )

(City and Guilds, 1993)

Q9. A local council is planning to build a new road. They will use information technology at many stages of the planning. Some of the systems available to them are:

> CAD (Computer Aided Design)
>
> Data logging
>
> Database
>
> DTP (Desk-top publishing)
>
> Spreadsheet
>
> Word-processing

Choose from the list above the most sensible system for each job below. Write your answer against each job. (Use each item ONCE only).

Counting cars using existing roads	
Making an information booklet	
Analysing a questionnaire	
Designing a bridge	
Estimating the costs	
Writing to contractors	

(SEG, 1993)

Q10. Many supermarkets now use computerised systems to add up sales, produce till receipts and check stock levels.

Not all shops use computerised systems like the one described above. Explain why such a system would be unlikely to be used in a small greengrocer's shop.

(NEAB/WJEC)

ANSWERS TO EXAMINATION QUESTIONS

A1. A – output

B – output

C – main processor

D – input

E – communications

A2. (a)

A	monitor	output
B	printer	output
C	mouse	input
D	keyboard	input
E	processor	processing
F	disc drive	backing storage

(b) (i) keyboard

(ii) mouse

(iii) disc drive

(iv) printer

A3. Monitor (visual display unit), keyboard, printer, processor box (contains hard disc and floppy disc drive).

A4. (a)

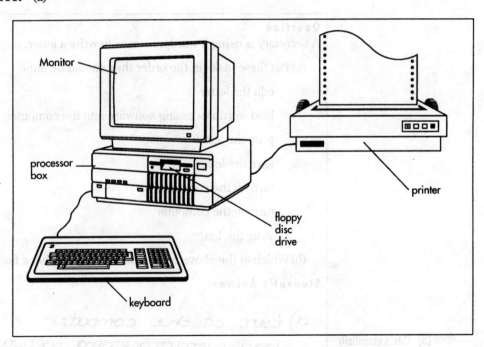

Fig. 4.9

(b) Some examples of things a computer is used for are:

■ store information

■ print information

■ control robots and other devices

■ run a spreadsheet

A5. Bleeper – output

Button – input

Red light – output

A6. Spreadsheet

Compiler

A7. Mouse, printer

A8. Load and run the software

Load the data file

Edit and insert corrections

Print a copy

A9. Data logging

DTP

Database

CAD

Spreadsheet

Wordprocessing

A10. The cost of setting up the system would be too expensive for a small shop. The small volume of data to be processed does not need a computer to process it as it would not take very long to complete using manual methods.

A STUDENT'S ANSWER WITH EXAMINER'S COMMENTS

Question

A secretary is using a wordprocessor to write a letter.

(a) Put these tasks in the order they should be done

edit the letter

load wordprocessing software into the computer

print the letter

save the letter

turn off the computer

turn on the computer

write the letter

(b) Which of the above tasks would be done using a floppy disc or a hard disc?

Student's Answer

a) turn on the computer
load word processing software
into the computer.
edit the letter
save the letter
print the letter
write the letter
turn off the computer

b) save the letter

❝❝ (a) This is essentially correct, however, the student has placed 'write the letter' after 'print the letter'. It should appear before 'edit the letter'.

(b) This is correct but not complete: 'load wordprocessing software into the computer' should also be included. ❞❞

REVIEW SHEET

Review sheets are provided at the end of most chapters to reinforce the principles studied, and will help you to test yourself. After completion, detach them from the book and add them to your revision file. They provide a useful overview of these topics, and will help with revision nearer to the exam.

1. The use of a computer and other equipment to store, process and transmit information is called _____

2. The organisation of human and other resources, including IT, into a coherent system for the purposeful storage, processing and transmissions of information is an

   _____

3. What is hardware?_____

   _____

   _____

4. What is software?_____

   _____

   _____

   _____

   _____

5. Write down the names of three input peripherals.

   (a) _____ (b) _____

   (c) _____

6. Write down the names of three output peripherals.

   (a) _____ (b) _____

   (c) _____

7. Which of the following are backing storage?
   CD-ROM
   floppy disc
   hard disc
   keyboard
   monitor
   tracker ball

8. What is RAM used for? _____

   _____

   _____

   _____

9. Why do you need to save files on backing storage?_____

   _____

   _____

   _____

   _____

10. Use these words to complete the sentences.
    analogue
    digital
    analogue to digital convertor.

    Computers are_____. Sensors are_____. When a computer reads a sensor it has to use an_____ to convert the signal from the sensor into a form it can understand.

11. State whether the following are true or false.

    a. A floppy disc is a piece of software.

    b. You can write a computer program using Logo.

    c. The operating system is always present when a computer is being used.

    d. The eight bit binary number 00000011 is the same as the denary number 3.

    e. The hexadecimal number A is the same as the denary number 11.

12. Write down the ASCII for the character W_____

13. Write down the character that is represented by the binary code 100 0111 in ASCII.

    _____

14. Using the glossary, write down the meaning of:

    analogue_____

    byte_____

    control character_____

    disc_____

    digital_____

    megabyte_____

    stripe card_____

    volatile memory_____

DATA CAPTURE AND INPUT

QUESTIONNAIRES

VERIFICATION

MARK SENSING AND OCR

BAR CODES

KIMBALL TAGS

MAGNETIC INK CHARACTER RECOGNITION

MAGNETIC STRIP CARDS

VOICE RECOGNITION

SOUND SAMPLING AND MUSIC

JOYSTICKS

MOUSE

TRACKER BALL

GRAPHICS PAD

PENS

SCANNERS

VIDEO DIGITISERS

SENSORS

VALIDATION

GARBAGE IN, GARBAGE OUT

GETTING STARTED

Data Capture is collecting data and its input to a computer. We try to make sure that the data we collect is accurate and that it is input to the computer without mistakes. There are various methods of doing this. Different methods of data capture are related to the different *peripheral devices*, i.e. hardware, used to input the data to the computer.

There are *two* very important concepts that should be thoroughly learnt in connection with the careful monitoring of data capture and input. These are verification and validation.

Verification ensures that data is recorded accurately.

Validation is a check that the data is realistic.

ESSENTIAL PRINCIPLES

Data capture is the collection of data and its input to a computer. There are a wide variety of different methods. Some of these are described in this chapter.

1 ▷ QUESTIONNAIRES AND OTHER FORMS

Getting people to fill in a questionnaire or form is one way of collecting data. An example of a form that might be filled in when reading an electricity meter is shown in Fig. 5.1.

ELECTRICITY BOARD

Account Number	B 025741X	
Customer	MR J.B. Priestley	
Address	5 Mill Bank Drive	
	Hexham	
	HX2 4PD	
Previous Meter Reading	5 7 2 1 4	
New Meter Reading		

Instructions

1. Fill in the New Meter Reading.
2. Check that it is BIGGER than the previous Meter Reading.
3. If any details have changed, fill in the new details in the boxes on the right hand side.

Fig. 5.1 A data capture form used to read an electricity meter

When designing a questionnaire or form we:

66 Useful steps in constructing a questionnaire 99

a) Use simple language so people can easily understand;
b) Say clearly and unambiguously what is needed;
c) Give examples if these would be helpful;
d) Provide enough space for the answer;
e) Provide help in answering if possible;
f) Collect all the information that is needed, but no more;
g) Avoid asking questions that may not be answered truthfully;
h) Record information in a way which will help computer input.

A questionnaire or form used for data capture is known as a **source document**. The data on a source document must be transferred to a computer-readable medium *before* it can be input to a computer. This can be done in several ways, for example:

a) Using 'key-to-disc' – the data is entered at the keyboard and saved on a magnetic disc.
b) Using 'key-to-tape' – the data is entered at the keyboard and saved on a magnetic tape.

2 ▷ VERIFICATION

In order to be sure that the data has been accurately transferred from the source document to the computer-readable medium, the data is '**verified**'.

To verify data we use the 'double-entry' method:

66 The double entry method 99

a) Transfer the data to the computer-readable medium.
b) Transfer the data to the computer-readable medium again.
c) Compare the results of a) and b). If these are the same then we have transferred the data accurately. If they are not the same then we have made a mistake and must correct it.

Data Collection

↓

Source
Document

↓

Enter data

← Errors

↓

Verify data

↓

Data
input to
computer

Fig. 5.2 Verification

This process is illustrated in Fig. 5.2.

The purpose of verification is make sure that what is written on the source document is accurately transferred to the computer-readable medium.

The process of transferring the data from the source document to a computer-readable medium using a keyboard, is expensive. It is necessary to employ many people and to buy expensive equipment. For this reason, methods of data capture and input have been developed that *avoid* the need to key and verify data. Some of these are described below.

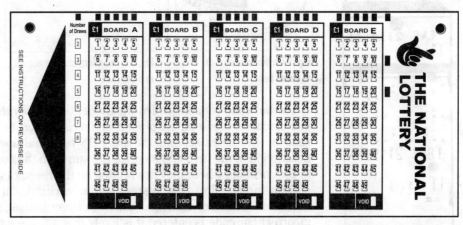

Fig 5.3 A Mark Sensing form
© Camelot Group Plc

---

3 › MARK SENSING AND OPTICAL CHARACTER RECOGNITION (OCR)

Mark Sensing and OCR *avoid* the need to key-in and verify data

In **Mark Sensing**, marks are made on a specially designed form or questionnaire using a pencil (see Fig. 5.3). The position of the mark on the form or questionnaire gives it meaning. By shining a light onto the paper and recording the intensity of the reflected light returned to it, a *mark sense reader* attached to the computer reads the data directly into the memory of the computer. This avoids the need to key-in the data. There is no verification of the input data. Mark Sensing is often used for multiple choice exam papers and to make it easier for Sales and Delivery employees to record the sale or delivery of goods.

For **Optical Character Recognition (OCR)** written or printed text is read using a special reader, or scanner, that works in a similar way to a mark sense reader. In OCR it is not the position of the marks on the paper that gives them meaning but the *shape* of the different characters and numbers. OCR can be used to read the pages of a book or a typed A4 sheet directly into the computer. The text input can be wordprocessed. This enables libraries to transfer their books to the computer and offices to store letters on a magnetic disc.

4 › BAR CODES AND LIGHT PENS OR LASER SCANNERS

Bar Codes and **Light Pens** or **Laser Scanners** are most often found in use in supermarket information systems. The light pen or laser scanner is used to *read* the bar code. The bar code is used to *identify* a specific item, e.g. an 850 gram can of baked beans. For an example of a typical bar code see Fig. 5.4. When shopping is taken to the checkout the cashier passes the items over a scanner which will read the bar code. A bar code is printed on most of the items stocked. If there is no bar code on the item then the price is entered on a cash register in the usual way. The cash register and scanner used are connected to a central computer and are known as a Point of Sale terminal (**POS terminal**).

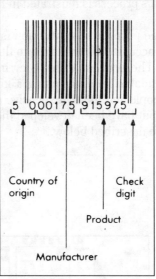

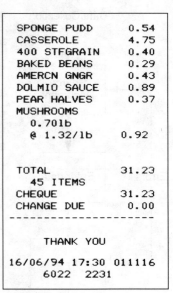

Country of origin

Check digit

Product

Manufacturer

Fig. 5.4 A bar code on a can of baked beans

Fig. 5.5 The information contained in a bar code

Fig 5.6 Receipt printed at a POS terminal

The bar code contains codes which identify the *country of origin*, the *company* which manufactured the item, the *product* and a *check digit* (see Fig. 5.5). This information is read by the laser scanner at the POS terminal and sent to the computer. The description of the item and its price are stored in the computer and instantly sent back to the checkout where they are printed on the receipt (see Fig. 5.6).

Data input using this system is not verified. The likelihood of entering the occasional wrong or damaged bar code is very small, so this is not a problem. If an incorrect bar code is entered it is likely that a *validation check* (see below), using the check digit or matching the input bar codes against a list of valid bar codes, will highlight such errors.

This information system also provides detailed information on what has been sold, which is useful to the supermarket for stock-keeping and re-ordering. Staff operating the checkout need less training, can work faster and can be paid less as the job is made easier. Fewer staff are also needed at the checkout. The customer is provided with more detailed information on purchases made. Unfortunately it is likely that the goods will not have individual price labels; this will make shopping more difficult as price comparisons cannot be made in different parts of the store.

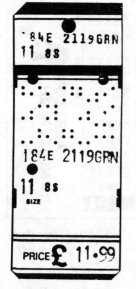

Fig. 5.7 A Kimball tag

5 ▷ KIMBALL TAGS

Kimball tags are small punched cards (see Fig. 5.7). They are most commonly found in clothes shops. They usually have printed on them information that identifies the garment they are attached to, e.g. description, size, colour, price and other details. This data is also recorded on the Kimball tag by means of punched holes in a special code. When a garment is sold, the Kimball tag is retained by the shop. The data on the Kimball tag can be input directly to the computer using a *Kimball Tag Reader* attached to the POS terminal. Otherwise, the tags can be collected and posted to the central computer installation for processing at a later date. Kimball tags have essentially the same function as bar codes, but they can hold more data. As with bar codes, the data input cannot be verified. Since Kimball tags can be torn easily this could also be a problem. However, they are helpful in keeping accurate stock records.

6 ▷ MAGNETIC INK CHARACTER RECOGNITION

Magnetic Ink Character Recognition (MICR) is most commonly used with bank cheques (see Fig. 5.8). MICR is only possible with a very restricted font. The font in use in the UK, has only 14 possible characters, including the digits 0 to 9. Numbers are printed in magnetic ink along the bottom of the cheque. These numbers are codes which identify the bank, the customer's account and the cheque. They can be read directly into the computer. When paying for goods in a shop, the customer fills in a cheque in payment for the goods bought. When the cheque is filled in the amount is written on the cheque by the customer. The customer gives the cheque to the shopkeeper who deposits the cheque at the bank. The MICR reader at the bank cannot read the amount written by the customer in normal ink. This must be typed onto the cheque in *magnetic ink* before it can be processed. The MICR reader will read the information on the cheque directly into the computer.

Cheques can be quite badly damaged before it is necessary to enter the data in some other way. There is no verification of input data. However, data can be fast – up to 2000 cheques per minute are possible. When the cheque is processed, money will be transferred from the customer's account to the shopkeeper's account.

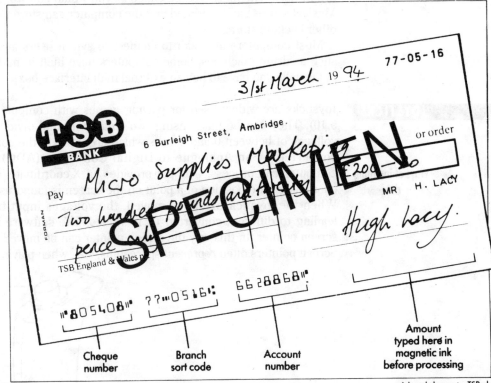

Fig. 5.8 MICR used on a bank cheque

| Cheque number | Branch sort code | Account number | Amount typed here in magnetic ink before processing |

Acknowledgements: TSB plc

7 ▶ MAGNETIC STRIPE

A **magnetic stripe** is a short length of magnetic tape sealed into the surface of a plastic card (see Fig. 5.9). Plastic cards containing magnetic stripes are used by banks and credit card companies to make sure that the owner is credit-worthy. These magnetic stripes carry enough information to allow a computer to identify the owner so that their credit limit can be checked.

Plastic cards are also used as phone cards. Some telephones accept phone cards instead of cash. The number of units unused is recorded on the card. When the user makes a telephone call the units used are deducted from those left on the card and the new total recorded on the card.

Fig. 5.9 A magnetic stripe card

8 ▶ VOICE RECOGNITION

Using a microphone as input device, computers can be programmed to recognise a limited range of spoken input. This is **voice recognition**. At present, the method is unreliable, although its long-term potential is promising. It would be a useful method of input for workers whose hands are occupied, or for disabled people with little hand movement.

9 ▷ SOUND SAMPLING AND MUSIC

Natural sound can be input and recorded in digital form on a magnetic disc. The sound can be processed. It may be used as part of a musical composition or in sounds for video games.

Music itself can be input, processed and re-played using a computer connected to a synthesiser. The music can be edited as you would edit words using a wordprocessor. Musical scores can be printed and the computer can store the music on floppy disc or other backing storage.

Most computers use midi to connect to synthesisers and other midi-instruments, such as drum machines. Some computers have built in midi-ports, e.g. the Atari ST, but usually you have to buy an external midi interface box.

10 ▷ JOYSTICKS

Ways of inputting data

Joysticks are widely used for playing games with computers in the home (see Fig. 5.10). They can be made using two small potential dividers (*pots*). These provide voltages of between 0 and 5 volts which are input to the computer. The voltages are converted by an Analogue to Digital Converter (ADC) to numbers which the computer can process. One pot provides an X-coordinate, the other provides the Y coordinate. The position of a point on the screen is found using its (X,Y) coordinates. When the joystick handle is moved, the voltages input to the computer change, leading to different converted (X,Y) values. The software responds by moving the screen pointer. In this way the screen pointer can be moved to any part of the screen. Screen pointers often represent spaceships, etc., when playing a computer game.

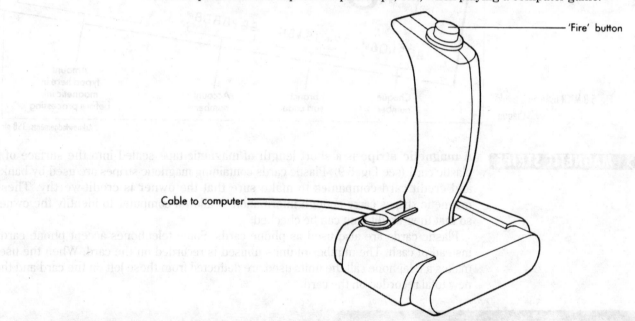

'Fire' button

Cable to computer

Fig. 5.10 A joystick

11 ▷ MOUSE

A **mouse** is now very common with microcomputers (see Fig. 5.11).

A mouse is a small hand-held input device with a ball fitted underneath. When the mouse is moved, the signal created by the movement of the ball is transmitted to the computer. This controls a pointer on the screen which moves in a direction corresponding to the direction of the mouse.

There are usually 2 or 3 buttons on the mouse.

Pull-down menus are accessed by pointing at them with the mouse. They consist of lists of features which can be *selected* by *pointing* at them *and clicking* a button on the mouse.

Icons are pictures that suggest the feature they represent, e.g. a picture of a floppy disc may give the user the possibility of saving or loading files to/from a disc. The user can select the icon by pointing at it and clicking a button on the mouse.

The mouse has proved to be such a useful, easy-to-use and versatile input device that most computers are now sold with one. In these cases it is often difficult to use the computer *without* a mouse. Instead of entering commands to the computer using text command lines, there is a WIMP user screen (see Fig. 5.12) that allows the user easy access to the facilities of the computer using a mouse. **WIMP** stands for 'Windows, Icons, Menus, Pointers'. WIMP user screens are also known as Graphic User Interfaces (GUIs).

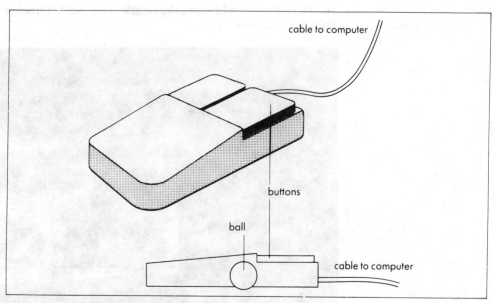

Fig. 5.11 A mouse

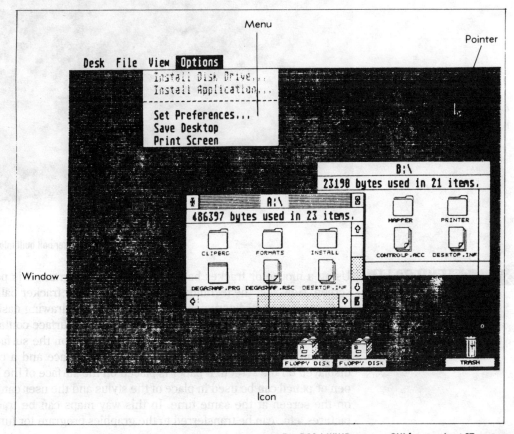

Fig. 5.12 A WIMP screen or GUI from an Atari ST computer

12> TRACKER BALL

A tracker ball (see Fig 5.13) works in a similar way to a mouse. There is a ball built into the underside of a mouse. When you move the mouse, this moves the ball and the pointer on the screen moves the same way. On a tracker ball the ball is built into the top of the device and it is exposed. You move the ball not the device. There are buttons next to the exposed ball that have the same function as mouse buttons.

You can use the tracker ball to access pull-down menus and select icons as you would with a mouse. You move the pointer on the screen by moving the ball and select a menu option or icon by clicking the buttons.

Tracker balls are commonly used with portable computers. When you are using a portable computer, you may have it balanced on your knees as you sit on the train or in your car. In these circumstances, it is difficult to use a mouse as there may not be a suitable flat surface to move the mouse on. A built-in tracker ball is ideal for use with a portable computer.

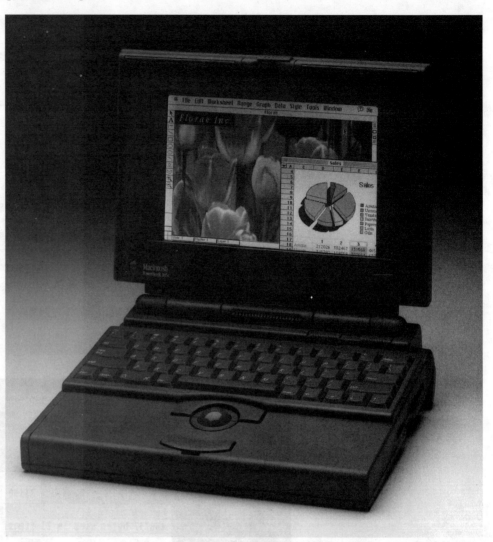

Fig. 5.13 A tracker ball built into an Apple Powerbook computer

13⟩ GRAPHIC PADS

Using a mouse or tracker ball and a graphics program, it is possible to draw on the screen. However, the technique of using a mouse or tracker ball is quite different from drawing with an ordinary pencil. In order to make drawing easier and more natural, a **graphics pad** can be used. This consists of a flat surface containing a touch-sensitive membrane (see Fig. 5.14). When the user presses on the surface using a rigid stylus, the membrane registers the pressure on the surface and a corresponding mark is displayed on the screen. If paper is placed on the surface of the graphics pad, a normal pen or pencil can be used in place of the stylus and the user can draw on the paper and on the screen at the same time. In this way maps can be traced and diagrams and pictures, etc., can be transferred to the graphics program for further enhancement.

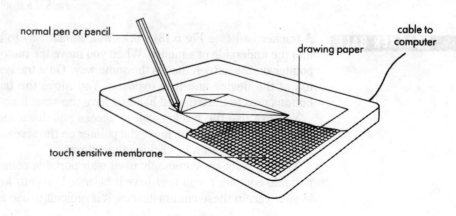

Fig. 5.14 A graphics pad

14> PENS

A Pen is used with a 'Palmtop' computer or Personal Digital Assistant (PDA), see Fig. 5.15. PDAs are very small computers about the size of a filofax. They are effectively computerised filofaxes but are much more powerful. They can hold a wide range of information and access it very quickly. They can recognise handwriting and change it to text. They can also be used to operate a WIMP User Interface or GUI. Instead of moving a mouse to control the pointer on the screen, you touch the screen with the pen in the place you are pointing at. There are no buttons on the pen but there is an icon on the screen that is used to select menu options and other icons. You can use the pen to access pull-down menus and select icons as you would with a mouse.

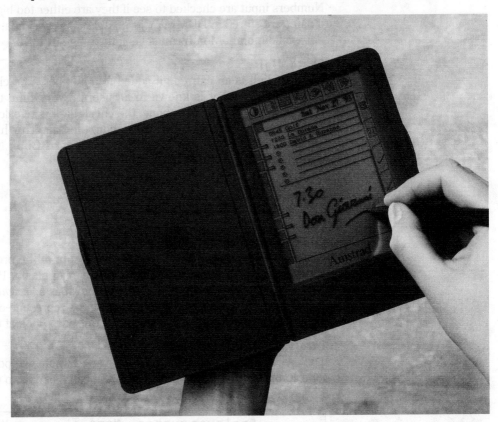

Fig 5.15 An Amstrad Pen Pad PDA

15> SCANNERS

Scanners are used to digitise printed text, diagrams and photographs into the memory of the computer. They can be hand-held but are more usually about the size of a desk-top photocopier. Some scanners will scan, print and act as photocopier! Using the associated software, a digitised representation of the scanned image can be saved onto disc. This can then be loaded into a graphics program or Desk Top Publishing (DTP) program where it can be enhanced and printed as part of a magazine or booklet.

16> VIDEO DIGITISERS

Video digitisers convert a video signal into a digitised representation in the memory of the computer. They consist of hardware to intercept the video signal and specialised software. Each frame in the video signal is digitised. At the press of a button, or in response to a pre-programmed sequence, the digitised image is saved onto disc. This can be done for a single frame, or a series of frames. Saving the digitised image of a video frame on disc is known as 'frame grabbing'. Using a video digitiser it is possible to capture a single frame from a video and print it as a picture in a magazine. A series of frames can have graphics or cartoons added using a graphics program. This technique is used to make TV adverts, Pop-video sequences, etc.

17> SENSORS

Sensors are often attached to micros. There are many types of sensors and they have a wide variety of uses. They can be used to record temperature, humidity, light intensity, etc. A combination of sensors could be used to control a greenhouse, keeping the conditions suitable for optimum plant growth. Sensors usually produce a voltage which must be converted to a digital signal using an Analogue to Digital Converter (ADC). The digital signal is interpreted as a binary number which can be used by the software to monitor or display a graph of the 'sensed' condition.

18〉 VALIDATION

66 *Common validation checks* 99

All data entered into a computer for processing is validated if at all possible. **Validation** is a check to make sure that **all** the data to be processed is realistic. Some common validation checks are described below:

Table lookup

The input data, for example a bar code, is checked against a table of *all* the bar codes that are used. If it is not in the table, then it is not acceptable.

Range Check

Numbers input are checked to see if they are either too big or too small. For example, if dates are stored in DDMMYY form, 021293 is a valid date, but 213492 is not, as 34 is not a valid month. Months must lie in the range 01 to 12.

Check digit

A check digit is an extra digit added to a number. The check digit is calculated in a prescribed way that is known to all users. Every time the number is transcribed, possibly read over the telephone, the check digit is re-calculated. If the correct check digit is *not* obtained from the calculation, then an error has been made and the data must be re-checked. The **International Standard Book Number (ISBN)** contains a check digit in the rightmost position.

ISBN	0	631	90057	8
Weight	10	987	65432	1

The check digit has a value that makes the sum of the products of the digits and the weights exactly divisible by 11. In the above example $0 \times 10 + 6 \times 9 + 3 \times 8 + 1 \times 7 + ...$ $+ 8 \times 1$ is exactly divisible by 11. This is known as a '*weighted modulus* 11' check digit. It can take the values 0 to 9 and 10 (which is represented by an X). You will find an ISBN on every published book including this one – look at the back cover!

Totals

The use of totals is best explained using an example. Suppose we are doing the payroll for a company. We may have the following batch of data to process:

Employee number	Name	Hours worked
34532	Jones	34
55234	Patel	37
89686	Singh	29
45378	Hardcastle	27
76859	Stratton	40
301689		167

In the example the employee numbers and the hours worked have been totalled. The total hours worked is a meaningful total. It is the total length of time worked by all these workers. This is known as a **control total**. The total of the employee numbers is meaningless. This is called a **hash total**. However, provided the details for this group of workers is kept together in a batch, neither of these totals will change. If the totals are re-calculated and they are *not* the same, then the details for some of the workers are either missing or have been changed. This example uses only a few workers to illustrate the use of totals. In large companies with many workers, totals help keep track of all their details.

19〉 GARBAGE IN, GARBAGE OUT

It is most important to be certain that the data input for processing is correct. When data is captured on a source document, it must be verified to ensure that what is written on the source document is accurately transferred to a computer-readable medium. When data is input for processing, it should be carefully validated to make sure that it is realistic. If incorrect data is input, then the result of any data processing may be wrong . . . **GARBAGE IN, GARBAGE OUT**.

EXAMINATION QUESTIONS

Q1 Ring TWO items that can be used to collect data for pupil records.

mouse   keyboard   line printer
optical mark reader   screen   ROM

(MEG, 1993)

Q2. Give two ways in which typewritten text can be input to a computer.

(City and Guilds, 1993)

Q3. Name the three items that are printed in magnetic ink on a cheque.

(City and Guilds, 1993)

Q4. A gas board issues its meter readers with a document for each meter to be read.

REF. NO:	DATE:
NAME:	MAX: MIN:
ADDRESS:	READING: ☐☐☐☐☐ CODE: ☐ Insert N if no reading available Insert R if reading outside range

Items in certain fields will be printed by the computer before the document is issued to the meter reader.
(a) Identify three items that will be printed before issue to the meter reader.

(b) Identify two items that might be filled in by the meter reader.

(SEG, 1993)

Q5. Many small railway stations now have automatic machines to issue tickets.
(a) Tick ONE change in everyday life caused by this:

Fewer staff are needed in the booking office	
Tickets are more expensive	
Trains run to time more often	

(b) Tick ONE way data is held on the ticket so it can be read by automatic ticket barriers.

Bar codes	
Magnetic stripes	
Raised carriers	

(SEG, 1993)

Q6. The traffic light system of a large town is to be computerised. The lights at many junctions are to be controlled by a single central computer.

(a) Give two types of input that would be required for the system.

(b) Give two benefits that introducing the system would have.

(SEG, 1993)

Q7. One type of error that could be made when data is typed into a computer system is a transcription error.

(a) A transcription error can be detected by a verification check. Explain how this check is carried out.

(b) A date can be validated as well as verified. A date is to be input in the form 25 APR 1994 (a two digit day, followed by a three letter month, followed by a four digit year). Describe the validation checks that could be carried out on dates in this form.

(SEG, 1993)

Q8. The Office Junior has sent off the following invoice which she produced on the Accounts Package.

Fieldsend Garden Produce	Invoice 234567
Fieldsend Farm, Hanglenth,	
Lincoln LN2 4RT	
Dated: 27 May 1994	Terms: Nett Monthly
John Smith Fruit Wholesalers	
345 Meadow Drive	
Derby DE9 6TG	
GOODS SUPPLIED	
22 boxes strawberries @ £10 each £220.00	

(a) What will be the result of this mistake for the buyer of the strawberries?

(b) What steps could have been taken to make sure that mistakes of this type do not occur?

(RSA, 1993)

Q9. (a) What method of data capture would be most suitable for recording the information in each of the following situations? In each case tick the most suitable method.

Situation	Most suitable method of data capture			
A book has been returned to a library after a loan	Bar-Codes	OMR	Magnetic Strip	OCR
The answers given by pupils in multiple choice exam questions	Bar-Codes	OMR	Magnetic Strip	OCR
Reading account numbers when customer pays gas bill	Bar-Codes	OMR	Magnetic Strip	OCR

(b) Give one other situation where a different method of data capture is used other than those listed above. Explain how the data is captured and why this method is the most suitable.

(c) A point of sale system in a supermarket includes a scanner attached to each till to read bar codes.

The bar code on a tin of peas contains the item code and a check digit.

(i) Why does it not contain the price?

(ii) What is the purpose of the check digit?

(iii) The till receipt contains the name of the item and its price. How is this information obtained?

(iv) What name is given to the mode of operation used to produce the receipt?

(NEAB/WJEC, 1993)

Q10. QUESTION DATA

A computer company called Soft Options has just bought a list from Zamco which details names and addresses of companies in the Somerset area. Soft Options wants to identify a list of companies which:

- have more than 500 employees
- use the Wordprocessing software WORD or WORDPERFECT
- have a budget of £5000

Soft Options will target these companies in a sales promotion.

Design a questionnaire to collect the information for Soft Options.

(City and Guilds, 1993)

ANSWERS TO EXAMINATION QUESTIONS

A1. OMR reader
Keyboard

(MEG, 1993)

A2. You can type it in using a keyboard
You can scan it using OCR software.

A3. The sort code, the account number and the cheque number are printed on a cheque before it is filled in. The amount is printed on the cheque after it has been filled in.

A4. (a)

Ref. No.	Max.
Name	Min.
Address	

(b) Date
Reading
Code

A5. (a) Fewer staff are needed in the booking office
(b) Magnetic stripes

A6. (a) Road sensors.

Push buttons for pedestrians.

These tell the IS how many cars are using the system and where the cars are. Pedestrians wanting to cross the road can be fitted in with traffic flows.

(b) Some benefits are:
- The speed of the traffic can be controlled.
- The distribution of traffic can be monitored and controlled so that hold-ups are avoided or minimised.

A7. (a) A verification check consists of:

Step 1: 2 different people enter the data.

Step 2: The computer cross-checks the data entered by one person against the data entered by the other person.

Step 3: Differences are identified and checked against the original data. The data in the computer is edited until the cross-check identifies no differences.

(b) The two-digit day should be:
- two digits, e.g. 01 not 1.
- larger than 00
- no more than 28, 29, 30 or 31 depending on the month

The three letter month should be:
- exactly 3 letters, e.g. APR not AP or APRIL.
- one of JAN, FEB, . . . , NOV, DEC.

The four digit year should be within a realistic range depending on the application.

A8. (a) They will be alarmed at this over charging.

(b) All invoices over a set amount could be checked by a senior employee.

A9. (a) Library – bar codes

Multiple choice exam – OMR

Gas bill – OCR

(b) Situation: Processing Bank Cheques.

Method of data capture: MICR.

Suitable because: Cheques can be read more quickly and accurately. It is relatively difficult to alter the data on the cheque.

(c) (i) The price is not in the bar code because the price changes. The bar code identifies the product and the price is obtained from the computer. The price held on the computer can easily be changed.

(ii) To enable the computer to check that it has read the bar code accurately.

(iii) The bar code identifies the item. The name and price of the item are stored on the computer with the bar code. The computer uses the bar code to find the name and price. It then prints them on the receipt.

(iv) The computer system is 'on-line' and 'interactive'.

A10. The questionnaire should collect this information:
- the company's name and address
- the number of employees
- the wordprocessor used
- the annual budget

There should be instructions on how to fill in the form and boxes to fill in. The budget could be grouped into 5 or 6 ranges, e.g. £5,000–£6000, and tick boxes provided.

There should be an explanation of why the data is being collected and the person filling in the form should sign and date it.

STUDENT'S ANSWERS WITH EXAMINER'S COMMENTS

Question data

A newspaper uses a computer to store details of its photographic library. Each photograph has information stored under the following headings; Description, Subject, Date, Negative Number, Photographer, Filmtype.

The dates are read into the computer in the following format:
DDMMMYY e.g. 15DEC92

(a) Each of the following dates has been rejected by a validation program. State which validation check has been used to discover each error.

AUG2166 *the month is in the wrong place*

3JAN71 *too short*

31SEP62 *there are only 30 days in September*

(b) Produce a comprehensive list of test data to test the date on this program.

13Feb91

19Dec92

12Jan84

(City and Guilds, 1993)

Examiner's comments

(a) These answers are correct but do not show that the student knows which errors a computer can detect. Better answers would be:

AUG2166 — the two leftmost characters should be digits.

3JAN71 — each date should be 7 characters in length.

31SEP62 — the two leftmost digits are out of range. In this case they should be between 01 and 30, inclusive.

(b) Part (b) is poorly answered. to construct useful test data you need to have a clear idea of the validation checks you are testing. Generally speaking you should test extreme values and one or two acceptable values for each validation check.
For example, if you were testing a validation check to ensure the date had the correct length, you could use this test data:

30SEP6 — an extreme value, just too short

30SEP62 — an acceptable value

05JAN93 — an acceptable value

15FEB955 — an extreme value, just too long

Other validation checks that should be tested would check that:

- the two leftmost characters are numbers
- the middle three characters are alphabetic
- the two rightmost characters are numbers
- the day is within range for the month
- the month is one of JAN, FEB, ... DEC
- the year is within a sensible range for the application

Clearly, a complete answer is quite extensive. In the exams, your answer may not be complete but should show that you understand validation checks and how to construct the data to test them.

REVIEW SHEET

1. Design a form to be filled in by pupils so that their school will have all the information it needs about them. The information on the form will be input to a computer.

2. Which of these items of information are stored in a bar code?

   ■ check digit _____
   ■ country of origin _____
   ■ manufacturer's code _____
   ■ name of the product _____
   ■ price _____
   ■ product code _____
   ■ sell by date _____

3. When a customer pays for goods by cheque in a shop:

   ■ What items of information are stored on the blank cheque?
   _____
   _____

   ■ What items of information are written on the cheque?
   _____
   _____

   ■ What item of information is typed on the cheque by the bank after the shopkeeper has paid it into the shop's bank account?_____
   _____

4. Which of these are likely to be magnetic stripe cards?

   ■ bus pass _____
   ■ credit card _____
   ■ library card _____
   ■ theatre ticket _____

5. Describe a situation where it would be helpful if a computer could understand you when you spoke to it and it replied by speaking back to you in the same language.
   _____
   _____

6. Describe how you would use a joystick when you play a game on a computer.

_____

_____

_____

7. Draw a diagram of a GUI you have used and label these features.

  ■ icon   ■ menu   ■ pointer   ■ window

8. Describe how you would use a mouse to operate a GUI. _____

_____

_____

9. A tracker ball could be described as an 'upside down mouse'. Is this description accurate? Explain your answer._____

_____

_____

10. If a Palmtop computer is to be used as a computerised filofax, which of this software would it need to have?

  ■ communications software   _____
  ■ database   _____
  ■ Desk Top Publishing graphics _____
  ■ spreadsheet   _____
  ■ wordprocessor   _____

11. Complete these sentences:

(a) A_____ can be used to measure the temperature in a greenhouse.

(b) To convert a photograph into a form that could be used by a computer you would use a_____

12. Code the date, the 19th of December 1993 in YYMMDD form.

_____

13. Which of these is a valid date coded in YYMMDD form?

  012393   _____
  891213   _____
  1994 May 16th _____
  19910516   _____
  921329   _____

THE MEMORY FILES & BACKING STORAGE

THE MEMORY

FILES

BACKING STORAGE

SECURITY

GETTING STARTED

Programs and data are stored in the computer's memory while the programs are edited or run and the data is processed. The memory is made up of both RAM, which is **volatile**, and ROM which is non-volatile. Programs and data may be stored in **files**, which are identified by their **filename**. Files are **saved** on backing storage and may be loaded into the memory. A data file may be divided into **records**, each containing several related **fields**. The fields are in the same order in records of the same type. Fields may be **fixed length** or **variable length**. Sometimes a record will contain a **key field** which identifies the record.

If a record can only be found by accessing *all* the preceding records and if the records are in no particular order then the file is a **serial access file**. If the records are also **sorted** into an order, possibly on the keyfield, then the file is a **sequential access file**. In a **random access file** it is possible to read or write a particular record without accessing other records beforehand.

A file is **created** and **saved** on backing storage using the **filename** to identify it. The file may be **merged** with other files to make one file. To bring the data on the file up-to-date, we **update** or **amend** the file. When the file is no longer needed it can be **deleted** by removing it from backing storage. A list of all the files on a particular disc or tape is called a **directory** or **catalogue**.

A **Database Management System (DBMS)** is software and data files organised to allow easy interrogation of the data by **searching** for records, having first defined a **search condition**.

Backing storage is non-volatile, long-term storage, usually on magnetic disc, magnetic tape or CD-ROM. Magnetic discs range from floppy discs for use with most microcomputers to hard discs that are used on more powerful microcomputers and mainframe computers. Magnetic tape cassettes are sometimes used with small microcomputers; cartridges are used with tape streamers for file backup; reel to reel magnetic tapes are used with mainframe computers. CD-ROM is used to store high volumes of on-line data and for multimedia applications.

The data held on computer systems must be kept **secure**. The loss of data is prevented by taking a regular **backup** of all data files. Unauthorised users are excluded by giving each user a **user identification number** and a **password**. In addition, **physical security** is ensured by employing security guards, etc.

ESSENTIAL PRINCIPLES

1 > THE MEMORY

Programs and data are stored in the main memory of the computer, while the programs are edited or run (executed) and the data is processed.

RANDOM ACCESS MEMORY (RAM)

In a microcomputer the main memory is **Random Access Memory** (RAM). RAM can be *written to* and *read from*. This memory is **volatile**, which means that the programs and data stored in it will be lost when the computer is switched off.

READ ONLY MEMORY (ROM)

Microcomputers frequently contain **Read Only Memory** (ROM). ROM, as its name suggests, can *only* be read. It is non-volatile and so retains its contents when the computer is switched off. ROM is usually used in microcomputers for programs which it is convenient to have available at any time, in particular when the computer has just been switched on. In many microcomputers the Operating System is in ROM. When the computer is switched on, the Operating System in ROM runs immediately. In order to change the Operating System, the actual ROM chip must be removed and another inserted. To do this the computer must be dismantled. This is usually the case for those microcomputers with a small amount of RAM memory. Where larger amounts of RAM are available it is usual to load the Operating System from disc into RAM before using other software. This allows the user to run different Operating Systems if required.

❝ Uses of RAM and ROM ❞

Unfortunately, the contents of ROM cannot be altered, so it is unsuitable for data that must be changed.

BATTERY BACKED RAM

Some microcomputers save the date and time on **Battery Backed RAM**. This is a small amount of RAM memory powered by a battery. The contents of Battery Backed RAM can be altered, but because it is powered by a battery, these contents are not lost when the computer is switched off. Battery Backed RAM is expensive and is suitable for storing only very small volumes of data. The batteries will run out periodically and must be renewed. Backing Storage, e.g. magnetic disc, must be used to store larger volumes of data when the computer is switched off.

2 > FILES

Data is kept on backing storage as a **file**. To store data on backing storage we save it. When we **save** data, the data is copied from the memory of the computer onto backing storage. To get the data back once the file has been saved, we load the file into memory. When we **load** data, the data is copied from backing storage into the memory of the computer.

Each file is given a **filename**, which identifies the file and so must be different from any other filename. The filename is used when we need to save or load the file, read data from, or write data to, the file.

FILE STRUCTURE

Where a file contains data it may be divided into **records**. A data file contains one or more records. A record is a collection of related data and contains several **fields**. A field is a single item of data. Fields within records of the same type will be in the same order. Each record will usually contain a **key field**. The key field is different in each record in a file; often it is an identification number that identifies the record and, in the case of personal data, also identifies the person. The key field is often used to determine the *location* of the record in the file. For example, a Sequential File may be sorted into ascending order using a *numerical key field*.

Example: A school's pupil information file.

> 85123: SHARP: LOUISE: 820601: 109 HAVELOCH ST.: THORNTON: BRADFORD
> 85145: PATEL: SANDIP: 811223: 12 HOLLY DRIVE: QUEENSTOWN: BRADFORD
> 86234: MOORSIDE: JAMES: 820913: 3 STONES LANE: ALLERTON: BRADFORD

The data is taken from an entirely fictitious file of pupils attending a Bradford School.

- Within each record there are seven fields.

- There are three records; one for each pupil.

- The fields are in the same order in each record.

Using the first record as an example, we have:

85123	pupil number (key field)
SHARP	family name
LOUISE	first name
820601	date of birth i.e. the 1st of June 1982
109 HAVELOCH ST	street
THORNTON	town

A Colon (:) has been used to separate the fields. In practice, the end of a field would be indicated by an End of Field Marker inserted by the software. How this is done need not concern us here, but an End of Field Marker is needed because there can be **variable length fields**. For example 'family name' may vary considerably in length from record to record. Without such a marker, confusion may arise as to where *exactly* the field ends. Other fields, such as 'date of birth' are described as **fixed length** because they have the same length in every record.

The pupil number is the key field. It is different for each pupil and identifies both the *record* and the *pupil*. The three records are sorted into ascending order on the key field.

Notice how the date is coded in YYMMDD format. This means that the first two digits starting at the left hand side represent the year, the next two digits represent the month and the last two digits, the day. The day, DD, always occupies two digits. For example, the 13th day would be coded as 13; the 6th day as 06. The month, MM, is coded so that January is 01, February is 02, November is 11, etc. If the year, YY, is 1989, this is coded as 89. The date is coded like this for several reasons. Firstly, it saves storage space when the file is saved on backing storage. Secondly, as the date is coded as a number in YYMMDD format, the records can be easily sorted into date of birth order. Thirdly, validation is easier. Simple range checks can be used to make sure the date is valid, i.e. DD lies between 01 and 31 inclusive, MM is between 01 and 12. A type check could be used to make sure the date only has numbers in it.

SERIAL AND SEQUENTIAL FILES

Every file contains records. The order in which records are stored, and the way the records can be accessed, varies.

In a **serial file** the records are not stored in any particular order.

In a **sequential file** the records are sorted into some order, usually on a key field.

In both serial and sequential files, it is only possible to access a record by first reading through *all* the previous records on the file.

RANDOM OR DIRECT ACCESS FILES

In a **random access file** it is possible to read the required record, or the data block containing the record, without first accessing other stored data. In other words, we can access the required record *directly*. For this reason random access files are also called **direct access files**.

Random access files, serial files and sequential files are all found on magnetic disc.

On magnetic tape, only serial files and sequential files are used. Random access files cannot be used on magnetic tape, since it is always necessary to start at the beginning of a magnetic tape and read through it until the required file, and then record, is found.

FILE OPERATIONS

Files are **created** when they are first set up and given a filename. A file may originally be a serial file which is then **sorted** into some order, e.g. ascending numeric on a key field (see the example above).

If we want to find a particular record, we **interrogate** or **search** the file until we find it. The **search condition** may be very simple such as 'name is Jones'. It may be more complex, for example, 'name is Jones AND age is less than 16'. Any record that satisfied the search condition will be accessed.

When we have two or more files containing records with the *same* field structure we may want to **merge** them into one file. This can be done by joining them end-to-end to give a serial file and then, if necessary, sorting the file to give a sequential file. If the files to be merged are sequential files in the same order, then it is possible to merge them and keep the original order by interleaving the records in the correct order.

When the data in a file is out of date because there is new data to be added, or changes are to be made to one or more of the records, we **update** or **amend** the file, making a completely up-to-date file. If we no longer need a file and wish to remove it from the disc, we **delete** the file. If we want another identical copy of a file, we **copy** the file. If we want to change the filename, we **rename** the file.

To get a list of all the files on a disc we look at the **catalogue** or **directory**. This is a list of all the files on a disc.

| 3 > BACKING STORAGE |

Backing storage is long-term storage, that is non-volatile. Data stored in the memory will be lost when the computer is turned off. However, if this data is first saved on backing storage, it is kept intact when the computer is turned off. When it is needed again it can be loaded into the memory from the backing storage.

MAGNETIC DISCS

Magnetic discs vary considerably, depending on the size of computer they are used with. However, they all provide faster access than the corresponding magnetic tape.

Data is stored on a magnetic disc on concentric **tracks** (see Fig. 6.1). Each track is divided into **sectors**, each separated by **inter-sector gaps**. A sector is the unit of data read from or written to the disc by the computer in a single read or write operation.

When you *format* a disc, it is divided into tracks and sectors on which files can be stored. Formatting a disc which has already been used may also delete any files already on the disc.

❝ Formatting a disc ❞

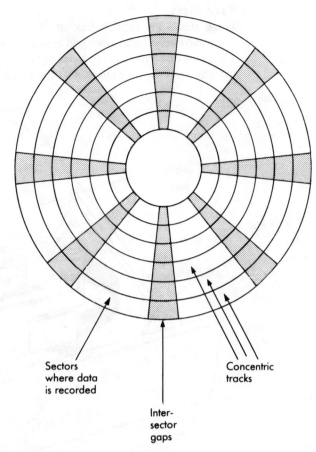

Fig. 6.1 The surface of a magnetic disc. There are typically 80 tracks and 10 sectors on a $3\frac{1}{2}$ inch floppy disc.

Floppy discs

These are flexible, circular, plastic discs coated with a magnetic material. They are contained in a protective sleeve (see Fig. 6.2). The read/write heads access the disc through the read/write hole. The heads are actually in *contact* with the surface of the disc as it spins. This reduces the life span and reliability of the floppy disc. The disc is gripped by the drive through its central hole, and spun at approximately 350 revolutions per minute. The index hole is used by the disc drive to locate the start of each track. A $5\frac{1}{4}$ inch floppy disc can store 320K of data; $3\frac{1}{2}$ inch floppy discs store 720K or more.

>> The write protect mechanism >>

The write protect mechanism is used to protect files on the floppy disc. When the write protect mechanism is on, you cannot save files on the disc, delete files saved on the disc nor alter files saved on the disc.

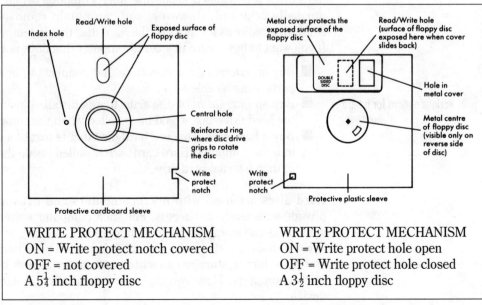

Fig. 6.2 Floppy discs

Hard discs

Hard discs are rigid, inflexible discs. They may be single or stacked as in Fig 6.3. The read/write heads move in unison, floating just above the surface of the hard disc. There is one read/write head for each surface of a disc. When the hard disc is switched on, the disc spins at a uniform, high speed.

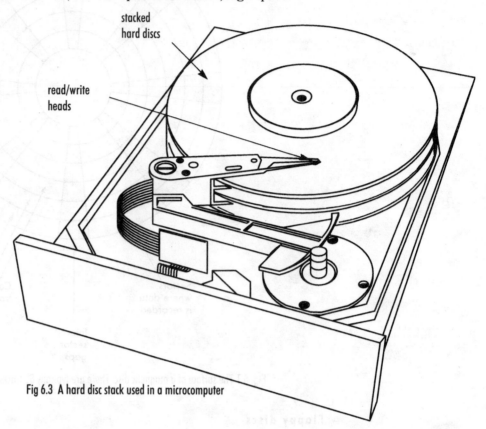

stacked
hard discs

read/write
heads

Fig 6.3 A hard disc stack used in a microcomputer

⁶⁶ Nature of the hard disc ⁹⁹

The read/write heads are so close to the disc's surface and the disc is spinning so fast that a speck of dust is sufficient to cause a 'head crash' that will destroy the disc. For this reason, hard discs must be used in absolutely clean conditions or sealed into the disc drive unit.

To access a particular sector the read/write heads move to the track it is on. The heads then remain stationary while the disc is spinning. The required sector is accessed as it passes underneath the read/write heads.

Hard discs for microcomputers are not usually visible when you are using the computer. There may be a light that comes on when the hard disc is accessed. Most hard discs are installed inside the microcomputer when it is assembled and are not normally removed. However, you can obtain removable hard discs. These are somewhat bulky as it is not just the hard disc that is removed.

If you want to buy a hard disc for a computer that does not have one, you can:

■ Buy an *external hard disc drive* that connects to one of the computer's external ports using a cable.

⁶⁶ Various options for a hard disc ⁹⁹

■ Buy an *internal hard disc drive* that is installed inside the computer. This is like the hard drive that would be installed when the computer is assembled.

■ Buy a *hard card*. This is a hard disc that is part of a circuit board that is plugged into the computer. Hard cards are installed inside the computer and are easier to fit than internal hard drives.

Hard discs are used with microcomputers and networks as they are robust and provide sufficiently fast access. For such computer systems, hard discs provide high volume on-line storage at an economic price.

Hard discs are also used with mainframes. These hard discs are more expensive and have larger storage capacities and faster access times than those used with microcomputers. However, they are essentially the same type of backing storage device.

MAGNETIC TAPE

Magnetic tape is a low cost backing storage media. Files stored on it can only be accessed serially or sequentially. Access is relatively slow. Data is stored on magnetic tape as illustrated in Figure 6.4.

Uses of Magnetic tape

The **header label** identifies the tape. The **Inter-Block Gap** separates the Data Blocks. A **Data Block** is the unit of data read from, or written to, the tape by the computer in a single read or write operation. The trailer label is the last on the magnetic tape and gives information such as whether the file continues on another tape.

It is not possible to both *read data from* and *write data to* a file on magnetic tape at the same time.

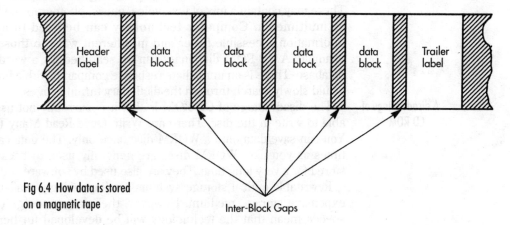

Fig 6.4 How data is stored on a magnetic tape

Inter-Block Gaps

The computer cannot read the entire magnetic tape into its memory as it is possible that the volume of data on the tape file would be more than the memory available. The computer accesses the data on the tape a block at a time. When a block has been read, it is processed before another block is read.

Cassette tapes

These are used to a limited extent with microcomputers for recording software. An ordinary tape recorder can be used with a home microcomputer. Cassettes used in this way are a cheap backing storage medium. Unfortunately, saving or loading programs or data on cassette is extremely slow and unreliable.

Tape cartridges

Magnetic tape is also available as a **magnetic tape cartridge**. These are reel-to-reel tapes encased in a plastic case for ease of handling. They are a larger version of the popular audio cassette. They are particularly useful for backing up hard discs when used with microcomputers and network file servers.

Reel-to-reel tape drives

Mainframe computers use reel-to-reel magnetic tape to store very large amounts of data at a low cost. It is possible to store around 100 million characters on a magnetic tape 3600 feet long, priced about £20 (a cost of 0.00002p per character).

CD-ROM DISCS

CD-ROM is the use of Compact Disc (CD) technology for backing storage for computers. CD-ROM can be used to store very large amounts of data on a relatively robust backing storage medium that can be accessed at speeds comparable with magnetic discs.

Advantages of CD ROM

An advantage of CD-ROM discs is their very high on-line storage capacity. A CD-ROM disc can store up to 1000 Mbytes of data. This could be up to 500,000 A4 pages of text, 2000 high resolution colour pictures, 25 hours of recorded speech or a mixture of these.

Another advantage of CD-ROM is the robust nature of the discs. A CD-ROM disc is 12 cms in diameter. This is a relatively compact and easy to handle way of storing such high volumes of data. CD-ROM is an optical medium. It is read by a laser beam which scans tiny pits on the surface of the disc. Consequently the risk of damage when the disc is accessed is reduced as there is no contact between the read mechanism and the disc. The discs are coated with a protective layer that allows them to be handled without erasing the data or damaging the disc. The robust nature of CD-ROM makes them suitable for the long term storage of data and for data in frequent use.

CD-ROM drives can be used with most microcomputers. They are similar in size to an audio CD drive. They can be installed next to the floppy disc drive or an external drive can be plugged into one of the computer's ports using a cable. Stacks of CD-ROM drives can be attached to networks.

CD-ROM is a developing technology. The ability to store large volumes of data means it is suitable for storing very large reference works such as dictionaries, encyclopedias, thesauruses, library catalogues, component parts catalogues, etc. These may contain a mix of text, voice, music, photographs, videos, etc. This is known as multimedia. Computer technology can be used to make this vast store of information accessible faster and in different ways to those traditionally used. For example, A CD-ROM dictionary can be searched for a word as you would search a database. There is an immediate response compared with a book dictionary where you would slowly search through the dictionary turning pages.

66 A disadvantage of CD ROM 99

The disadvantage of CD-ROM is that it is currently not usual for most users to be able to write to the disc. There are Write Once Read Many (WORM) discs available. You can save data onto a WORM disc once only. The data can then be read as many times as you like. WORM discs are generally used to backup files that need to be stored for a very long time. They are also used by software and multimedia developers.

Rewritable optical storage systems are increasingly available but these are still an expensive storage medium. However, their large storage capacity and fast access speeds mean that the technology will be developed further. These discs may well replace magnetic discs and tapes in the future.

4 ▷   SECURITY

Data saved on backing storage is valuable. It has cost time and money to collect and store the data. The data may be of great commercial value to a business. Consequently, it is most important to ensure that the data is **secure**.

BACK-UPS

The most important security precaution against loss of data files or programs through accident, malicious damage or theft is to keep extra copies of them. These extra copies are known as **back-ups**.

Magnetic tape is ideal where we need to record large amounts of data and where we have no need to access the data very quickly, or very frequently. It is also a low-cost storage medium. For these reasons magnetic tape is ideal as a back-up medium for other magnetic media such as discs.

Both discs and tapes are unreliable storage media and occasionally programs or data recorded on them will be corrupted or lost in some other way. When data is corrupted it is changed so that it is meaningless. When we back-up a disc onto magnetic tape all the data and programs on it are copied, from the disc to the tape. When the data on the disc becomes corrupted, the data and programs can be restored by copying them from the backup tape to the original disc. It is very important to make sure that all programs and data are backed-up.

In *large mainframe* computer installations reel-to-reel tapes will be used as the back-up medium. For microcomputers magnetic tape cartridges are used. Tape cartridges are used with a **tape streamer,** a peripheral designed to allow easy copying of all the programs and data on a disc onto the tape cartridge. They are particularly useful with hard discs where it is necessary to make frequent, regular back-ups of 120 Mbytes or more of programs and data.

66 The ancestral back-up system 99

Where it is very important to be sure that programs and data are always safe from corruption, the ancestral back-up system is used (see Fig. 6.5).

■ The **son** is the copy of the programs and data currently in use. This will be backed-up on a regular basis, perhaps daily.
■ The **father** is the most recent copy of the son.
■ The **grandfather** is the copy of the son that was taken before the father.

It is usual to keep the son copies on site where they are easily accessible. The father copies are likely to be stored in a fire-proof safe nearby, probably in the same building as the computer but not in the same room. The grandfather copies should be stored elsewhere, possibly in another town or city. This system is a very effective way of making sure it is always possible to restore corrupted programs and data (unless you are extremely careless or unlucky!)

It is also possible to use magnetic discs as a back-up medium. This is frequently done with microcomputers. The ancestral system for back-ups is still effective, but floppy discs are used instead of magnetic tape cartridges.

USER IDENTIFICATION AND PASSWORDS

Another precaution against data loss or damage is to restrict the use of the computer software by only allowing registered users to make use of the computer. This is done by giving each user a unique identification code, the User Id, and associating a particular password with it.

A password is a special sequence of characters, known only to a particular user, that must be presented to the computer system before it will allow access to the system. If every user keeps their User Id and password secret, it is unlikely that anyone else will gain entry to the system.

PHYSICAL SECURITY

No data file, program or computer system is safe unless it is physically secure. Premises must be made accessible only to registered users. Security guards should be employed and premises must be kept under lock and key. Registered users should have identification cards or similar and these should be checked regularly.

Computers can be key locked so that they cannot be operated unless they are unlocked by someone who has the right key. Floppy discs, etc. should be locked in a secure cabinet, not left lying around.

NETWORK CABLE SECURITY

Computer network cable should be installed in an inaccessible location to prevent unauthorised connection to the network. The cable should be shielded from the electromagnetic fields generated by electric wires, to prevent corruption of data on the network cable.

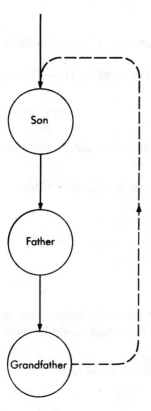

Fig. 6.5 The ancestral system for back-ups

EXAMINATION QUESTIONS

Q1. You can buy this computer.

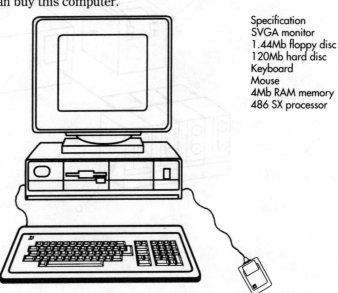

Specification
SVGA monitor
1.44Mb floppy disc
120Mb hard disc
Keyboard
Mouse
4Mb RAM memory
486 SX processor

(a) What backing storage does the computer use?

(b) Which type of disc has the fastest access time?'

(c) Explain why you would save your data on backing storage instead of in RAM memory.

(d) The computer's memory can be upgraded from 4Mb to 8Mb. Describe an advantage in upgrading the memory.

(SEG, 1993)

Q2   An advertising agency uses information systems to prepare text and graphics for brochures and other advertising material.

(a) Which three of the following applications packages would be suitable for this?

    A   communications
    B   desk-top publishing
    C   painting and drawing
    D   accounting
    E   payroll
    F   word processing

(b) The information system used includes four different types of storage. Two of these are CD-ROM and RAM. What two other forms of storage would be most suitable in this system?

(c) Explain why each of the following types of storage device is necessary.

    (i)   CD-ROM

    (ii) RAM

(NEAB/WJEC, 1993)

Q3.   The diagram shows a mainframe computer system.

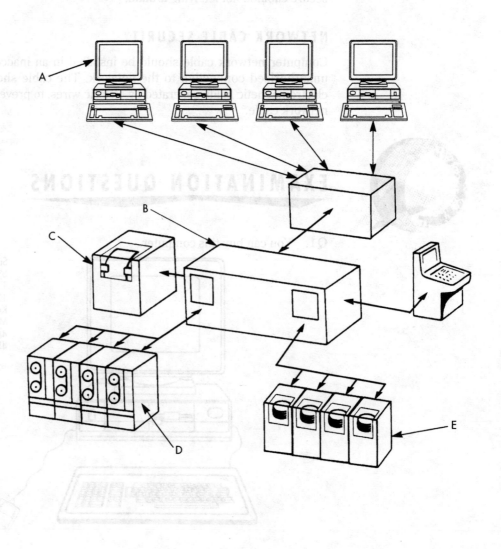

Select from this list of words the name of each of the units marked.

Line printer
Magnetic disc unit
Magnetic tape unit
Main processor
Terminals

(SEG, 1993)

Q4. Why is software stored on a ROM chip and not on a RAM chip?

(City and Guilds, 1993)

Q5. A doctor's surgery keeps manual medical records of its patients. These are to be transferred to a computer system.

(a) The hardware and software arrive in the surgery. Select THREE steps which will be necessary before the computerised system replaces the manual system. Write the three steps in the correct order.

design the computer
system testing

staff training
create files

program design
examine the patients

(b) The system uses direct access to records.

(i) Explain what this means.
(ii) Explain what is meant by serial access to records.

(MEG, 1993)

Q6. The Magi-micro has 512K RAM. How many bytes and bits does the RAM contain?

(City and Guilds, 1993)

Q7. (a) Explain the meaning of serial access and direct access. For each give an example of a backing store device which can use that method of access.

(b) Programmers often spend more time maintaining programs than writing new ones. Give three reasons why program maintenance is necessary.

(c) Systems analysis consists of various steps. Describe the two steps:

(i) Feasibility study

(ii) Implementation.

(NDTEF, 1993)

Q8. ROM and RAM are two different types of memory found in the IAS of a computer's CPU.

(a) What do these abbreviations stand for?

(i) ROM

(ii) RAM

(iii) IAS

(iv) CPU

(b) Describe the differences between ROM and RAM and give an example of the use of each.

(NDTEF, 1993)

Q9. Put a ring round the correct answer from each group of three terms in the passage below.

Example: A keyboard is (A COMMUNICATION /AN INPUT/ AN OUTPUT) device.

In a large company with 25 000 employees, the payroll system would usually use (A BATCH/AN ON-LINE/A REAL-TIME) processing system to produce payslips. The computer operator first loads the (CASSETTE/MAGNETIC/ PAPER) tape unit with the payroll master (FIELD/FILE/RECORD) and the (DISC/TRANSACTION/UTILITY) file. A blank tape for the (BACK-UP/NEW/ OLD) master file is also loaded. (BLANK/PRE-PRINTED/RECYCLED) stationery will be loaded into the (PLOTTER/PRINTER/TYPEWRITER).
The (APPLICATION/SOURCE/UTILITY) program is then (ERASED/RUN WRITTEN).

(SEG, 1993)

Q10 A program is stored on a floppy disc.

    (a) Describe what has to be done so that the program can be run on a computer.

    (b) The computer has a hard disc. Describe what has to be done so that the program can be run without using the floppy disc.

ANSWERS TO EXAMINATION QUESTIONS

A1. (a) Floppy disc and hard disc.

    (b) Hard disc.

    (c) Data saved in RAM is lost when the computer is switched off. Data saved on backing storage is permanent.

    (d) A bigger memory enables larger programs to be run. Large programs are often large because they have extra programming to make them easier to use. The larger the memory, the more data can be loaded into it. This can reduce the number of disc accesses and speed up program execution.

A2 (a) B,C,F

    (b) Floppy discs and a hard disc.

    (c) (i) CD-ROM—strictly speaking, this is not required for DTP but would be useful for storing high volumes of clip art.

        (ii) RAM— This stores the programs and data while they are being used.

            Without RAM no processing could be done.

A3. A – terminals
B – main processor
C – line printer
D – magnetic tape unit
E – magnetic disc unit

A4. The software stored on a ROM chip cannot be altered and can be used as soon as the computer is switched on. It isn't lost when the computer is switched off. Software stored on a RAM chip is lost when the computer is switched off. It has to be loaded into RAM before it can be used.

A5. (a) create files
system testing
staff training

    (b) (i) Go straight to a record without reading intermediate records.

        (ii) Read through each record in turn until the correct one is found.

(MEG, 1993)

A6. 512 K bytes   =   1024 × 512 bytes

                   =   524288 bytes

1 byte   =   8 bits on most microcomputers
So

512K   =   1024 × 512 × 8 bits

                =   4194304 bits

Approximate answers might be acceptable, for example:

512K   =   512,000 bytes

                =   512,000 × 8 bits

A7. (a) Serial access: to access a record, the computer has to read all the records from the beginning of the file up to the record being accessed.
Direct access: the computer can go straight to the record being accessed.

The method of access found on backing storage:		
types of access	disc	tape
direct access	✓	✗
serial access	✓	✓

     (b) Program maintenance is necessary because:

- all the errors in the program may not be found during testing.
- the program may be changed so that it does additional tasks.
- the program may be re-written to improve its speed doing some tasks.

     (c) (i) Feasibility study: A brief study to find out if the information system proposed is realistic and to estimate the development costs.

         (ii) Implementation: The acquisition of hardware and software, the training of staff, the documentation and the bringing into operation of the information system.

A8. (a) (i) Read Only Memory   (iii) The Immediate Access Store (the memory)

         (ii) Random Access Memory   (iv) The Central Processing Unit

     (b) Differences:

ROM	RAM
Can only be read	Can be read and written to
Non-volatile	Volatile

Used for:

ROM: Used to store programs that need to be available as soon as the computer is switched on. These programs may run automatically, e.g. The Operating System.

RAM: Used for the computer's main memory. The computer stores programs and data in RAM while they are being processed.

A9. a batch
magnetic
file
transaction
new
pre-printed
printer
application
run

A10. (a) There are several possible answers, e.g.:

- switch on the computer
- put the floppy disc in the disc drive
- load the program into the computer
- run the program.

(b) Copy the files on the floppy disc to the hard disc, i.e. install the program on the hard disc.

STUDENT'S ANSWER WITH EXAMINER'S COMMENTS

Question

MARVELLOUS MAGI-MICRO

Yours for only £300. The new Magi-Micro comes with a

16-bit processor
processor speed 16MHz
Monochrome monitor - medium resolution
10 MB hard disk
3.5″ floppy disk drive
512K RAM
MS-DOS
A ROM chip containing a boot file
Integrated wordprocessor, spreadsheet, database and graphics software and a choice of a quality printer, either an ink jet or daisy wheel printer.

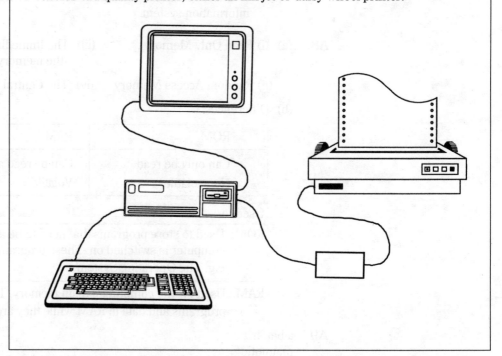

Look at the advertisement for a microcomputer.
Explain briefly:

a) the difference between RAM and ROM

b) the uses of RAM and ROM

c) compare the two disk storage systems, describing their uses and relative advantages

d) the terms: medium resolution and boot file in relation to the magi-micro

e) how an inkjet printer works.

(City and Guilds, 1993)

Student's answer

a) RAM means Random Access Memory. ROM means Read Only Memory.

b) RAM is used for the computer's memory. ROM is used to store programs that are run immediately the computer is switched on.

c) Floppy discs store less data than hard discs. Access to the data is slower on a floppy disc than a hard disc. They are both used to store programs and data.

d) The boot file is stored in ROM. It runs as soon as the computer is switched on and starts up the Operating System. A medium resolution monitor shows more detail on the screen than a low resolution monitor and less than a high resolution monitor.

e) An inkjet printer squirts jets of ink at the paper.

Examiner's comments

(a) True but trivial. A more complete answer would be:
ROM is non-volatile and the information held on it can only be read.
RAM is volatile. Information can be read from it and written to it.

(b) Both RAM and ROM are part of the computer's memory.
RAM is used for the main memory of the computer. It stores programs and data that are being used.
ROM is used to store programs that are needed as soon as the computer is switched on, e.g. the boot file, which starts up the Operating System.

(c) A good answer. In addition, floppy discs are usually removable whereas hard discs are not usually removable.

(d) A good answer.

(e) True, but the examiner also wants to be told that an ink jet printer forms characters, etc. using a dot matrix print head.

REVIEW SHEET

1. A school keeps a file of information about all the pupils at the school.

(a) What information should be kept about each pupil? Give reasons for your choice.

_____

_____

_____

_____

(b) Each pupil has their own record on the file. Describe the fields that should appear in each record.

_____

_____

_____

_____

_____

2. In a warehouse. the Master file contains details of all the goods in stock at the start of the day. This file is sorted into numerical order using a stock identification number.

Each day, the details of all the goods delivered to and sent out from the warehouse are saved on a Transaction file. The stock identification numbers of goods on the transaction file are in no particular order.

Using these words, complete these paragraphs. You can use the words more than once.

> direct access
> disc
> tape
> sequential
> serial

(a) The Master file is a_____ file as it is sorted into some order. The Transaction file is in no particular order so it is a_____file.

(b) Both the Master file and the Transaction file could be saved on magnetic_____or magnetic_____

(c) You can store_____ and _____files on magnetic tape or magnetic disc.

(d) You cannot store_____files on magnetic tape.

3. Use these words to complete these sentences.

> backup
> delete
> load
> rename
> save
> search
> sort
> update

(a) When you_____a file on disc, you keep it for use in the future.

(b) Information stored on disc can be used after you_____it into the computer.

(c) You can find the information in a file by doing a_____

(d) You can arrange information into order by doing a_____

(e) If you_____ the information on a file you will have changed it so that it is up-to-date.

(f) When you _____a file, you make another copy of it.

4. Draw a labelled diagram of a floppy disc. Using the diagram explain how the write protect mechanism works and its purpose.

5. State whether the following are true or false.

(a) Hard discs can store more information than floppy discs._____

(b) You can update information saved on a CD-ROM. _____

6. CD-ROM is used to store the same type of information as a hard disc but it is also used to store video and music.

Select two of these statements as the main reasons for this.

■ Hard discs are magnetic but CD-ROM is optical. _____

■ You can read the information from both CD-ROM and a hard disc at about the same speed. _____

■ CD-ROM can store more information in more compact form._____

■ CD-ROM are lighter and more portable than hard discs. _____

OUTPUT

GETTING STARTED

The type of output generated is determined by the use to which it will be put. For interactive systems a **monitor** screen is best. These can be *low* , *medium* or *high resolution* and may vary in size.

For permanency, a **printer** using **continuous fan fold** stationery or single A4 sheets is satisfactory. The stationery may be pulled through the printer by a **tractor feed** or pushed through by a **friction feed**. Depending on the speed and quality of printout required a **character**, **line** or **page** printer will be used. The printer mechanism may be **impact** or **non-impact**. Because a printer is a slow peripheral a **spooling** queue may be used and also a **buffer**, so that the computer can be used for other tasks while the printer is in use.

Printed paper is bulky and in the long term will deteriorate. Computer output on **Microfilm** or **Microfiche** is more compact and lasts longer, so it is ideal for distribution, storage and reference.

Graph plotters are used for high quality drawings as the limited graphic capabilities of most printers are inadequate. Where printed output would not be understood, or to emphasize commands from the computer, **speech synthesis** may be used, as the spoken word communicates more effectively.

MONITORS

PRINTERS AND HARD COPY

BUFFERS & SPOOLING

COMPUTER OUTPUT ON MICROFILM (COM)

GRAPH PLOTTERS

SPEECH SYNTHESIS

CONTROL INTERFACES AND ACTUATORS

ESSENTIAL PRINCIPLES

Output generated by computers is familiar to most people even if they have little contact with computers in other ways. A visit to a travel agency, a motor spares stockist or an estate agency may bring us into contact with screen output. Electricity Boards, Gas Boards, Local Councils and a variety of other bodies, all send out bills which have been printed by computer. Libraries often store their indexes on microfiche; historians will use a computer to store plans and maps. This chapter contains a brief, but systematic, review of computer generated output.

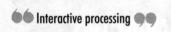

1 ▷ **MONITORS**

❝❝ Interactive processing ❞❞

❝❝ Types of monitor ❞❞

When using a computer it is likely that you will receive information about the activities taking place in the computer by reading the output on a screen. This screen is known as a **monitor**. A monitor looks very much like a television set. In response to the output you may be asked to provide some input. The input prompt to attract your attention, so that you will reply to the request for data as quickly as possible, is a flashing **cursor**. The cursor may be a small square that appears on the screen. The input will then be used by the computer. This cycle of input, processing and output will continue while the computer is being used. This is **interactive** processing, so called because the user interacts with the computer. Interactive processing is very similar to having a conversation with the computer, but instead of *hearing* the conversation we *see* it on the screen.

Most microcomputers must have a monitor attached before they can be used, as they are almost always used interactively. A monitor is probably the most common output peripheral in use with computers. With home computers it is very common to use a television as a monitor. Television sets do not usually give as clear a picture as a monitor, but they can receive TV programmes, which is not possible on a monitor.

Monitors can be **high**, **medium** or **low resolution**. The level of resolution is measured in **pixels**. A pixel is the smallest area of the screen that can be changed by the computer. A pixel can be thought of as a dot that makes up a picture, similar to the dots that make up a photograph in a newspaper.

HIGH RESOLUTION

This means that it is possible to display a very detailed picture on the screen. In high resolution the screen may display, for example, 640 by 400 pixels, though higher densities are possible. High resolution monitors are used when we want very detailed and accurate screen displays. They are particularly useful for Graphic Design, Computer Aided Design and related applications. It is also possible to buy high resolution screens that are much bigger than normal screens. For example, in Desk Top Publishing there may be a need to view a whole A4 (the size of this page is A4) or A3 (twice as big as A4) page on the screen for it to be readable. Extra large, high resolution screens make this possible.

MEDIUM AND LOW RESOLUTION

These monitors provide less detailed screen displays than a high resolution monitor but they are also correspondingly cheaper. If high resolution is not required for a particular application, then a medium resolution monitor could be adequate. A typical medium resolution monitor will display 640 by 200 pixels, much less than the high resolution screen. A low resolution display may be only 320 by 200 pixels. A low resolution display is generally suitable for television sets, which can be used to good effect with computer games at home.

2 ▷ **PRINTERS AND HARD COPY**

Printed output from a computer is called **hard copy**. Some printers use paper that is **continuous** in the sense that there are many sheets joined together. These sheets are joined by perforations that make the sheets easier to separate. The paper is folded into a box in a **fan-fold**. Down the sides of the paper are rows of **sprocket holes** which are used to pull the paper through the printer (see Fig. 7.1).

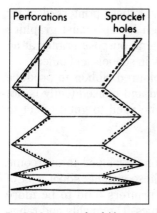

Fig. 7.1 Continuous fan-fold printer stationery

Computer stationery may be plain or can be **pre-printed** with other details beforehand. Companies sending out invoices or bills often pre-print their computer stationery with their logo and other details before the computer is used to add the details for each customer (see Fig. 7.2). This method is often used to produce individualised bills and advertising material that address the customer by name. Where several copies of the printed output are needed, perhaps for sending to the customer and filing in the office, it is possible to print on **multipart** computer paper. Multipart stationery consists of several layers of continuous fan-fold stationery with a layer of carbon paper between. Printing takes place as usual to produce a top-copy, but other copies are produced through the carbon paper. When using multipart stationery it is necessary to use an **impact** printer. This has a print head that physically hits an inked ribbon onto the printer paper. The impact transfers the ink on the ribbon to the paper. Printers that use ink jets or a thermal print head do not have print heads that hit the paper. These are **non-impact** printers.

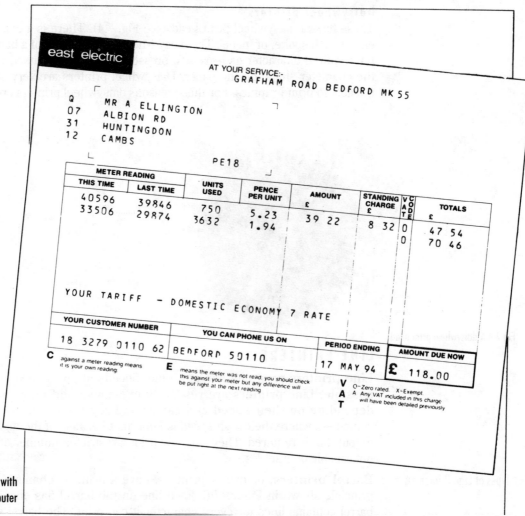

Fig. 7.2 A pre-printed bill with details printed on it by the computer

CHARACTER PRINTERS

Character printers print one character at a time. They are the slowest type of printer. Their speed is measured in **cps**, i.e. characters per second. Speeds of between 80 and 200 cps are usual. Character printers are relatively cheap and can be purchased for £200 or less. They are often used with microcomputers where their slow speed is unimportant, because of the low volume of printed output, and their low cost makes them attractive.

Dot matrix printers

These form each character by printing part of a 7 by 5 matrix (see Fig. 7.3). Most dot matrix printers are impact printers. They have a print head consisting of a matrix of steel pins that are projected or withdrawn to form the shape of the character. The printout produced by these printers is either **draft** print which is of a low quality, or **Near Letter Quality** (NLQ). In NLQ mode each character is printed twice, producing a much better quality printout.

 Types of Character Printer

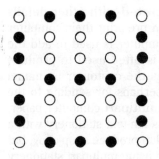

Fig. 7.3 The number 8 formed by a dot matrix print head

The flexibility of the shape formed by the print head makes these printers ideal for printing graphics, though the quality is not good enough for specialist graphics applications. This type of dot matrix printer is a good general purpose printer at an economic price (around £200) and they are used extensively in schools and offices.

Impact dot matrix printers can also be used with a coloured ribbon to produce printout in several colours. The colour cannot be blended and consequently is not sufficiently adaptable for good quality artwork, but can be used to good effect to emphasise simple graphs and bar charts.

Ink jet printers

These are non-impact dot matrix printers which have been developed to overcome some of the limitations of the impact dot matrix printer. These printers shoot a jet of ink at the paper to form the printed character. Ink jet printers tend to be more expensive, but produce much better quality print and graphics. The quality and range of the colour printing possible is also improved.

Daisywheel printers

These have a daisywheel print head (see Fig. 7.4). There is a character shape on the end of each spoke, or 'petal'. The daisy wheel spins in front of a hammer which strikes the required character as it passes, pressing it against an inked ribbon which prints the character shape on the paper. Daisywheel printers are very slow, noisy, and are not able to print graphics. For these reasons daisywheel printers are now rarely used.

Fig 7.4 A daisywheel print head

LINE PRINTERS

Line printers print one line at a time. Speeds of up to 2000 lines per minute are possible. Line printers are relatively expensive and may cost £1,000 or more depending on their speed and capacity. They are often used with mainframe computers where their high speed is important because of the high volume of printed output that is required. They can only print a restricted number of characters and are not capable of graphics.

Barrel printers, or drum printers, have a print mechanism that works on the principle shown in Figure 7.6. Each line on the barrel has one character only. The barrel contains lines for every character it can print. The barrel spins once for each line printed. There is a hammer for each print position. The hammer strikes the paper against the ribbon and the barrel, thus transferring the printed character to the paper. The line is built up as shown in Figure 7.5.

❝ Types of Line Printer ❞

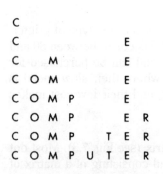

Fig. 7.5 The build up of a line containing the word 'COMPUTER' when using a barrel printer

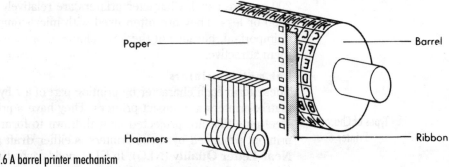

Fig. 7.6 A barrel printer mechanism

Chain printers

These also build up one line at a time. The print mechanism used is shown in Figure 7.7. The chain rotates, so that the required character will at some stage pass the print position. Commonly used characters may appear on the chain more frequently than other letters in order to speed up printing.

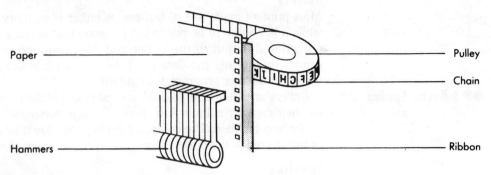

Fig. 7.7 A chain printer mechanism

Laser Printers as a type of Page Printer

PAGE PRINTERS

Page printers set up a page and then print it. The most common type of page printer is a **laser printer**. These range from small desk-top printers used with microcomputers to large, free standing printers used with mainframe computers. Speeds range from 4 pages per minute to 200 ppm; costs vary from £500 to £20,000 or more. Laser printers are able to produce a wide range of type fonts and graphics. They can print in black and white or colour. It is difficult to distinguish between the best quality colour laser printing and a colour photograph.

Laser printers work by directing a laser beam at an electrostatically-charged surface. The shape of the characters is 'etched' onto the charged surface to make a template of the shapes to be printed. This is then used to transfer ink to the paper. In most cases ordinary paper can be used.

Benefits of laser printers

Laser printers are popular as they are flexible, fast and quiet. However, the cost of printing is quite high compared to most other printers. As a result, their use may be restricted in schools and colleges. It is more economical to print draft copies of work on dot matrix printers, only printing the final copy on a laser printer.

PRINTER PAPER FEED MECHANISMS

The **tractor feed** is the most common type of paper feed mechanism. It consists of two toothed wheels, one positioned at each edge of the paper that engage the sprocket holes in the edge of the paper and pull it through the printer (see Fig. 7.8).

Types of paper feed mechanism to printers

On some printers used with microcomputer systems the tractor feed is either not used, or can be removed. Instead, a **friction feed** is used. This consists of a hard rubber roller, the same width as the paper, that presses against the paper and pushes it through the printer. A friction feed mechanism is not suitable for large volumes of printout on continuous stationery but is very useful if printout on a single sheet of standard A4 is required. The sheet can be fed into the printer by hand. This is a slow and cumbersome method, so **single sheet feeders** have been developed. These supply single A4 sheets to the printer, which are then pulled through the printer by the friction feed. This method is increasingly used in small offices where there is no requirement for high volumes of printout, but letters are often printed on single sheets of paper.

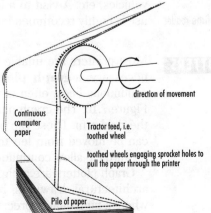

direction of movement

Continuous computer paper

Tractor feed, i.e. toothed wheel

toothed wheels engaging sprocket holes to pull the paper through the printer

Pile of paper

Fig. 7.8 A tractor feed mechanism

3 > BUFFERS AND SPOOLING

All printers are slow compared with the speed of the processor in a computer. If a program needs to use a printer this can prevent other programs and users from making use of the computer. It may mean a long wait while the computer is printing before other work can continue.

Buffers

Most printers make use of **buffers**. A buffer is memory that is used to store output while it is waiting to be printed. A program that needs to use the printer will transfer any printed output to the buffer and then continue processing immediately. The printer then prints the data from the buffer while the program that produced the output, or another program, is being run.

66 Buffers and Spooling 99

Buffers are often able to hold several pages of data waiting to be printed, but even so, their capacity is limited. If there is a large volume of printout to be done then the buffer may be filled. The computer cannot continue until all the data has been printed or transferred to the buffer. This causes the processor to wait for the slower printer.

Spooling

Waiting for the printer can be avoided by **spooling** the printer output. In spooling, all printed output is first saved as a data file on backing storage. Output to backing storage peripherals such as magnetic disc is very fast. Once the data file has been saved, the program can continue processing. The data file now joins the queue for the printer. Printing takes place when the data file reaches the head of the queue. This may take some time on a computer system with high volumes of printed output. The printout may not be done until quite a long time after the program has finished processing.

Buffers are almost always found in use with printers. Even inexpensive printers used with microcomputers have build-in buffers. Spooling is used with mainframe computers and networks of microcomputers.

4 > COMPUTER OUTPUT ON MICROFILM

Where it is necessary to keep a record of activities, high volumes of output may need to be kept for perhaps several years. Such records may need to be consulted infrequently, or there may be a legal requirement to keep them. Records printed on paper will take up a large amount of storage space and tend to deteriorate quickly. Instead of storing the output printed on paper it is possible to make a copy of the page on microfilm, as it would have appeared had it been printed. This is Computer Output on Microfilm (COM) .

66 Advantages of COM 99

Microfilm takes up much less storage space and does not deteriorate as quickly as paper. Microfilm is generally available as a roll of film 16mm or 35mm wide. The only disadvantage of microfilm is that a special reader must be used, but the expense of this is more than compensated for by lower storage costs.

COM is also useful where large volumes of information are needed at a variety of locations. A common example of this is the book catalogue in a library. Printed output is again unsuitable because it is bulky, difficult to access and easily torn. Microfilm is not used because it is made up as a roll. Instead, the roll is converted into flat sheets of **microfiche** measuring 105 × 148mm. The microfiche catalogue can be copied many times and be made available at any location, provided a **microfiche reader** is available (see Fig. 7.9). Microfiche is easily packed and sent through the post. For this reason it is also suitable for applications such as spare parts catalogues for motor vehicles, etc. A visit to a local library, or a motor spares dealer, to see microfiche in use is highly recommended.

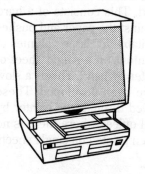

Fig. 7.9 A microfiche reader

5 > GRAPH PLOTTERS

Most printers are unable to print high quality precision graphics. Where these are necessary, a **graph plotter** is used. Graph plotters are very slow, but can draw continuous lines, often in several colours. A **flat bed graph plotter** is illustrated in Figure 7.10. The graph plotter illustrated has three interchangeable pens mounted on the rigid arm. These can be lowered for drawing, one at a time, as required. The pens can be moved from left to right, while the rigid arm can be moved backwards and forwards to allow continuous lines to be drawn on the paper.

Graph plotters are a highly specialised output device. They are especially useful for architectural drawings, building plans and Computer Aided Design applications, where a high quality precision drawing is required, but the volume of output is low.

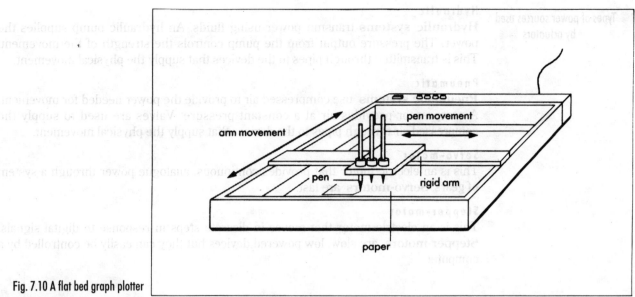

Fig. 7.10 A flat bed graph plotter

(labels in diagram: pen movement, arm movement, pen, rigid arm, paper)

SPEECH SYNTHESIS

6

Speech synthesis can help the disabled to use computers.

For some applications printed output, on the screen or on paper is inappropriate. It may be that only a few instructions are required in a situation where reading would be difficult. In any event, some people have difficulty reading, perhaps through disabilities of one form or another. Attempts have been made to get the computer to produce sounds similar to normal speech; this is speech synthesis.

Software that attempts to reproduce speech is available for most microcomputers. For example, you can type in a sentence and the computer 'reads' it through a built-in loud speaker. This type of software associates a sound with a particular combination of letters in the words. It usually produces recognisable speech but it does not have the quality of human speech. There are difficulties with words like 'bough' and 'thought' where the same 'ough' spelling has different sounds associated with it. Where only a limited number of words are used, human speech can be recorded in digital form and reproduced by the computer. This is often done in computer games.

CONTROL INTERFACES AND ACTUATORS

7

Computers use **control interfaces** to communicate with and control a range of devices that perform physical actions (see fig. 7.1). Control interfaces often simply switch on or off some electrical device, such as, a heater or a fan. However, control interfaces can also be used to control sources of mechanical power. By communicating with and controlling sources of mechanical power, computers can perform physical tasks. For example, a robot can be made to pick up an object.

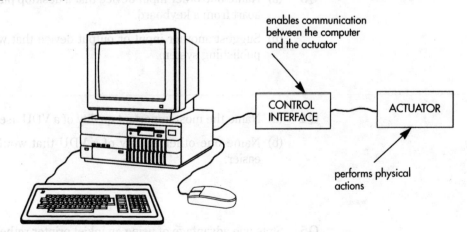

enables communication between the computer and the actuator

CONTROL INTERFACE

ACTUATOR

performs physical actions

Fig. 7.11

The construction external to the computer that enables a power source to be used to perform particular physical actions is called an **actuator**. A computer will signal the control interface which communicates with the actuator, telling it what to do.

The following are some *power sources* used by **actuators**. They make the actuator perform a mechanical task.

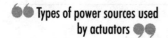

Hydraulic

Hydraulic systems transmit power using fluids. An hydraulic pump supplies the power. The pressure output from the pump controls the strength of the movement. This is transmitted through pipes to the devices that supply the physical movement.

Pneumatic

Pneumatic systems use compressed air to provide the power needed for movement. A compressor provides air at a constant pressure. Valves are used to supply the compressed air through pipes to the devices that supply the physical movement.

Servo-motor

This is an electric motor that provides continuous, analogue power through a system of gears. **Servo-motors** are fast.

Stepper-motor

This is an electric motor that moves in discrete steps in response to digital signals. **Stepper-motors** are slow, low powered devices but they can easily be controlled by a computer.

EXAMINATION QUESTIONS

Q1. Ring TWO items used for output from a computer.

screen   light pen   keyboard   graph plotter   mouse   joystick

(MEG, 1993)

Q2 Ring ONE output device which would be most suitable for producing electricity bills.

daisywheel printer   screen   line printer   graph plotter

(MEG, 1993)

Q3 (a) Name one other input device that a desktop publishing system would need, apart from a keyboard.

(b) Suggest another input or output device that would be useful for a desktop publishing system.

(City and Guilds, 1993)

Q4 (a) Name the most important quality of a VDU used for desktop publishing.

(b) Name one other quality of a VDU that would make desktop publishing easier.

(City and Guilds, 1993)

Q5 State one advantage of using an inkjet printer rather than a daisy wheel printer.

(City and Guilds, 1993)

Q6 What are the advantages and disadvantages of using a laser printer instead of a dot matrix printer (9 pin, impact)?

Q7

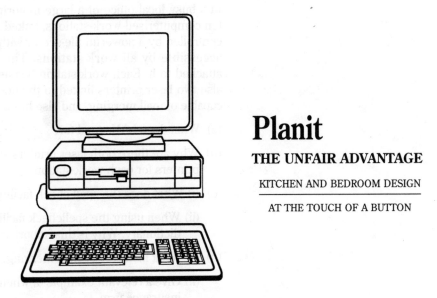

Planit

THE UNFAIR ADVANTAGE

KITCHEN AND BEDROOM DESIGN

AT THE TOUCH OF A BUTTON

A kitchen design firm uses a computer system to help in planning new kitchens for clients.

The client will choose the style of units that is required.

A surveyor will then measure up the kitchen.

A designer will work out how best to fit the units into the kitchen, and then plan the routes of pipework and wiring.

(a) Name one input device (apart from a keyboard) that the designer could use, and explain why it is suitable.

(b) A high quality plan needs to be drawn by the computer for when the kitchen is being fitted. Name an output device that would produce a high quality plan of the kitchen, and explain why it is suitable.

(c) Describe some other tasks (apart from the actual design of the kitchen) for which the company might use the computer.

(SEG, 1993)

Q8 Information systems sometimes accept spoken input and use a voice synthesiser to speak to users.

(a) Name an input device used for voice recognition and an output device used for voice synthesis.

(b) Describe a situation where voice synthesis and voice recognition are an essential part of the information system being used.

Q9 A small company uses a computer.

(a) The company wishes to run two programs.

Program A involves reading names, addresses and dates of birth to print personalised birthday cards.

Program B involves complicated calculations to predict sales figures for next year. The results are to be saved on disc.

How can a multiprogramming operating system help to run the two programs in the shortest possible time?

(b) Why does the company use a laser printer to print letters to its customers and a dot-matrix printer to produce employee wage slips?

(MEG, 1993)

Q10 Read the paragraph below, and then answer the questions:

In a busy local office of a large motoring insurance company there are about ten computerised work-stations, linked to each other by a LAN. The system is controlled by a powerful file-server with a 300 Mbyte hard disc drive, which is accessible by all work-stations. The file server also has a tape-streamer attached to it. Each work-station has its own dot-matrix printer, and there are also two laser printers linked to the network. The word-processing software is capable of mail merging, and also has a spell check facility.

(a) What does LAN stand for?

(b) Why are there both laser printers attached to the network and dot-matrix printers for each work-station?

(c) (i) What does the spell check facility do?

(ii) When using the spellcheck facility, you can add extra words to its dictionary. Why is this important?

(d) (i) What is meant by mail-merging?

(ii) Give a relevant example of when mail-merging might be used in this insurance firm.

(SEG, 1993)

ANSWERS TO EXAMINATION QUESTIONS

A1 screen
graph plotter

(MEG, 1993)

A2 line printer

(MEG, 1993)

A3 (a) A mouse is essential.

(b) A scanner would be useful. This would be used to scan pictures, etc into the DTP system.

A4 (a) High resolution, so that greater detail can be shown.

(b) A larger screen, e.g. an A4 screen, would be useful. Colour is often more useful than black and white.

A5 A daisy wheel printer can only print one font at a time, in one size, and cannot print graphics. An ink jet printer can print several fonts, in several sizes and can print graphics.

A6 A laser printer can print a wide range of fonts and graphics. It produces a high quality printout. Printing is fast and quiet. However, a laser printer is expensive to buy and to run. A dot matrix printer is cheap to buy and run. However, it produces a lower quality printout. Printing is slow and noisey.

A7 (a) A mouse could be used. It is easier to draw and plan diagrams on the screen using a mouse.

(b) A graph plotter could be used. Often graph plotters draw on A3 (large) sheets of paper. They draw smooth, continuous lines and can draw in colour.

(c) The company could use the computer for payroll; stock control; writing letters, reports, contracts, etc.; sales statistics; etc.

A8 (a) input : microphone

output : loudspeaker

(b) Voice synthesis and voice recognition are essential in circumstances where other forms of input and output cannot be used. For example:

■ for some disabled people

■ for workers who are using both hands to do their job and cannot break off to use keyboard input, etc.

A9 (a) Schedule the computer so that the processor is being used for the calculations in Program B whilst it is printing from Program A

(b) The company wants high quality impressive documents for its customers. These are not necessary for the small number of employees.

(MEG, 1993)

A10 (a) LAN = Local Area Network.

(b) The dot matrix printers, which are cheap to run, are used for work within the insurance company. The laser printers, which are expensive to run, are used for letters to customers, etc.

(c) (i) It checks that words are correctly spelt.

(ii) You may want to add words not in the dictionary, e.g. names, technical terms and abbreviations, etc.

(d) (i) You set up a standard letter and a data file. When you mail merge them you produce personalised letters.

(ii) You could send personalised letters to customers advertising your insurance services.

STUDENT'S ANSWER WITH EXAMINER'S COMMENTS

Question

Output from computers can be presented in many different ways

(a) software to log data in a science laboratory can present this data on a screen or as hard copy. State one advantage and one disadvantage of these two methods.

You can see the data on the screen but you have to wait for the hardcopy.

(b) In publishing systems it is necessary to combine text and various forms of graphics.

(i) Why is it often necessary to import graphics files into a DTP package?

(ii) Why is it becoming increasingly easy to do this?

(i) You can't create good graphics in DTP software (ii) It is built into the software.

(NEAB/WJEC, 1993)

Examiner's comment

❝ The student's answer is too vague and too brief. It lacks some significant details that would clearly show that the student understands the topics being examined.

(a) An advantage of displaying the data on a screen is that you can see what is happening when it is happening. A disadvantage is that data displayed on a screen is not permanent unless it is saved on disc or printed.
An advantage of printing the data is that you have a permanent record of what has been logged. A disadvantage is that you do not necessarily have the data in a form that can be later analysed by computer unless it is input once again.

(b) (i) DTP software has a restricted range of graphics functions compared with graphics software.

(ii) Difficulties in importing graphics arise because of different and incompatible file formats. Most software can now import and export files in a much wider variety of formats so it is more likely a compatible format will have been used. Common formats are: WMF, GEM and PIF, etc. ❞

REVIEW SHEET

1. Complete the sentences using these phrases:

> high
> resolution
> interactive
> low resolution
> picture
> text

(a) When you use Desk Top Publishing software, you should use a_____ monitor as this is better for detailed work.

(b) Wordprocessing can be done on a_____ monitor as you can easily read text on any type of screen.

(c) Sometimes, when you use a computer, it is like having a conversation with it. This is _____processing.

2. Computers can speak.

(a) Describe a situation where a computer spoke to you.

_____

_____

_____

(b) Describe a situation where speech is the best form of communication from a computer.

_____

_____

_____

(c) Do computers really understand what they are saying?

_____

_____

_____

(d) Can computers have a conversation with you like you would have with your friends?

_____

_____

_____

3. Use these words to complete the sentences.

> character
> page
> perforations
> sprocket
> tractor

(a) Putting paper in a printer with a _____ feed can be complicated. You must make sure the teeth go into the _____ holes.

(b) A dot matrix printer prints one _____ at a time. This can be very slow. Laser printers print a _____ at a time. These can be much faster.

(c) Sheets of continuous computer paper can be separated by tearing them along the _____. The _____ holes down the side can sometimes be removed in a similar way.

4. If you were using CAD software, you might choose to use a graph plotter instead of a printer. Why?

_____

_____

_____

5. Which of these printers give the best quality printout?

     dot matrix

     ink jet

     laser

_____

6. A new washing machine is guaranteed for five years if you fill in a form and send it to the manufacturers.

(a) Design the form.

(b) Imagine you have just bought a new washing machine. Fill in the form you have just designed.

(c) Label the form to show which information will be:

     pre-printed on the form

     written on the form

7. Describe how a library catalogue stored on microfiche is used. What are the advantages in storing the catalogue on microfiche?

_____

_____

_____

_____

OPERATING SYSTEMS AND NETWORKS

OPERATING SYSTEMS

GRAPHICAL USER INTERFACE (GUI)

STANDALONE MODE

NETWORKS

NETWORK SECURITY

GETTING STARTED

The **Operating System** (OS) is a program that supervises the running of other programs and helps the user manage the computer system. The operating system provides a standardised environment in which programs can easily access the hardware, making them *portable* between different computers running the same OS.

An Operating System will also maintain security by checking **User Identification Numbers** and the corresponding *passwords*. However large or small a computer, in order to use it an operating system must be available.

Graphical User Interfaces (GUI) make it easier to use a computer. You can access the Operating System functions using a mouse and Windows, Icons, Menus and a Pointer (WIMP).

Microcomputers are often used in **standalone** mode. On some microcomputers you can run more than one program at the same time. This is *multitasking*.

Microcomputers can be attached to a network and used as **network stations**. The microcomputers may be attached directly to the computer network or may communicate with it over the telephone network using modems.

There are several different shapes of computer networks. A mainframe computer may be the centre of a star network; microcomputers can be connected to form a **line network** or a **ring network**. A **Local Area Network (LAN)** has permanent cable links between all the network stations and other hardware connected to the network, whereas a **Wide Area Network (WAN)** will make use of temporary links, such as telephone lines, to make network connections. LANs will be confined to a building or room in contrast to WANS, which may be international.

Networks create **security** problems because of the large number of users. Access to networks can be restricted by user identification numbers and passwords; physical security measures; shielding the network cable; data encryption; keeping a log of network usage.

ESSENTIAL PRINCIPLES

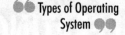

> **1**   OPERATING SYSTEMS

WHAT IS AN OPERATING SYSTEM?

The **Operating System (OS)** is a program. It must be available in memory when a user program is run. Unless an OS is present a computer cannot normally be used. In the vast majority of computers the operating system is loaded into the memory from disc. In some microcomputers the OS is present in a ROM chip, thus leaving all the **RAM** memory free for user programs and data.

●● Types of Operating System ●●

IBM PCs and compatibles, such as RM Nimbus computers, use the MS-DOS operating system. Another OS commonly used with microcomputers is CP/M, which is used on the Amstrad PCW series and the Atari ST range. UNIX is an increasingly popular OS for mainframe computers.

WHAT DOES THE OPERATING SYSTEM DO?

■ **The OS supervises programs while they are running.** The operating system looks after programs while they are being run, making sure no problems arise and helping to overcome them if they do. The OS tries to keep programs running if at all possible.

■ **The Operating System makes the hardware easy to use.** User programs run on the OS, which runs between the user program and the hardware (see Fig. 8.1), making it possible for the user program to access the hardware using simplified standard routines provided by the OS. For example, when you press a key on the keyboard a very complex process involving electronics and Operating System software leads to that character appearing on the screen. We would find it tedious to have to directly program this process every time we press a key. The computer would be practically unusable without standard OS routines to ensure key presses resulted in corresponding character displays on the screen.

●● Functions of the Operating System ●●

All access to the hardware from the user programs should be through the standard routines provided by the operating system.

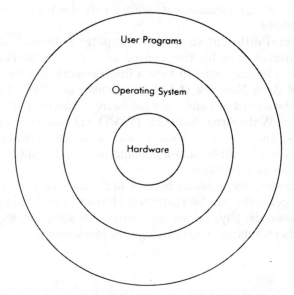

User Programs

Operating System

Hardware

Fig. 8.1 The OS runs between the user programs and the hardware

■ **The OS helps the user decide what to do.** The operating system supervises the running of user programs and will display messages telling the user what to do. For example, if the printer has run out of paper the OS will attract the user's attention to this; if the program needs some data, the OS will display a message asking for the data to be provided and may tell the user which file and which disc is needed.

■ **The OS makes programs portable from one computer to another.** Operating Systems provide a standardised environment, enabling user programs to use peripherals, such as disc drives, by giving the same instructions on any computer running that Operating System. The disc drives could be of different makes and work differently and the computers could also be different, but still the OS would allow standard instructions to be used. Ideally, this makes programs portable, in other words, they should run on any computer running the OS they were written to be run on.

■ **The Operating System provides utilities to manage the computer system.** When using any computer system it is important to be careful and tidy so that, for example, you do not lose files or get one file confused with another. The OS provides the necessary utilities to enable the system to be well managed.

For discs, there will be instructions to format the disc and to delete, rename or copy files saved on the disc. When a disc is formatted a skeleton framework is set up of the sectors and blocks on the disc in which data and programs will later be saved. On a new (unformatted) disc this framework is not present. The disc must be formatted before it can be used.

A file is *deleted* by removing it from the disc. A **renamed** file will have its filename changed, but not the data in the file. A file can be *copied* from one disc to another, so that a copy of the file exists on both discs.

The OS will maintain a **directory** (or *catalogue*) of a disc, which is simply a list of the filenames of all the files on a disc. This directory is itself saved on the disc.

■ **Operating Systems optimise the use of resources.** In larger computers the OS will arrange the use of hardware and software resources, so that maximum use is made of them and all users get a fair share. Users can be given **priorities**, so that if resources are in short supply the operating system can restrict access to users with a *low* priority and make the resources available to those with a *high* priority. A **log** will be kept by the OS which records *who* is using the computer, *how long* they used it and *what* they did. This gives enough information so that users may be charged for the resources they have used.

■ **The OS maintains security.** On larger computers and networks each person who is allowed to use the computer will have a User Identification Number usually known as the **User Id**. Each user also has a password which is known only to the user. The OS keeps a register of all the User Ids and passwords and will only allow registered users who give the correct password to use the computer.

Hackers, who are not registered users, will sometimes discover how to break into the system, often by guessing a User Id and the password. However, their activities will be recorded on the log by the OS and they can usually be traced and identified.

2 ▶ GRAPHICAL USER INTERFACE (GUI)

GUI or WIMP (Windows, Icons, Menus, Pointer) systems have been developed to make it easier for users to make use of a computer. They enable the OS and other programs to be run without the need to type in complex text operating system commands. Text OS commands are often difficult to remember and it is easy to make mistakes when typing them in at the keyboard. WIMP user interfaces bypass these problems by using a mouse instead of a keyboard. (See Fig. 5.11)

WINDOWS

Windows are rectangular areas of the screen which contain information relating to one task (see Fig. 5.12). If a microcomputer supports multitasking, it is possible to run different tasks in different windows, displaying the results on the screen at the same time. For example, a wordprocessor can be run in one window and a database in another, at the same time. This allows data to be transferred from, say, the database to the wordprocessor, by moving it between the windows. It is also possible to open windows on different parts of the same task, for example, different parts of a wordprocessing document and transfer text between them.

99 Features of GUI systems 99

ICONS

Icons are pictures that represent objects, e.g. floppy discs, or operations that can be performed, e.g., a picture of a dustbin may be used to allow files to be deleted.

MENUS

Operations are also made available through **menus**. Menus contain lists of menu options that can be chosen.

POINTER

A **Pointer** is used to point at icons and menu options. It is controlled by moving a mouse about a flat surface. The movement of the pointer on the screen corresponds to the movement of the mouse on the flat surface. An icon or menu option can be selected by *pointing* at it and *clicking* one of the buttons on the mouse. When an icon or menu option is selected, the operation it represents is performed. Usually all the operations available can be accessed using a mouse, without the need to type in text OS commands at the keyboard.

3 › STANDALONE MODE

Microcomputers which are not linked to other computers are being used in **standalone mode**. Often, they will have peripherals, such as printers and disc drives, attached to them but they will not be linked to other computers most of the time. Most programs that are run on standalone microcomputers are interactive.

❝ Multitasking ❞

In general, microcomputers run one program at a time, but it is becoming common for a computer to run several programs at the same time. On a microcomputer, running several programs at the same time is called **multitasking**. For example, when using my wordprocessor I may wish to refer to a database to extract information to be put in an article I am writing. If the microcomputer I am using will only run one program at a time I have to save the article on disc, exit from the wordprocessor, load the database, extract the information, save the information, exit from the database, load the wordprocessor, get the document I was using and load the information I extracted from the database! A lengthy process!

If the microcomputer supports multitasking, I simply load the database, extract the information and transfer it into the article. I am able to do this because the wordprocessor and the database will run on the same computer at the same time.

4 › NETWORKS

Computers can be linked together to form networks. There are several ways in which these connections can be made. The shape of the network chosen is determined by the way in which the links are made and the size of the computers attached to the network.

STAR NETWORK

❝ Multiaccess ❞

A **Star Network** is common when a mainframe computer is being accessed by many users (see Fig. 8.2). When many users access a computer at the same time, this is known as **multiaccess**.

Users access the network using network stations attached to it. A network station is usually a microcomputer with additional hardware and software to enable it to communicate over the network. Network stations are also referred to as 'terminals'.

❝ Network stations ❞

A network station can be connected directly to the computer network or it can communicate with another computer over the telephone network.

Where a network station is connected directly to the computer network, the additional hardware is often called a 'network board' as it is frequently available as a circuit board that plugs into the computer. The additional software is referred to as 'network software'. This software enables the network station to send and receive data over the computer network.

Where two or more computers communicate over the telephone network at national or international distances, communications software and a **modem** are required.

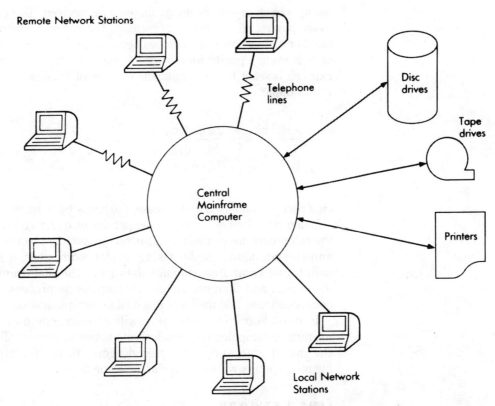

Fig. 8.2 A Star Network

A modem (*mo*dulator/*dem*odulator) converts the digital signal output by the micro-computer to an analogue signal that can be transmitted along the telephone lines. A modem also converts the analogue signals sent along the telephone lines to digital signals that the computer can process (see Fig. 8.3). The diagram shows two similar microcomputers communicating but, in fact, provided the appropriate communications software is available, any two computers can communicate.

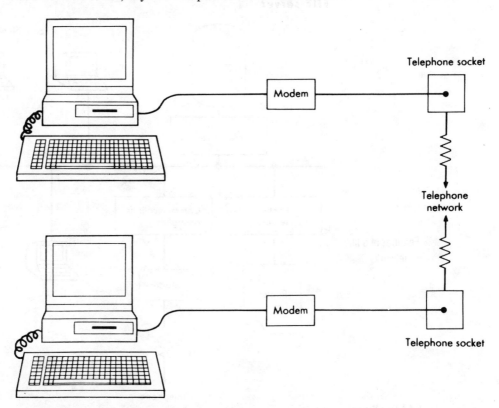

Fig. 8.3 Computers communicating using the telephone network

Communications software

Communications Software is a program that can transmit and receive data via the modem and the telephone system. The telephone system is not a reliable means of transmitting data, so when the data is transmitted, it is checked. The modem does a

parity check automatically as the data is received. To perform a parity check using **even parity**, all the bits representing the received character are added up. If the number of 1s is even the data has been transmitted accurately. To ensure the number of 1s is even, a **parity bit** is added to the bit pattern representing the character. This extra bit is set at 1 or 0 to make the number of 1s even.

For example:

even parity bit	bit pattern
1	101 0010
0	011 0011

Odd parity is also used. In this case, the parity bit is set to make the number of 1s odd.

Using the telephone system is expensive as a charge is made for the length of time the computers are connected. A microcomputer can be used both as a network station and in standalone mode. Using a microcomputer, it is possible to access the mainframe computer, transfer data from the mainframe to the microcomputer, disconnect and then use the microcomputer to process the data. This reduces the connection time and the costs involved in communications.

In most Star Networks there will be microcomputers connected to a central mainframe computer via the telephone network; others will be in the same building as the mainframe and connected directly to it. Not all of these terminals and microcomputers will be on-line at the same time.

LINE NETWORK

A **Line Network** is used to link several microcomputers, allowing them to communicate with each other and to share data and peripherals (see Fig. 8.4). Each microcomputer uses its own processing power and it is likely that each will be running a different program.

File server

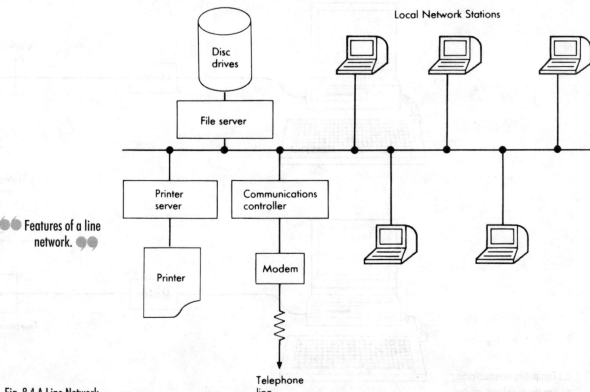

66 Features of a line network. 99

Fig. 8.4 A Line Network

66 File servers let computers share programs & data 99

On most line networks there will be a **file server**, i.e. a computer that organises the sharing of files saved on common backing storage by all computers connected to the network. Files will be stored on a hard disc capable of storing very large volumes of data and accessing it very quickly. By sharing a hard disc, each network station is given access to greater volumes of on-line data at a more economic cost. Most of the programs run by microcomputers connected to the network will also be stored on the hard disc and loaded and run as required.

Printer server

A printer server is a microcomputer that organises access to the printers attached to it for all the stations on the network. The printer server has one or two printers attached to it. These printers can be used by all the network stations. It is more economical to buy a printer server and the one or two printers attached to it than to buy a local printer for every station on the network. Local printers would not be in use all the time as printing is done for only a short period of time after the output has been prepared on the network station. The printers attached to the printer server will be in use more often as all the network stations use them.

When a network station uses a printer attached to the printer server, the printed output may not be printed immediately. Printed output is spooled to the printer, that is, it is temporarily saved on the hard disc on the fileserver where it joins the queue for printing. When it reaches the head of the queue, it is printed. If the printing was directed to a printer, the user would have to wait until the printing had been completed before control returned to the network station. However, because the printed output is saved to the network hard disc before printing, the network station user does not have to wait long before control returns. Saving to the network hard disc is much faster than waiting for output to be immediately printed.

The advantages of sharing a network printer are that it is more economical; a better quality printer can be purchased; control returns to the network station faster. The disadvantage is that the printout is not available immediately. It may be necessary to wait some time for printouts.

Communications controller

Microcomputers connected to the network may also wish to *communicate* with other computers that are not on the network using a shared modem and telephone lines. A **communications controller** will be necessary to ensure that data is sent to the appropriate network station. In some Line Networks the file server, printer server and communications controller may be a single microcomputer doing all of these tasks. The RM Nimbus networks that are widely used in education are examples of Line Networks.

RING NETWORKS

A **Ring Network** is similar to a Line Network, except that the ends of the line are joined to form a ring (see Fig. 8.5).

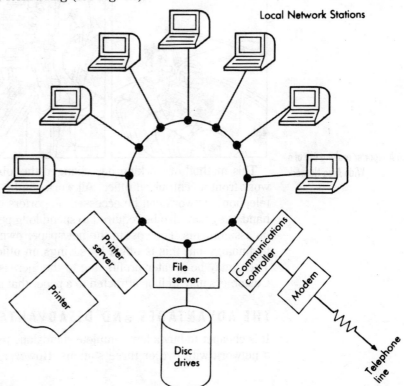

Fig. 8.5 A Ring Network

On a line network data is sent in both directions along the network whereas on a ring network data is sent in one direction only. Consequently ring networks generally communicate faster. However, it is often easier to extend line networks as only a single cable is needed to each new network station. This is useful where the complete network cannot be planned in advance because of the need for possible future expansion or where network stations are widely dispersed.

Features of a Ring Network

LOCAL AREA NETWORKS (LAN)

Features of a Local Area Network

A **Local Area Network** or LAN is a network where all the different hardware connected to the network is permanently linked by a cable, so that there is no need to use a modem and telephone line to communicate with other network stations. LANs are likely to be Line Networks or Ring Networks. A LAN will be located on one site, possibly in a building such as a school or an office block, perhaps even in a single room.

WIDE AREA NETWORKS (WAN)

Features of a Wide Area Network

A **Wide Area Network** or WAN is a network where all the hardware on the network is not permanently linked, perhaps due to the wide geographical distribution of network stations. WANs are likely to make use of a modem and telephone lines for regular communications with other parts of the network. A common example of a WAN is a mainframe computer that is accessed from terminals via the telephone system in a Star Network.

Since the telephone network is world wide, it is possible and not uncommon for WANs to be international. For example, a newspaper reporter can write articles on a wordprocessor running on a lap-top computer powered from a car battery while sitting in a car parked at a remote location (see Fig. 8.6). The article can be saved as a wordprocessing document on a disc. When it is possible to use a telephone, perhaps from a public call box, the reporter can use the telephone system to make a temporary connection between the lap-top computer and the WAN used by the newspaper. Once connected, the reporter can send one or more articles, previously prepared for publication, in a few seconds.

Fig. 8.6 A reporter making use of a Wide Area Network

This method of working has changed the job of a reporter. There is less need to work from a centralised office. All work can be done in any location from where the telephone network can be accessed. Reporters can now work at home. On the other hand, they may also be required to spend long periods away from home when working on assignments. The cost to the newspaper owner is greater investment in computer technology but this is offset by savings on office accommodation and clerical staff. There may be greater profits due to the increased speed at which news is reported. Customers may well be attracted to a paper that prints news ahead of its rivals.

THE ADVANTAGES AND DISADVANTAGES OF NETWORKS

It is cheaper to buy a few complete standalone microcomputer systems, than to set up a network with two or three stations. However, once the initial cost of setting up a network has been paid, it can be cheaper to add extra stations to a network than to buy standalone microcomputer systems. Expensive peripherals can be shared on a network where the cost of purchase for a standalone system might be too great, e.g. laser printer, graph plotter.

Programs and data stored on a hard disc connected to the network can also be shared. This may be more economic than buying single copies of software packages for a number of standalone systems. Networks enable users to share data. If this data is kept up-to-date, then they will coordinate their work better and it will be of a higher standard.

5 > NETWORK SECURITY

Networks create **security** problems because of the increased number of users sharing the system. These problems can be overcome in several ways.

■ User Identification Numbers and passwords restrict access to the use of the software and data stored on the network;

■ Physical access to network stations should be restricted by employing security guards and door locks operated by magnetic stripe cards, or by entering a password on a key pad lock;

❛❛ How to overcome security problems ❜❜

■ The network cable should be shielded to prevent unauthorised connection. The data on the network should be encoded to obscure its meaning (i.e. data encryption);

■ The Operating System should keep a log of users and their activities so that hackers can be detected and traced.

All these measures should be used to deter unauthorised use of the network.

EXAMINATION QUESTIONS

Q1. A secretary is doing the firm's accounts. He logs onto the network and enters his password. He presses the correct letter to select a spreadsheet program from a list on the screen. He then loads in the correct file, enters new data and recalculates the sheet, obtains a printout and saves the new version. In this current system all operations have to be done using the keyboard.

Which of the following is the OPERATING SYSTEM directly responsible for. Tick the appropriate boxes.

(a) Asking for the password ☐

(b) Entering an invoice number ☐

(c) Displaying a negative amount in red ☐

(d) Calculating a new total ☐

(e) Controlling data sent to the printer ☐

(f) Selecting a save option ☐

(NEAB/WJEC, 1993)

Q2. Tick TWO ways of protecting personal data:

Laser printing	
Locking discs away	
Sorting data	
Using a data bank	
Using a password	

(SEG, 1993)

Q3. Describe how, in a modern office system, computers can be connected and managed on a network.

(MEG, 1993)

Q4. An order-processing system uses on-line processing, telephone lines and modems.

(a) What is the modem used for?

(b) What is on-line processing?

(c) Some of this information stored on the system is coded. Give TWO reasons why information is coded on a computer file.

(MEG, 1993)

Q5. Describe how a computer hacker might do more harm than an office burglar.

(MEG, 1993)

Q6. Three different types of systems software are the operating system, utility programs and translation programs.

(a) Give three jobs of an operating system.

(b) Name two utility programs and explain briefly what they do.

(c) A low-level language program needs to be translated into machine code before it is executed. Name the translation program that carries out this task.

(d) Name two high-level languages.

(e) High-level languages also need to be translated so that they can be executed. This can be done in two different ways. Name two different types of translation program used with high-level language programs and explain the differences between them.

(SEG, 1993)

Q7. QUESTION DATA

A daily newspaper has a local area network which links all the computers in their London Headquarters. The Headquarters consists of a newsroom, an editorial office and a printing works. The paper also has a wide area network linking it to a regional office in Edinburgh and an overseas office in New York.

(a) The local area network is linked using direct wire connectors.

How might the wide area network be linked between:

(i) Edinburgh and London.

(ii) London and New York.

(b) Describe how use of LANS has affected work in this daily newspaper.

(City and Guilds, 1993)

Q8. State two functions which would be carried out by the operating system.

(City and Guilds, 1993)

Q9. A school uses a database system to handle records of pupils.

(a) Give ONE benefit to the school staff of using a computer system.

(b) Describe THREE particular routines that the database software provides.

The office staff use a mouse and windows to interface with the database software.

(c) Write down **TWO** features that you associate with such a graphical user interface.

(d) Give **ONE** advantage of using such an interface instead of a traditional command-line environment.

(MEG, 1993)

Q10. Sainsbury's commission a new product from Sprayway Ltd, a facial mineral water spray.

Sainsbury's launch the product in selected branches throughout the North-East of England on a trial basis.

(a) Explain how the Sainsbury's head office in London are likely to receive the sales information that they require to assess whether the product should be stocked throughout all of their stores.

(b) What information would the Sainsbury's head office be looking to extract from their sales database, in order to decide whether to stock the facial spray throughout all of their stores?

(c) How else could Sainsbury's have collected sufficient information about the sales of the facial spray to make their stocking decision if they were unable to use information technology?

(d) State **TWO** advantages information technology would give Sainsbury's in making such stocking decisions.

(ULEAC, 1993)

ANSWERS TO EXAMINATION QUESTIONS

A1. The Operating System is directly responsible for (a) & (e).

A2. Locking discs away/using a password.

A3. Three from:
Computers would be cabled together connected to a common file server;
Computers would share a high quality printer or have local printers;
Software would be stored on the file server and shared between users;
Each user would have a secure area to prevent unauthorised access of data.

(MEG, 1993)

A4. (a) To translate signals from the computer into signals which can be transmitted over the telephone system.

(b) User is in direct contact with the computer.
Computer responds to user input.

(c) Two from:
To save space in the computer's memory;
To save data entry time;
To process the data faster.

(MEG, 1993)

A5. Four from:
Personal data might be viewed and acted upon/sold;
Personal data might be altered;
Personal data might be destroyed;
Software might be deleted;
Viruses could be introduced into a system and spread.

(MEG, 1993)

A6. (a) ■ Controlling input and output.

■ Providing system security using passwords and user identification numbers.

■ Keeping a log of who uses a computer network.

(b) Format – used to format a disc so that it can be used on the computer.

Copy – makes a copy of a named file.

(c) Assembler.

(d) COBOL
BASIC

(e) High level languages are converted using Compilers and Interpreters. Compilers translate the whole of the source program into machine code (the object program) before the object program is executed. Interpreters translate one line of the source program at a time and execute it before continuing to translate the rest of the source program.

A7. (a) (i) telephone line or micro wave

(ii) satellite link

(b) LANs, especially those linked via WANs, enable:

■ reporters to send articles to the newspaper from around the world.

■ the newspaper to communicate with it's employees faster, using E-mail.

■ all employees can share resources on the network, including on-line databases, etc.

A8. An Operating System:

■ controls the input and output.

■ deals with errors while the computer is running.

■ provides system utilities, e.g. format.

A9. (a) Faster access to pupil information

(b) Three from:
Searching for specified information
Different layouts for printed output
Sorting data into a variety of orders
Specifying what data to display
Any other functions

(c) Two from:
Windows to position on the screen
Icons to select applications
Mouse control of the pointer
Pointer on the screen

(d) One from:
Very little typing
Fewer commands to memorise
Ability to drag data from one application to another
Easy transfer of data
Any suitable advantage

(MEG, 1993)

A10. (a) Sales information about the product sales is likely to be recorded in electronic form as the product is sold. This information will be sent to Head Office in electronic form across a WAN.

(b) The sales information about the new product will be extracted from the sales information about all products. The Head Office will want to know how much of the product has been sold, where it was sold, at what times it sold most and if different pricing affected sales.

(c) They could manually record the sales of the new product. One method is to have a sales assistant handing out the product and recording sales. This method is often used to promote new products.

(d) The advantages of using IT are:

■ the information is collected and sent to Head Office much faster.

■ the information is reliable, comprehensive and accurate.

■ the information from all the stores is available.

STUDENT'S ANSWER WITH EXAMINER'S COMMENTS

Question

A school is setting up a new computer resource base, with 16 stand-alone computers, for pupils.

The school could have installed a network, but decided against this option. Discuss the possible reasons for this decision.

(NEAB/WJEC, 1993)

Student's Answer

The network in our school is always breaking down. None of the computers work and we cannot do our work on the computers. This could be why the school didn't have a network.

Examiner's comment

❝ That is one good reason to avoid installing a network. There are others:

■ information stored on a network is less secure.

■ it can be difficult and expensive to link computers in different rooms in the school.

■ computers using a network can be slowed down if the network is heavily used.

■ if pupils' work is stored on the file server, the amount they can store will be limited.

There are also many good reasons to install networks that are not mentioned here! ❞

REVIEW SHEET

1. State whether the following statements are true or false.

(a) An Amiga computer has a different operating system to an IBM computer.

_____

(b) Database software cannot be run unless the operating system is also used.

_____

(c) Wordprocessing software can be run without using the operating system.

_____

(d) A portable program can be run on any computer.

_____

(e) GUIs make IT more difficult to use.

_____

2. Use these words to complete the sentences:

icon
menu
mouse
pointer
window

(a) If you open more than one_____ _____, you can look at different parts of a wordprocessing document at the same time.

(b) In a graphics package, you will find an _____that allows you to draw on the screen as if you were using a pencil.

(c) You can choose from a _____by pointing and clicking a button on the_____.

(d) If you move the mouse a _____ moves on the screen in the same way.

3. Draw a diagram of a computer network you are familiar with. On the diagram, label this hardware:

■ a network station

■ the file server

■ printers

■ hard discs

4. A school is intending to buy some computers for Information Technology. These alternatives are being considered:

■ Setting up a computer room with 20 standalone computers each with a local printer, a hard disc and a floppy disc.

■ Setting up a computer room with 20 computers in a LAN. They would share the network printers and hard disc. Only a few of the computers would have floppy discs.

■ Buying 20 portable computers each with a hard disc and a floppy disc. Four portable printers would be bought.

(a) Discuss the advantages and disadvantages of each alternative.

_____

_____

_____

_____

_____

_____

(b) Estimate the cost of each alternative.

_____

_____

_____

(c) Propose your own ideal set up.

_____

_____

(d) What software would you advise the school to buy?

_____

_____

5. WANs often use the global telecommunications network.

(a) Describe how a journalist would use a WAN.

_____

_____

(b) What advantages does the use of a WAN have to a journalist.

_____

_____

6. Which of the following can be used to prevent hackers using a network?

■ regular backups of important files _____

■ user identification numbers and passwords _____

■ store all the data on CD-ROM _____

■ a log of who is using the network _____

■ car park permits _____

CHAPTER 9

COMMUNICATING INFORMATION

AUDIENCE

WORDPROCESSING

GRAPHICS

DESK TOP PUBLISHING (DTP)

ELECTRONIC MAIL

MULTIMEDIA

CONFERENCING

GETTING STARTED

When we **communicate information** we try to be clear, simple and interesting and to present the information being communicated in a straight forward and logical manner. We take into account the extent to which our audience is likely to understand the information and seek to interest them in what we are communicating.

IT can extend and enhance the effectiveness of our communication skills. All IT software is to some extent used to communicate information. In this chapter we focus on the IT software that is mainly used for communicating information, that is:

■ **Wordprocessing** software is used to prepare and print articles, reports and other documents. Letters can be personalised and address labels printed for envelopes.

■ **Graphics** software is used to draw pictures, produce posters, illustrate articles and design textiles and industrial products.

■ **Desk Top Publishing** combines wordprocessing and graphics in the format typical of a newspaper with text in columns, photographs and other illustrations.

■ **Electronic Mail** is sent from one computer to another, using a network. The sending of mail by this method is faster and more convenient than using the traditional paper, envelope and stamp method.

■ **Multimedia** is the presentation of text, graphics, sound and video in a format that could be described as interactive DTP. Multimedia is often based on CD-ROM backing storage technology.

ESSENTIAL PRINCIPLES

❝❝ Communication is the key ❞❞

IT extends and enhances our ability to *communicate*. In this chapter, we look at software that is mainly used to communicate information, e.g. software for wordprocessing, graphics and Desk Top Publishing (DTP). This software does not replace traditional methods of communication, it extends and enhances them. It is most important to remember that using IT is no substitute for a clear, simple, interesting presentation of the information being communicated in a straight forward and logical manner. Your use of IT should improve the effectiveness of your communication skills. It may not teach you those skills.

❝❝ Nature of the wordprocessor ❞❞

For example, **wordprocessors** do not replace hand writing, although they may very well replace manual and electronic typewriters. Wordprocessors extend what we can do and allow us to do what we already do in new, better ways. Wordprocessors are not being used to their full potential if they are just used for making a neat copy of work that has already been written out. They should be used for drafting and re-drafting text. For example, writing a long essay (or a book!) involves planning the way in which large volumes of written material are presented. Sometimes you will want to move a sentence or a paragraph to a new position in the essay. If you have hand written or typed your essay, this can be difficult. You may have to re-write or re-type sections or cut out a section and stick it in somewhere else. With a wordprocessor, you can simply move the text to its new position. You can include pictures, diagrams and other graphics in some wordprocessors. These could be drawings that you have done yourself using graphics software. They could be photographs or printed diagrams from books that you have scanned into the computer. Desk Top Publishing (DTP) software will enable you to re-arrange the text and graphics you have produced into a layout similar to that of a newspaper or magazine.

These facilities can be very useful for developing and producing coursework for GCSE exams. They are also widely used throughout commerce and industry to improve productivity and effectiveness.

1 ▷ AUDIENCE

❝❝ Think about the audience ❞❞

When you are communicating information, by whatever means, it is important to consider the effects of what you do on your **audience**. You should do this for all forms of communication by whatever media you are using.

You will need to take into account the extent to which your audience understands the material you are communicating. For example, if you are explaining how a Nuclear Power Station works, your explanation to children in primary school would need to be more straight forward than if you were giving an explanation to a group of A-level Physics students. If the complexity of the material presented does not match the understanding of your audience, they will be bored, confused and annoyed. It is unlikely they will enjoy your explanation.

As the purpose of communication is to *inform* your audience, they should not fall asleep because your means of communication is dull. If you can use humour and metaphor effectively, your audience might be more interested in the material you are communicating. The use of colour images instead of black and white; video instead of still pictures; sound and music as well as pictures can motivate audiences.

Teachers in schools have to consider their audience when planning their lessons. How often have you been bored because the lesson was too easy or frustrated because the material was too hard? Which teachers do you find interesting? Why? If you remember these experiences when you are trying to communicate information to your audience you may produce more effective work yourself.

2 ▷ WORDPROCESSING

Wordprocessors, i.e. computers running wordprocessing software, have now largely replaced the traditional, mechanical or electronic typewriter. Wordprocessors can do any task carried out on a typewriter. They also make such tasks easier, and have additional, more powerful facilities.

A wordprocessor will typically consist of a microcomputer, monitor, mouse, disc drive, printer and wordprocessing software. Many, but not all, wordprocessors can be operated either from the keyboard alone or using the keyboard and a mouse. A mouse improves the ease and speed of operation of a wordprocessor. The quality of the printed output is determined by the type of printer used. For high quality output, high speed graphics and a wide variety of character styles or fonts, a laser printer is needed. For inexpensive, low quality printout, a dot matrix printer is appropriate.

❝❝ Wordprocessing software ❞❞

Wordprocessing software is extensive and varied. There is very often a choice of wordprocessors for a particular computer and many wordprocessors will run on several different makes of computer. It may interest the reader to know that this book was written using the 1stWord wordprocessing software running on an Atari ST microcomputer (see Fig. 9.1). This software is also available for other computers, e.g. the Archimedes and the IBM PC. A wide variety of other wordprocessing software can be run on the Atari ST, e.g. WordPerfect, Text Pro, K-Word, STwriter, etc.

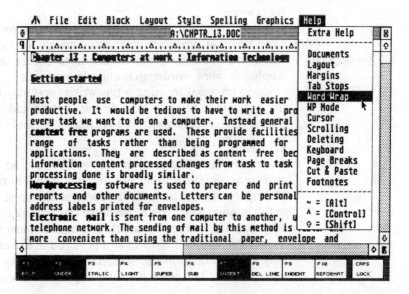

Fig 9.1 The screen displayed by the 1stWord wordprocessor running on an Atari ST

WHAT A WORDPROCESSOR CAN BE USED FOR

Wordprocessors can be used to prepare a wide variety of printed material. The range of tasks that can be done is so extensive that only a few can be mentioned here. These are some of the tasks that a wordprocessor could be used for:

❝❝ Some uses of the wordprocessor ❞❞

■ writing a letter, memo, news sheets, leaflet, brochure, essay, article, book, etc.
■ preparing a curriculum vitae (c.v.), questionnaire, work sheet, exam paper, etc.
■ keeping a list of names and addresses so that they can be printed out on sticky labels which can then be stuck on envelopes.
■ printing personalised letters to be sent to customers, patients, subscribers, donors, etc.
■ helping disabled people communicate, particularly the deaf.

WHAT WORDPROCESSORS DO

Different wordprocessors do the same tasks but may be operated in different ways. Some wordprocessors will have more facilities and be easier to use than others. The facilities described below are available on most wordprocessors. You should look for these facilities on the wordprocessor you use and make sure you can use them.

Create a document

❝❝ Creating a document ❞❞

A document is a file of words or text to be processed, for example, an article or a letter. When a new document is needed it is **created**. When you are creating a document, the screen displayed will be blank to begin with. The text is typed into the document from the keyboard and appears on the screen as it is typed. The point at which you are entering text on the screen will be marked by a cursor. This may be a solid rectangle, the size of one character, that may be flashing. The end of the document may be marked in some way, possibly by a horizontal line across the screen. If you want to keep the document you have created then you will have to save it (see below).

What You See Is What You Get (WYSIWYG)

WYSIWYG or What You See Is What You Get means that the document you see on the screen of the wordprocessor is exactly as it will look when it is printed. This is a most desirable feature. It is often difficult to visualise the printed format of a document if you are using a wordprocessor that does not display documents in WYSIWYG form on the screen.

❝ WYSIWYG ❞

Commands

All wordprocessors use **commands** in some form or another to operate the facilities provided. In some wordprocessors, commands can be operated using command menus. These are displayed on the screen underneath or above the document being processed. They can be accessed using the keyboard or, more conveniently, with a mouse. Each option selected in the Command menu may have its own sub-menu.

Wordwrap

When entering text, at the end of each line , as you type beyond the right margin, the word that you type in will be automatically carried over onto the next line. This is **wordwrap**. You need take no action to ensure that wordwrap takes place. In most wordprocessors, wordwrap is entirely automatic.

❝ Wordwrap ❞

If you are used to using a typewriter, you may be inclined to press <RETURN> at the end of each line. Do NOT do this. You should only press <RETURN> at the end of a paragraph. Pressing <RETURN> marks the end of a paragraph.

Scrolling

Since it is likely that a document will be too big for all of it to be displayed on the screen at the same time, the document will **scroll**, that is, if you are viewing an existing document, text will disappear at the top of the screen while more text appears at the bottom, when you move down the document. You will notice the opposite effect when moving up the document. You have not lost the text when it is not displayed on the screen. The entire document is stored in the memory of the computer but we can only see part of it on the screen. Scrolling takes place automatically when you are entering text. You need not take any action to ensure it happens at the appropriate time.

❝ Scrolling ❞

Moving around a document

When you have entered the document, you may want to **move around it** to view and edit it. To do this you can use the cursor control keys or 'arrow keys'. However, this will be quite slow, particularly if you want to move from the start of a long document to the end. Your wordprocessor may provide quicker ways of moving around a document. For example, it is not uncommon to press the <PGUP> key to move up the document one screen and to press the <PGDN> key to move down a document by one screen.

❝ Cursor control keys ❞

Delete, insert and edit text

When a document has been entered, it may have mistakes in it, eg. spelling mistakes, or you may decide you want to re-write parts of it. You can delete or insert text by editing it on the screen. Delete means 'remove existing characters'; insert means 'put in new characters'. Editing text is done by a combination of deleting and inserting text. All wordprocessors allow text to be edited.

Control characters

Your document may contain 'invisible' characters that you have entered at the keyboard but do not see on the screen. These are known as **control characters** as they are used to control the operation of the word processor. The most obvious of these is the character that represents a single press of the <RETURN> key, though there will be others to represent different style and format commands. You might find it useful to know where you have pressed the <RETURN> key in your document as this key is pressed at the end of a paragraph and to insert blank lines. Many wordprocessors will allow you to chose whether to display the control characters on the screen.

❝ Control characters ❞

Block delete, move and copy

You can define a block of text then delete it, move it to a different position in the document or make another copy of it in a different position, perhaps in another document. A block can be a character, a paragraph or the whole document. A block is defined by highlighting it using the mouse or a combination of function keys. The ability to delete, move or copy large blocks of text is a very useful facility when re-drafting or re-writing large documents.

Text style

Various **style** facilities are available in most wordprocessors to improve the appearance of the text. For example, text can be underlined, bold or italic or a combination of these. You can have different sizes of text or different fonts. The size of a character is measured in points. A **font** is a particular style of forming the letters printed. Some text styles are illustrated in Fig. 9.2.

> **Different fonts**

You can change text style before entering the text. All text subsequently entered will be in the style chosen. You can change text style after you have entered the text by highlighting the block to be re-styled and then selecting the new style.

Times New Roman font, 10 point, normal

Times New Roman font, 14 point, normal

Times New Roman font, 18 point, normal

Times New Roman font, 22 point, normal

Times New Roman font, 14 point, italic

Times New Roman font, 14 point, italic, underlined

~~Times New Roman font, 14 point, strike through~~

Arial font, 10 point, normal

Arial font, 14 point, normal

Arial font, 22 point, normal

Arial font, 14 point, normal, italic

Arial font, 10 point, normal

Arial font, 14 point, underlined

~~Arial font, 14 point, strike through~~

Fig 9.2 Different styles of text

Format

Formatting facilities control the layout of text in the document. There will be a variety of formatting facilities, for example, text can be centred on a line; margins can be justified so that the right and left margins are aligned; text can be indented; text can be printed in several columns instead of the usual across the page format; the width and length of the page can be altered; page headings and page numbers can be automatically inserted.

Frames

In some wordprocessors it is possible to draw a simple, rectangular **frame** or border around text to emphasis it. However, it is more usual to put in features that enhance the presentation of a document using DTP software.

Search and replace

The **search** facility is used to find particular words or character strings in a document. The **search and replace** facility is used to find a particular word and replace it with another. For example, if a word has been spelt incorrectly, every occurrence of the word can be located and the incorrect spelling automatically replaced by the correct spelling.

Spelling check

The spelling of words can be checked against an extensive dictionary which can be added to or changed as you wish. Spellings can be checked as you type in the words or you can check the whole document when you want to. It is also possible to check grammar, though grammar checkers are less common and less reliable than spelling checkers.

Save and load documents

When a document has been created it can be **saved** on backing storage, eg. magnetic disc. The computer can then be switched off but the document will not be lost as there is a copy of it on the disc. When the document is needed at a later date, it can be **loaded** from the disc into the computer.

Printing

Documents can be **printed** on a printer connected to the wordprocessor. The quality of the printed output from a wordprocessor is determined by the type of printer used. For high speed, good quality and a wide variety of character styles, fonts and graphics a laser printer is needed; for inexpensive, lower quality printout a dot matrix printer is appropriate.

Many inexpensive dot matrix printers will now print a variety of fonts, in draft and Near Letter Quality (NLQ). Draft printing is fast, but low quality as you can easily see the dots that form each character. NLQ is much better quality than draft. You cannot easily see the dots that form each character and there may be more than one font available.

MAIL MERGE

Companies regularly send letters to customers in which the content of each letter is the same but the name, address and other limited details change.

A **standard letter** contains the part of the document that does not change from letter to letter. The data in the standard letter that does change can be indicated using markers. A **marker** will be replaced by data read from a separate data file. For example, a standard letter can be merged with a data file of customers' names and addresses to print an individualised letter for each customer.

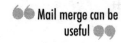 Mail merge can be useful

To use mail merge to send a personalised, standard letter to customers, you proceed as follows. However, you should note that although the principles of doing a mail merge are the same in all wordprocessors, the actual methods of doing it will differ, perhaps considerably.

1. Create a standard letter with markers

You should note that different wordprocessors use different ways of inserting the markers. The standard letter should be saved on disc. An example of a standard letter is shown below:

DIY Magazine
25 Wakefield Rd.
Halifax HX2 5GR
25/6/94

Dear <marker 1>,

I am writing to remind you that your annual subscription is due later this month. I am sure you have enjoyed DIY Magazine this year. You can look forward to a host of interesting articles and other features in the coming year that will help you keep your home at <marker 2> in good shape.

Please renew your subscription as soon as possible.

Yours sincerely,

Daniel Merlin
Circulation Department

---

2. Create a data file

Next, build up a file of data to replace the markers when the letters are printed. Different wordprocessors do this in different ways. The data file corresponding to the above standard letter is shown below:

marker 1, marker 2
John Smith, Stanbury
Rizwan Malik, Bradford
Bodan Jovanovich, Halifax
Jennie Jones, Oxenhope

3. Do the mailmerge

You now have a standard letter and a data file and are ready to do a mailmerge. To print the personalised standard letters, you will have to identify the standard letter and the data file, then activate the mail merge. The letters will be printed for the customers whose details are stored in the data file. In this example, four letters would be printed as there are four records in the data file. One example of a personalised letter printed using mail merge is shown below. Notice that the markers have been replace by the data.

DIY Magazine
25 Wakefield Rd.
Halifax HX2 5GR
25/6/94

Dear Bodan Jovanovich,

I am writing to remind you that your annual subscription is due later this month. I am sure you have enjoyed DIY Magazine this year. You can look forward to a host of interesting articles and other features in the coming year that will help you keep your home at Halifax in good shape.

Please renew your subscription as soon as possible.

Yours sincerely,

Daniel Merlin
Circulation Department

Exporting and importing

Exporting and Importing

Saving a document with the intention of loading it into, for example, DTP software, is known as **exporting** the document. Loading a document that has been prepared on, for example, a different wordprocessor, is known as **importing**.

You may be able to import a wordprocessed document into DTP software without modifying the form in which it is saved on disc. However, it is likely that you will have to ensure that the form in which the document is exported matches one of the forms in which the DTP software can import it. If you can match the form of an exported document with a form in which it can be imported, then all the control characters will be understood by the receiving software. This means that all text styling will be kept. If you cannot match the form of the exported and imported documents then the control characters will not be understood and text styling may be lost. Documents can always be exported and imported in ASCII form but, in this case, all text styling, etc. will be lost.

You can import graphics into some wordprocessors. You will need to be sure that the form in which the graphic has been exported matches a form in which it can be imported.

Some wordprocessors are supplied with a library of clip art, eg. Microsoft Word for Windows. Clip art is art work that has been prepared by a professional artist and saved on disc. A clip art library will contain useful graphics, such as, borders for restaurant menus, cartoon characters to put in newsletters, etc. Clip art can easily be imported into the wordprocessor it has been prepared for.

You may also be able to import a spreadsheet or a database into a wordprocessed document. This is useful for preparing business accounts, etc.

Quit

When you have finished using the wordprocessor, you will want to exit from it and switch off the computer. It is important to exit from the software using the commands provided as there will be a check built into the wordprocessor to remind you to save your document if you have not done so. If you do not save your document *before* quitting, it will not be available if you want to use it in the future.

How wordprocessing has changed the job of a typist

The job of an office typist has changed greatly due to the introduction of wordprocessors. Compared to using a manual or electronic typewriter, with a word processor, there is much less need to retype letters and less routine copy typing. More attention can be given to the presentation of work and more style and format facilities are available to encourage this. Correspondence does not have to be stored printed on paper in filing cabinets but can be saved on disc until needed. Consequently, much less manual filing of correspondence in filing cabinets is necessary and it is easier to locate the documents saved on disc.

Wordprocessors increase the productivity of typists, allowing them to complete *more* work of a *higher* standard. This may lead to fewer typists being employed. The operating of a wordprocessor demands different skills to those necessary to use a typewriter so that typists have had to retrain, learning new skills. Not all have easily adapted to the new technology. However, those that have learned wordprocessing skills benefit from higher pay and status. The client has also benefited due to the use of wordprocessors. Replies to letters can be quicker and more personalised. Correspondence will be more likely to be clearly printed and error free. The cost of the service is also likely to be held or reduced, allowing savings to be passed on to the customer.

3 ▶   GRAPHICS

Graphics software provides a means of drawing pictures on the computer screen. It varies in complexity and capability and must be carefully selected depending on the use to be made of it.

Most graphics software is 2-dimensional, i.e. there is no attempt to construct solid objects. For convenient use of graphics software a mouse is essential as a WIMP environment will almost certainly be used. The facilities available are likely to be represented by icons or be listed in pull-down menus. They can usually be activated by pointing at the appropriate icon or menu entry with the mouse-controlled pointer and clicking the button on the mouse to select them.

WHAT GRAPHICS SOFTWARE CAN BE USED FOR

Graphics software can be used to prepare a wide variety of illustrated material. The range of tasks that can be done is extensive. These are some of the tasks that can be done using graphics software:

- drawing a picture, diagram, cartoon, etc.
- drawing a map, a plan of a house, etc.
- designing patterns for wallpaper, textiles, etc.
- producing posters and other advertising materials

WHAT GRAPHICS SOFTWARE WILL DO

The facilities described below are available on most graphics software. You should look for these facilities on the graphics software you use and make sure you can use them.

- **Draw** on the screen
  A line can be drawn freehand on the screen by moving the mouse. The line corresponds to the movement of the mouse. Various types of standard line may be selected, e.g. straight or dotted, in a variety of patterns. You can choose different widths of line.

- **Colours**
  A variety of colours will be available on a colour monitor. There will be a range of standard colours to choose from and perhaps the facility to mix colours to produce a unique blend. These colours can be used in combination with other features of the software to draw coloured lines, for example.

- **Fill**
  Closed shapes can be filled with patterns. These patterns may be standard, or designed by the user, perhaps in several colours.

- **Airbrush**
  Fill patterns or colours can be applied in a texture that mimics the effect of an airbrush or spray gun. Different brush patterns can be selected or designed by the user.

❝❝ Common facilities of Graphic Design software ❞❞

■ **Text**
Words and characters can be typed in a variety of styles or fonts. It may be possible for the user to customise an existing font or design a new one.

■ **Circles and boxes**
Circles and boxes can be drawn. These may be in outline or they could be filled in with a colour or pattern.

■ **Blocks**
An area of the screen can be defined as a *block*. This block can then be moved or copied to another part of the screen. Blocks can be transformed by stretching, enlarging, reflecting or rotating them.

■ **Zoom**
Areas of the screen can be magnified, or zoomed in on, to allow very fine detail to be added or changed.

Pictures and Clip art

Pictures can be saved on disc and imported. These could be drawings; diagrams; plans; maps; images that have been scanned from a photograph; video frames that have been digitised. It is sometimes useful to have available a library of images (**clip art**) that have been prepared by a professional artist with a specific purpose in mind. For example, a circuit designer would find it useful to have a clip art library containing the symbols used in drawing electronic circuits; the secretary of a sports centre might find a clip art library of sports equipment useful. Clip art can be prepared on graphics software for importing to a wordprocessor.

Exporting and importing

Pictures may be **imported** for inclusion in a current composition; scanned images may be imported so that they can be enhanced or otherwise edited. The final image may be **exported** for import to a newsletter or an advert being prepared on DTP software.

Save and load documents

Pictures can be **saved** on backing storage and **loaded** when required.

Printing

Pictures can be **printed**. A laser printer will produce high quality graphics. A dot matrix printer will produce lower quality graphics.

Colour printing is still expensive, although ink-jet printers using 4 or 5 colours are available at a reasonable price. It is difficult to get an accurate printout on paper of the colour seen on the screen. The printout provided by a laser printer is adequate if a black and white print is acceptable.

Quit

When you have finished, you will want to exit and switch off the computer. It is important to exit from the software using the commands provided as there will be a check built into the graphics software to remind you to save your work if you have not done so. If you do not save your work before quitting, it will not be available if you want to use it in the future.

The above facilities should be available in most graphic design software. Using such facilities it is possible to do textile design (see Fig. 9.3), wallpaper design and produce high quality business cards and tickets for dances, etc. Typical systems are the RM Nimbus running PCpaint software, IBM PC compatibles running Paintbrush, Atari ST systems using DegasElite or Neochrome and Apple computers using MacPaint.

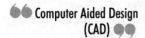
More specialised facilities of Graphic Design software

More specialised facilities are sometimes available for specific tasks. For example, some graphics software will accept images captured by a video camera when input via a video digitiser. These images can be changed or enhanced using the facilities of the graphics software. This technique can be used to add text to video film or to create a mixed sequence of video and graphic designs such as cartoons.

Computer Aided Design (CAD)

Three-dimensional objects can be designed with some specialised graphics software. These objects can be displayed on the screen as wire frame images, or as solid objects which can be rotated or viewed in plan and elevation.

In manufacturing, graphics software can be used to design products. A library of standard components can be provided so that the new design can be made up from existing manufactured parts as far as possible. It becomes relatively easy to redesign products as their designs are easily changed using graphics software without the need to redraw the entire design.

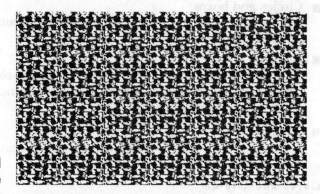

Fig 9.3 A textile design produced using graphics software

4 ⟩ DESK TOP PUBLISHING (DTP)

Desk top publishing software allows the user to produce printout in the style of a newspaper (see Fig. 9.4). That is, in columns with pictures and other graphics.

DTP software can be thought of as integrated wordprocessing and graphics, with additional features to enable pages to be laid out in columns and illustrations to be inserted where necessary. Different character sizes and fonts will be needed on the same page. Some facility to import photographs and video images will be required.

Often, DTP software will have only primitive wordprocessing and graphics facilities. The DTP software provides only the structure to manipulate documents into columns, etc. and to cut and position graphics as required. In this case the DTP software is relying on the user to use the specialised facilities of wordprocessor and graphics software to prepare documents and illustrations before importing these into the DTP software for placing in the desired page format. DTP software is run on a microcomputer system with a laser printer for high quality, fast printout. A mouse is essential, as DTP is inevitably run in a WIMP environment. A scanner will be needed to import photographs and possibly a video digitiser to capture video images.

Typical systems are Pagemaker and Timeworks on IBM compatible microcomputers; Pagemaker and QuarkXPress on Apple computers.

Fig. 9.4 Desk Top Publishing

WHAT DTP SOFTWARE CAN BE USED FOR

DTP software can be used to prepare a wide variety of good quality printed material with a range of text sizes, styles and fonts that includes graphics. DTP software is mainly used for constructing page layouts for newsletters, magazines, etc. where an attractive and interesting blend of text and graphics is important.

WHAT DTP SOFTWARE CAN DO

Different DTP software does the same tasks but may be operated in different ways. The facilities described below are available on most DTP software. You should look for these facilities on the DTP software you use and make sure you can use them.

Create and layout a page

DTP software is page based. It focuses on identifying which areas of a page will contain text and which will contain graphics. This is called **page layout**.

When a new page is **created**, one of the most important tasks to be done is to layout the page. To begin with the screen displayed will contain an outline of the page. The page itself will not have text or graphics on it. Text and graphics are placed on the page as it is constructed. They can be moved and the shape of the frame they are in adjusted, as required. The page layout may be changed at any time.

Text

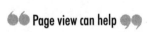
What DTP software can do

Text is typed onto the page from the keyboard or imported from a wordprocessing document. Text can be processed in DTP software as it can be in a wordprocessor, however, the screen view in DTP often makes this difficult. Text is usually best imported from a wordprocessor. The DTP software can be used to enhance the style of the imported text.

Graphics

Graphics are usually imported. The ability to generate graphics in DTP software is often limited in comparison with graphics software. You may be able to draw lines and put frames round text and imported graphics. However, DTP software will allow you to re-size a graphic and crop its overall size. This allows you to select a part of an imported graphic and change its size to suit your page layout. You can move graphics around on the page.

Page views

Page view can help

It is important that you should be able to *see* the page you are constructing before printing it out. However, laying out an A4 page using a standard monitor creates difficulties. If you display the whole page on the screen, you will not be able to see it in sufficient detail to read the text or make fine adjustments to the graphics. If you display only part of the page, you will not see the layout of the whole page. One solution to these problems is to provide menu options that allow you to move very quickly from a view of the whole page to a view of part of the page. A more expensive solution is to buy a larger, A4 monitor.

Page measurements and column guides

Most DTP software displays horizontal and vertical rulers to help you layout the page exactly. To help you place your text and graphics, column guides are provided. These save you working out where the columns should be placed. The aligning of text and graphics to the column guides can be done automatically.

Column flow

When placing text on the page, you may need to continue at the bottom of a column into the top of the next column. DTP software will handle the flow of text from the bottom of one column into the top of the next column.

Moving around a document

You may want to move around the page to view and edit it. To do this you can use the cursor control keys or 'arrow keys'. However, as most DTP software is operated using a mouse and a GUI, you may find that using the vertical and horizontal sliders in the GUI is faster.

Save and load documents

Pages can be saved on backing storage and loaded when required.

Printing

Pages can be printed. A laser printer will produce the high quality needed for DTP use.

Quit

When you have finished, you will want to exit and switch off the computer. It is important to exit from the software using the commands provided as there will be a check built into the DTP software to remind you to save your work if you have not done so. If you do not save your work before quitting, it will not be available if you want to use it in the future.

5 > ELECTRONIC MAIL

Using a modem and a telephone line, data can be transferred from one computer to another. Using this method of communication, computers can send documents, possibly prepared on a wordprocessor, to each other. These documents are then available to the user of the receiving computer. This is **electronic mail**.

Electronic mail is possible by transferring the document to an intermediate computer. This avoids the need for the sending and receiving computers to be in direct contact. Mail can be sent to an intermediate computer which is always available. At a later date this mail can be accessed by the receiving computer, whenever it is convenient to do so. This is the basis of most public electronic mail systems, e.g. Telecom Gold.

E-mail can be distributed from one sending computer to several receiving computers. This can involve an intermediate computer but may not do so. For example, companies can prepare their mail on a wordprocessor during the day. Each letter to be mailed is stored along with the telephone number of the receiving computer to which the document must be sent. At night, the computer automatically dials up the receiving computers and transfers their mail to them. This method of communication is used by some household appliance service departments to send details of the next day's work to service engineers who work in widely dispersed areas. Each service engineer has a microcomputer which must be ready to receive E-mail at a predetermined time during the night. At this time, the documents prepared at the central computer location during the day are transferred.

66 Advantages of Electronic Mail **99**

The advantage of E-mail is that large volumes of data can be transmitted quickly over the national and international telephone networks. This is much faster and , therefore, cheaper than voice transmission and complex reports, diagrams and pictures can be included.

6 > MULTIMEDIA

Multimedia is a developing means of communicating information. It is almost always associated with GUI systems. Multimedia combines wordprocessed text and graphics in a format similar to DTP with the addition of moving video and sound. Multimedia can be used to produce computer based learning materials, encyclopedias, etc. that have a richer, more comprehensive content than has previously been possible. Multimedia applications often use CD-ROM backing storage as they require fast access to very large volumes of data.

For example, consider an encyclopedia of birds. If the encyclopedia was in book form, it would contain written descriptions of the birds, habitat, etc. and still pictures of the birds. Multimedia provides this information and in addition will offer recordings of bird song and video of the birds flying, etc. This is closer to what we experience when we observe birds and can be expected to be of more help in identifying them. As the information is available on a computer, it can be copied into other computer software, such as a wordprocessor. Access to the information can be more like accessing a database than reading a book.

7 > CONFERENCING

66 The rise of conferencing **99**

Conferencing is conducting a meeting or conference using IT. If you want to join the conference, you log on to the central computer where the conference is being held. You do not have to meet with the other people involved in the same room at the same time. You can join the conference at any time and leave it when you want to. The central computer keeps a record of what everyone has said.

For example, suppose I wanted to join a conference about the GCSE exams, I would use my desk top computer to log on to the remote computer where the conference was being held. The conference could have been going on for several years. There would probably be a menu of seminars I could join. For example, there could be seminars on each of the different GCSE subjects and the various tasks GCSE boards have to do, such as, awarding the grades. I might choose to join the seminar on Information Systems. Within this conference seminar I would expect to find articles, questions, ideas, etc. about Information Systems. I would read through all this material, perhaps making my own comments. If I knew the answers to questions other people were asking, I would type them in. I might leave questions of my own for other people to answer. I then log off. I might return to the conference again in a few weeks to see if there is any additional material of interest to me. A conference could continue indefinitely. The computer stores all the contributions people make. You do not know who will join the conference and when they will join it.

An electronic conference proceeds more slowly than a live conference. It can bring together people from anywhere in the world who might not otherwise have the chance to meet. You have a chance to say what you want to, when you want to, at your own pace. No one can interrupt you. You can think carefully about what you want to say before typing it into the computer.

EXAMINATION QUESTIONS

Q1. Tick TWO advantages to school library staff of using a word processor rather than a typewriter.

	ADVANTAGE Tick ✔
The ribbon is changed automatically.	
It is quicker because the carriage returns automatically.	
It uses less paper.	
Work can be checked on the screen before printing.	
The keyboard is smaller.	
The printing is clearer.	

(MEG, 1993)

Q2. You are asked to include a picture on a letter. Which software would you use to combine text and graphics?

(City and Guilds, 1993)

Q3. In your letter you realise that paragraph 2 should follow paragraph 3. Which one of the following techniques would be the most efficient to carry out this correction? Put a tick inside the round brackets of one technique only.

text over writing   ( )

deleting and retyping   ( )

block move – cut and paste   ( )

(City and Guilds, 1993)

Q4.   In order to advertise the Xmas fayre, the secretary created the following poster using her wordprocessor:

> # XMAS FAYRE
> ## Come and visit *Santa*
> ## At
> ## Middlebridge School
>
> ## Sat. December 4th 1993
> ## 2.00pm start

To improve the appearance of this poster, it was decided to use a Desk Top Publishing package and the resulting poster is shown below.

Describe the changes to the poster which have been made by using the Desk Top Publishing package.

(NEAB/WJEC, 1993)

Q5. Chris has decided to purchase a Desk Top Publishing system to produce recipe books and leaflets.

  (a) Chris does not write good English. Describe, with examples, 2 ways in which software with good wordprocessing facilities would help him to produce better work.

  (b) Give examples of what a DTP set-up might be used for. What would it do that software with ordinary wordprocessing facilities would not do?

  (c) What hardware/software would be necessary for him to produce high quality hard copy.

(RSA, 1993)

Q6. (a) Give TWO advantages to viewers of using viewdata rather than teletext.

  (b) Give TWO advantages to the viewers that teletext has over viewdata.

(MEG, 1993)

Q7. Describe how teletext services benefit house-bound people.

(MEG, 1993)

Q8. There are many ways in which computers help newspaper reporters to prepare text for presentation to the printer.

  (a) Describe TWO such ways that have been used.

  (b) Describe how the job of a newspaper reporter has changed through developments in information technology.

(MEG, 1993)

Q9. A company employs door-to-door sales representatives. They enter their orders into portable computers during the day. The orders are transmitted to head office each evening.

  (a) Describe how the representatives would transmit their orders to head office.

  (b) Describe the operation of an electronic mail system which is used by the representatives.

(MEG, 1993)

Q10. In order to produce the monthly company newsletter in-house, the Personnel Department acquire Desk Top Publishing facilities.

Explain THREE facilities/functions of such a package that would help Christopher Monks to produce an effective newsletter.

(ULEAC, 1993)

ANSWERS TO EXAMINATION QUESTIONS

A1. It is quicker because the carriage returns automatically.

Work can be checked on the screen before printing.

(MEG, 1993)

A2. Desk Top Publishing (DTP) is the best software to handle text and graphics. However, some wordprocessors now permit the inclusion of graphics.

A3. Block move – cut and paste.

A4. Some changes made using DTP are, as follows:

- The text size and font has been changed
- A picture has been imported
- The text has been repositioned

A5. (a) Chris would find a grammar checker and a spelling checker useful. He could write using a large, clear font and print his work. He might be encouraged by the clear, neat presentation of his work with neither spelling nor grammatical errors.

(b) DTP could be used for producing posters, newsletters, etc.

DTP has these facilities that are not found in most wordprocessors:

- You can import graphics.
- You can layout a page in columns and easily place or re-position text and graphics on the page.

(c) A laser printer.

A6. (a) Two from:
Two way system
Enables people to make reservations
Pages transmitted when the user requests them
Thousands of pages
Access to electronic mail

(b) Two from:
Free service
No call charges
Can flip from TV to teletext
Provides subtitles
Shorter page numbers

(MEG, 1993)

A7. No need to leave house to find out information
Data updated regularly

(MEG, 1993)

A8. (a) Send complete story using a portable computer and a modem
Reporter types in story in office and stored on a central computer
Typesetting done by picking up all stories and putting them together using DTP

(b) Portable computer modem means more work can be done where the action is.
Teletext systems means that some information available by television rather than searching elsewhere.

Answers describing benefits of telex, fax, electronic data exchange.

(MEG, 1993)

A9. (a) Two from:
Connect the computer to a telephone line
Log in to the head office computer
Transmit data file to head office
Log off system

(b) Two from:
Reps log on to the system through the telephone and computer
Messages are left for other reps
Other reps have to log on and look at their messages

(MEG, 1993)

A10. Some facilities/functions of DTP that help produce a newsletter.

- You can place text and graphics in whatever position you wish and reposition them whenever you wish.
- You can apply a variety of text style features, e.g. bold, underline, different sizes of text, etc.
- You can create borders, tint backgrounds, etc. using the built-in graphic facilities.
- You can import clip art, scanned images, etc.
- You can import text from one or more wordprocessors or type it directly into the DTP software.

STUDENT'S ANSWERS WITH EXAMINER'S COMMENTS

Question

Middlebridge School are holding their annual Xmas fayre and the following text has been drafted using a wordprocessing package.

Dear parent/guardian
We are holding the school Xmas fayre on Saturday December 4th and we need volunteers to help with the stalls and donations of items to sell on the stalls. We plan to have the following stalls: Cakes, Sweets, Toys, Tombola, Books, Plants, White Elephant, Crafts.
As you know this is our main fund-raising event of the year and we plan to spend the money raised on increasing the number of computers within the school. Items can be left in the school office at any time and if you are interested in helping on the day please leave your name with the school secretary.
Yours faithfully
J. Smith
Headteacher

The Headteacher has decided that the sentence starting 'As you know . . . ' should be moved so that it becomes the last sentence of the letter.

Explain how you would do this without re-typing the sentence.

(NEAB/WJEC, 1993)

Student's answer

You would use the mouse. Then you would go to the end of the letter. Then you would move the sentence.

Examiner's comments

❝ This answer is probably correct but it is not expressed very clearly. Because the student avoids technical language, the answer appears vague. There are several acceptable answers to this question. This is one possible answer, giving a sequence of actions:

- Highlight the sentence
- Move the cursor to the new position, in this case, just after the sentence ending 'school secretary'
- Select the block move function. ❞

REVIEW SHEET

1. Which of these features of a wordprocessor are not available on a conventional manual typewriter?

    centring _____

    inserting text_____

    tab stops _____

    underlining _____

    wordwrap_____

2(a) Name a wordprocessor you have used. Is it a WYSIWYG wordprocessor? Which computer will it run on?

    _____

    _____

(b) Describe how you would use it to:

    (i) load a document _____

    _____

    (ii) move a block of text _____

    _____

    (iii) save a document _____

    _____

    (iv) type in text with different sizes and fonts _____

    _____

    (v) wordwrap _____

    _____

3. Which of these tasks that you can do with graphics software are more difficult when using coloured pencils and paper? Why?

    copying part of the picture several times within the picture
    colouring in evenly
    drawing a circle
    drawing a picture
    making several copies of the finished picture

    _____

    _____

    _____

4. Describe the tasks that you can do with Desk Top Publishing software that you cannot do with wordprocessing and graphics software.

    _____

    _____

    _____

5. What is clip art? What are the advantages and disadvantages of using clip art?

_____

_____

_____

6. Using these words, complete the sentences:

bigger
export
import
scroll
smaller

(a) When you _____ clip art into DTP software, you can use it on the page you are preparing.

(b) Font size 22 is _____ than font size 14.

(c) The information on the computer screen will _____ off the top and move on at the bottom as you move down a wordprocessing document.

7. What are the advantages of E-mail to an engineer, who works for a company based in Huddersfield, when he or she is sent to India to work on the construction of a hydroelectric dam?

_____

_____

_____

8. Describe an example of Multimedia that you have used.

_____

_____

9. Describe the advantages and disadvantages of conferencing to an IT teacher working in the Shetland Isles.

_____

_____

_____

10. Which of the following are true or false? Why?

■ You can only make one printed copy of a document prepared on a wordprocessor.

_____

■ If you do not save your work, when you switch off the computer it will be lost.

_____

■ There is no point in using DTP software as you can do all the work on a wordprocessor and graphics software, print it, cut it out, rearrange it and then photocopy it.

_____

■ Conferencing is not likely to be used very much because it is much more enjoyable to meet your friends for the weekend at a good hotel and have a relaxed chat.

_____

■ Wordprocessors are more difficult to use than manual typewriters.

_____

DATABASES AND HANDLING INFORMATION

GETTING STARTED

Computers are used for **information handling** activities where there is a large volume of data or the information needed is difficult or time consuming to access.

Databases help us search large volumes of information and sort it. We can set up search conditions and report on the results, summarising what we have found out. Databases usually handle text, but they can include pictures and sound.

Videotext is a simple means of handling page based information. Teletext is a type of videotext. Ceefax and Oracle are examples of teletext.

Expert systems help us organise our experience and knowledge so that we can identify and solve problems. For example, doctors can use expert systems to help them find out which illness a patient is suffering from.

ESSENTIAL PRINCIPLES

Information handling activities can be as simple as sorting out buttons into piles of similar sizes and colours. You are unlikely to use IT to do this. When there is a very high volume of information to handle or the information is complex, IT will increase the speed at which you can access the information in order to find answers to your questions.

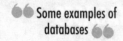

1 DATABASES

Files, Records and Fields

A **database** is an organised collection of structured data. The data will usually be structured in the form of files, records and fields.

A **file** is an organised collection of related records; a **record** is a collection of related fields; a **field** is an item of data within a record. Fields can contain various types of data, i.e. numeric data, character strings, etc.

For example, a squash club will have a **file** containing a separate record for each member of the club. Within each member's **record** will be **fields** for their membership number, name, address, date of birth, etc.

Databases enable the user to search through large volumes of data, selecting information using complex search conditions and displaying it on the screen or printing it in whatever format or order is required. Database software is often supplied to the user without files of data. The user is expected to create and maintain any data files required.

Some examples of databases

Examples of some of the large number of databases available for microcomputers are Quest on the RM Nimbus and the BBC Master, DBase on the IBM PC (and compatibles) and Superbase on the Atari ST.

WHAT DATABASES CAN BE USED FOR

Databases can be used for a wide variety of tasks. Typically there is a large volume of data which needs to be accessed quickly. Sometimes several records will be extracted from the database for viewing or printing.

These are some of the tasks databases can do:

Some uses of databases

- Car and vehicle records; nationally and, for example, of all the cars likely to be parked in the school car park.

- Criminal records; national and local police.

- Stock keeping; shops and warehouses of all types.

- Customer records; all types of business.

- Membership lists for sports clubs, etc.

- Estate agents' files of houses for sale.

- Recording information about hotels, etc. for tourists

- School records of pupils, staff, exam results, etc.

- Libraries: for book issues and catalogues.

- Census data; for statistical analysis by historians, etc.

- Information about plants, animals, etc. for biologists, etc.

WHAT DATABASES DO

Different databases do the same tasks but may be operated in different ways. Relational databases are programmable and can do the same tasks as flat file data bases but may be more difficult to use.

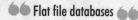

Flat file databases

Flat file databases are relatively straight forward and easy to use. They handle one data file at a time containing records with the same record specification and provide facilities to sort, search and print reports. They are not usually programmable. It is this type of database that is most often used up to GCSE. Examples are Grass for BBC and RM Nimbus computers, FileExpress for IBM compatibles, the database in Claris Works for Apple computers.

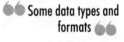
Relational databases

Relational databases are more complex to use. They offer the same features as a flat file database but, in addition, can handle more than one data file at a time. The data files may have different record specifications. They are always programmable. Different levels of access can be set for different groups of users. Menus can be written specifically for a group of users and passwords can control access. If you use a relational database at GCSE, it is unlikely that you will be expected to use the features of it that go beyond those available in a flat file database. Examples are Foxbase and Superbase for IBM compatibles.

Databases consist of information handling software and data files. In order to set up, maintain and search the data files and produce meaningful reports, the information handling software must have the facilities described below. They are available on most flat file databases. You should look for them on the database you use and make sure you can use them.

Create

The user must be able to **create** (i.e. set up) a data file in which data can be stored. This involves, at least, giving the file a filename and specifying the structure of each record in the record specification.

The **record specification** will include:

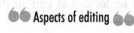
The record specification

- A list of the fields in each record in the order they appear in every record.
- For each field in the record:
  a unique field name
  a description of what the field contains
  the data type and format of the data
  the field length

A variety of **data types** and **formats** will be available. Some of the more common ones are:

Some data types and formats

- Character strings, e.g. 'Bradford City AFC'
- Numbers in integer form, e.g. 24, -6
- Numbers in real form, e.g. 238.67, -4.235, 0.56
- Number formats specify the number of decimal places, if a £ sign is needed, etc.
- Date formats specify how the date will be displayed, e.g. 5 JUN 94, 940605, etc.

Every record in a database should have a key field. A key field is unique and identifies the record. If the record was, for example, a customer record, the key field would also uniquely identify the customer.

Edit: Insert, delete and amend

Aspects of editing

Having created a record specification, it should be possible to **insert** (i.e. **enter**) a record. A data entry screen will be displayed showing the record specification. You enter data into the empty fields, setting up the record. The record is saved before you enter the data for another record. You can add records to the database at any time. When you have set up several records, you may want to **delete** (i.e. **remove**) some of them.

It should also be possible to **change**, (i.e. **amend**), the record specification. You may want to add an extra field or remove a field. This should not affect the existing data. You can also change the data that you previously entered into a field.

Data entry using a keyboard is slow and can be inaccurate. This may cause problems where there are large volumes of data to be input. Consequently, other methods of entering data are used where possible. For example, when setting up a library management information system, it is necessary to create a database containing details about all the books in the library. There will be a large number of books and a relatively large amount of text based information about each book to be input. An alternative method to entering this data using a keyboard is to read the ISBN numbers using a bar code reader. The ISBN bar codes read are then matched with those on a CD-ROM. The CD-ROM contains ISBN numbers for all the books published in Great Britain. All the other details about the books are also on the CD-ROM. A new database is created, using the information on the CD-ROM, that contains details about only the books in the library.

Search or interrogate

A database will often contain a very large number of records. You will want to **search** the database to get only the information you need. You can search or **interrogate** the data file for the information you want by defining a search condition or query. This search condition is used to select the required records.

Examples of search conditions are:

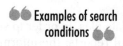
Examples of search conditions

- Name begins with 'CR'
- Number plate contains '4CH'
- Code is '23R-5X'
- Balance < 0
- Hair is NOT 'brown'
- Schoolcode = 37141 AND Examspassed contains 'Information Technology'
- Licence is 'provisional' OR vehicle contains 'cycle'
- Code NOT = 'Z-23' AND Credit is 500 OR Balance > 1000

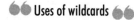
Uses of wildcards

You can often use *wildcards* in search conditions. Suppose we are trying to identify a car that has been in an accident. We noticed that the car was G registration and the number plate contained the characters '2' and 'L' in that order but possibly not together. A suitable search condition might be: Numberplate is 'G*2*L*'. The *'s are being used as wildcards. They indicate that there may be some or no characters in that position. All the number plates starting with 'G' and with a '2' followed by an 'L' will be selected. *'s are often used as wildcards, though different databases use other characters.

You will have to understand **precedence rules** if you want to use complex search conditions. These define in which order the logical operators AND and OR are evaluated.

For example, consider this sentence: John AND Shahid OR Jestin are going to the cinema.

This could mean:

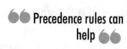
Precedence rules can help

1 John is going with one of Shahid or Jestin.
2 John and Shahid are both going without Jestin or Jestin is going alone.

Most databases interpret the sentence as in 2. above unless told otherwise. The easiest way to be sure you have expressed exactly what you intend is to use brackets. You would define the meanings expressed in 1. and 2. above as:

1 John AND (Shahid OR Jestin) are going to the cinema.
2 (John AND Shahid) OR Jestin are going to the cinema.

Search conditions tend to be written in slightly different syntax in different databases. You will need to find out how to set up search conditions in the database you are using. Using the search condition you set up, the file would be looked at and all the records that satisfy the search condition will be selected.

Sort

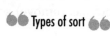
Types of sort

It may be helpful to **sort** the records selected using a search condition into some order, e.g. alphabetic order on the name, before reporting on the results of the search. Sorts can be ascending or descending. Ascending means upwards. An ascending alphabetic sort on names would put the names in the order A to Z. Descending means downwards. A descending alphabetic sort on names would put the names in the order Z to A.

Report

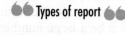
Types of report

Having searched the file, perhaps sorting the records selected, a **report** to the user on the results of the search is required. This report could be displayed on the monitor screen, saved as a file on disc or printed. In either case a report can be constructed that contains either all or some of the fields in each record selected. The report could be in record format (see Fig. 10.5), i.e. with the fields printed out in a format similar to the data entry screen, or in columns (see Fig. 10.7). In a report in column format, each row will contain the details extracted from one record. The format of a report should be under the control of the user.

Some databases will add up numeric fields and print group, page and report totals. Other calculations, such as averages, may be possible.

Bar charts, pie charts and line graphs can be printed from some databases. These can be used to display visual summaries of the information stored on the database.

EXAMPLE 1: MEMBERSHIP RECORDS FOR A SQUASH CLUB

This example of an **information system using a database** tackles the problem of keeping *membership records* for a squash club. The information system is also used to report useful summaries of information derived from the database. There are many other similar information systems that use databases.

The database used by the squash club contains information about a small number of fictitious members. Sufficient records have been set up to illustrate how such an information system would work. In practice a much larger volume of information would be handled.

The squash club has different classes of membership, i.e. young people, ordinary members (adults), un-waged (adults who are not in full time employment), honorary members and life members. Each membership class pays an appropriate subscription. Young people pay £5 per year; ordinary members, £20; un-waged, £10; honorary and life members do not pay a subscription.

The squash club has separate competition ladders for male and female members. The position of a member in the competition ladders is used to select teams for league matches and other competitions.

The database was set up so that the club treasurer could use it to keep track of members who have not paid their subscriptions. There are a variety of other useful tasks that the database can also be used for.

A flowchart can help

A flowchart showing how the information system is organised is shown in Fig. 10.1. The system is based on a flat file database.

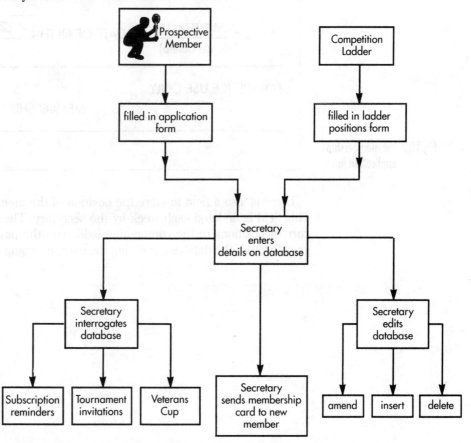

Fig 10.1
The information system used by a squash club

Input

Members fill in an **application form** (Fig. 10.2) when they join the squash club. This application form is used to collect the information needed about the new member. Notice that the form is as simple as possible. The order in which the information is asked for is repeated on the data entry screen for the database and in the record structure of the database. This assists accurate data entry and cross-checking.

The membership number is used as a key field to identify the member and the member's database record. The membership number is allocated by the secretary and written on the application form. The application form is then used as a data entry form when the new member's record is set up on the database for the first time.

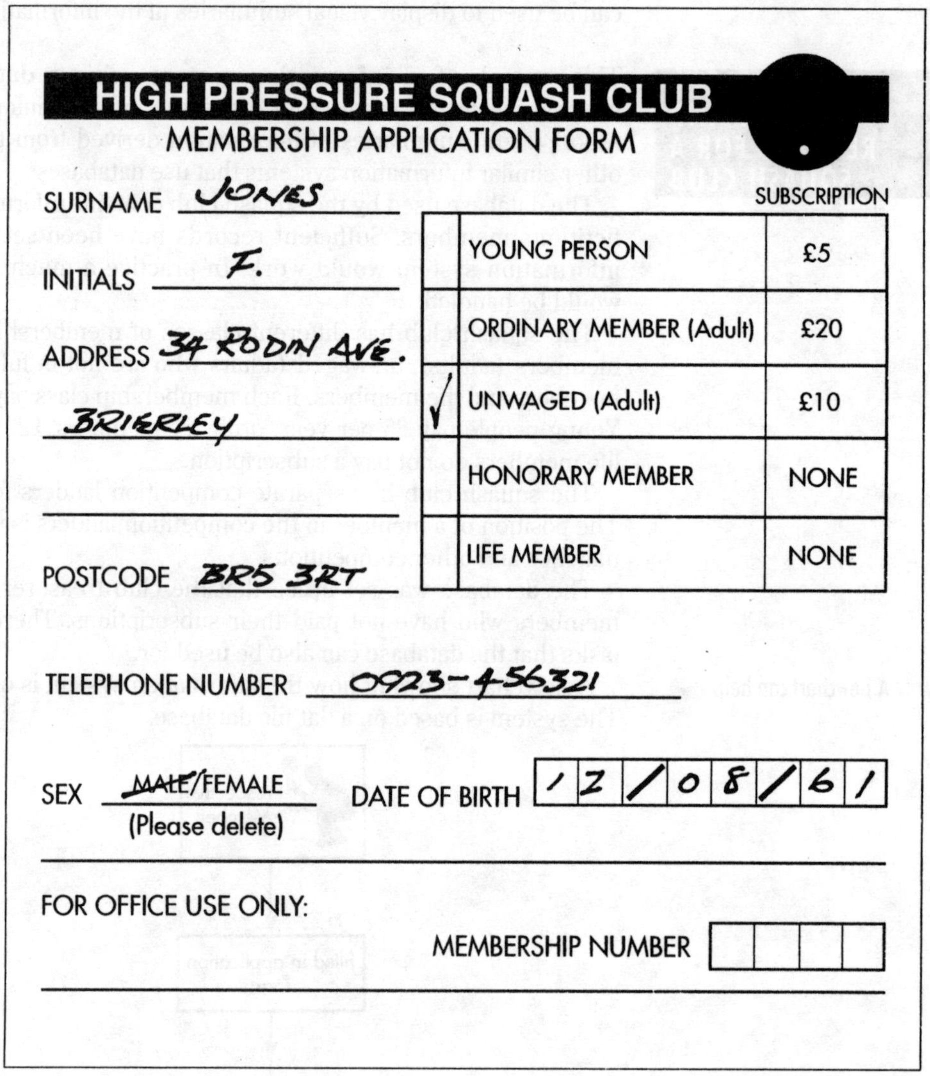

HIGH PRESSURE SQUASH CLUB
MEMBERSHIP APPLICATION FORM

SURNAME _JONES_

INITIALS _F._

ADDRESS _34 RODIN AVE._

BRIERLEY

POSTCODE _BR5 3RT_

TELEPHONE NUMBER _0923-456321_

SEX _MALE_/FEMALE
(Please delete)

DATE OF BIRTH _1 2 / 0 8 / 6 1_

	SUBSCRIPTION
YOUNG PERSON	£5
ORDINARY MEMBER (Adult)	£20
✓ UNWAGED (Adult)	£10
HONORARY MEMBER	NONE
LIFE MEMBER	NONE

FOR OFFICE USE ONLY:

MEMBERSHIP NUMBER [ ][ ][ ][ ]

Fig 10.2 The membership application form

There is also a field to store the position of the member in the competition ladder. This field is updated each week by the secretary. The secretary receives a list of the current positions in the competition ladder on the positions form (see Fig.10.3) and goes through the database updating the corresponding field.

POSITIONS FORM

WEEK COMMENCING

MEN'S COMPETITION LADDER

NAME	POSITION

WOMEN'S COMPETITION LADDER

NAME	POSITION

FILLED IN BY: _____

Fig 10.3 The position form

The record specification looks like this:

field name	description of field	data type	length
member	membership number	integer	4
surname	surname and initials	string	20
address	address and post code	string	40
phone	telephone number	string	20
date	date of birth in YYMMDD form	integer	6
sex	sex...M=male F=female	string	1
ladder	position in ladder	integer	2
class	subscription class: Y=young person O=ordinary member U=un-waged H=honorary member L=life member	string	1
subs	subscription outstanding	real, 2 decimal places	7

Notice that the membership class is to be coded as a single character. This will reduce the size of the file so that you can get more records on the available backing storage. There is no loss of meaning provided you know what each code stands for.

Each member of the squash club has a membership card (see Fig. 10.4). The membership card has on it the name of the member and their membership number. This identifies the member and reminds the member of his or her membership number. The information system generates the membership card from the membership record. The membership card may never be used in conjunction with the information system described here. However, it may be important to the squash club that members have some form of identification that they can carry with them. It is a feature of information systems that they can generate information, such as membership cards, that are useful in the social context which the information system supports but are not useful in relation to the system itself.

Uses of the membership card

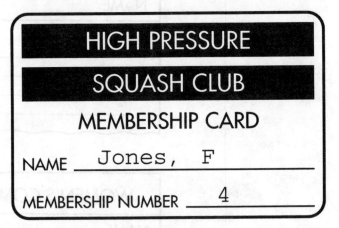

HIGH PRESSURE
SQUASH CLUB
MEMBERSHIP CARD

NAME ___ Jones, F ___

MEMBERSHIP NUMBER ___ 4 ___

Fig 10.4 The membership card

The secretary can enter membership data over several sessions. In the first session the record structure is created and data entered. At the end of the session the database is saved. The secretary begins all the following sessions by loading the database. Membership records can then be inserted, deleted or amended as members join the squash club, leave it or change their membership details respectively. At the end of each session the secretary saves the database again.

Fig. 10.5 shows all the records that have been entered into the example information system. The report is in record format.

Fig 10.5 A printout of all the records on the database

MEMBER	1
SURNAME	MASON, T
ADDRESS	56 HILL VIEW, APPLEBY, AP12 3DU
TELEPHONE	0234 453322
DATE OF BIRTH	730621
SEX	F
LADDER	4
CLASS	O
SUBS	£20.00

MEMBER	2
SURNAME	JONES, M
ADDRESS	34 RODIN AV., BRIERLEY, BR5 3RT
TELEPHONE	0923 456321
DATE OF BIRTH	821123
SEX	M
LADDER	2
CLASS	Y
SUBS	£5.00

MEMBER	3
SURNAME	JONES, P
ADDRESS	34 RODIN AV., BRIERLEY BR5 3RT
TELEPHONE	0923 456321
DATE OF BIRTH	590304
SEX	M
LADDER	6
CLASS	O
SUBS	

MEMBER	4
SURNAME	JONES, F
ADDRESS	34 RODIN AV., BRIERLEY BR5 3RT
TELEPHONE	0923 456321
DATE OF BIRTH	610812
SEX	F
LADDER	2
CLASS	U
SUBS	£10.00

MEMBER	5
SURNAME	GOWER, N
ADDRESS	6 STATION RD., STEETON ST4 6TY
TELEPHONE	0234 563987
DATE OF BIRTH	670502
SEX	M
LADDER	1
CLASS	O
SUBS	£20.00

MEMBER	6
SURNAME	DOWNS, S
ADDRESS	MOORSIDE, HILLCREST, BRADFORD BD7 4RT
TELEPHONE	0222 457342
DATE OF BIRTH	691001
SEX	F
LADDER	3
CLASS	U
SUBS	

MEMBER	7
SURNAME	SMITH, J
ADDRESS	13 CROSSLEY RD., APPLEBY AP2 4FG
TELEPHONE	0121 987980
DATE OF BIRTH	790906
SEX	M
LADDER	4
CLASS	Y
SUBS	£5.00

MEMBER	8
SURNAME	SCHACK, R
ADDRESS	3 WALTON RD., ALLERTON AL12 6BN
TELEPHONE	
DATE OF BIRTH	711209
SEX	M
LADDER	3
CLASS	O
SUBS	£20.00

MEMBER	9
SURNAME	WORTH, A
ADDRESS	45 REDMOND AV., THORNTON TH5 4ED
TELEPHONE	0223 454344
DATE OF BIRTH	750909
SEX	F
LADDER	5
CLASS	U
SUBS	£10.00

MEMBER	10
SURNAME	WORTH, N
ADDRESS	45 REDMOND AV.. THORNTON TH5 4ED
TELEPHONE	0223 454344
DATE OF BIRTH	720819
SEX	M
LADDER	5
CLASS	O
SUBS	£20.00

```
MEMBER          11
SURNAME         FORD, R
ADDRESS         34 LOW FOLD, ALLERTON AL3 5CX
TELEPHONE       0473 964213
DATE OF BIRTH   660529
SEX             M
LADDER          7
CLASS           H
SUBS
```

```
MEMBER          12
SURNAME         FORD, T
ADDRESS         34 LOW FOLD, ALLERTON AL3 5CX
TELEPHONE       0473 964213
DATE OF BIRTH   630421
SEX             F
LADDER          9
CLASS           O
SUBS            20.00
```

```
MEMBER          13
SURNAME         HILL, J
ADDRESS         22 GREEN LANE, THORNTON TH5 7UY
TELEPHONE       0788 777454
DATE OF BIRTH   640717
SEX             M
LADDER          10
CLASS           U
SUBS            £10.00
```

```
MEMBER          14
SURNAME         TODD, B
ADDRESS         16 MALT LANE, QUEENSBURY QU11 6MN
TELEPHONE       0344 343434
DATE OF BIRTH   780315
SEX             F
LADDER          10
CLASS           Y
SUBS            £5.00
```

```
MEMBER          15
SURNAME         PATEL, R
ADDRESS         34 SUNBRIDGE RD., STEETON ST8 4AS
TELEPHONE       0145 567788
DATE OF BIRTH   540302
SEX             M
LADDER
CLASS           L
SUBS
```

```
MEMBER          16
SURNAME         DEAN, B
ADDRESS         8 WAYSIDE CRES., THORNTON TH4 9SD
TELEPHONE       0282 882345
DATE OF BIRTH   760417
SEX             F
LADDER          7
CLASS           H
SUBS
```

```
MEMBER          17
SURNAME         WALKER, K
ADDRESS         7 HALLMARK AV., KEIGHLEY KY5 7GH
TELEPHONE       0123 567334
DATE OF BIRTH   820512
SEX             F
LADDER          8
CLASS           Y
SUBS
```

MEMBER	18
SURNAME	PEARSON, L
ADDRESS	19 JAMES ST., HALIFAX HX2 4RT
TELEPHONE	0434 899775
DATE OF BIRTH	700101
SEX	F
LADDER	1
CLASS	O
SUBS	

MEMBER	19
SURNAME	FARR, M
ADDRESS	FLAT 4, HIGHVIEW, QUEENSBURY QU4 8TH
TELEPHONE	0435 777656
DATE OF BIRTH	750721
SEX	M
LADDER	9
CLASS	U
SUBS	£10.00

MEMBER	20
SURNAME	SINGH, R
ADDRESS	23 CHERRY CRES., STANBURY ST5 6SK
TELEPHONE	0554 633344
DATE OF BIRTH	710919
SEX	M
LADDER	8
CLASS	O
SUBS	

MEMBER	21
SURNAME	KAUR, J
ADDRESS	34 BROADHALL AV., CROSSHILLS CR12 7YU
TELEPHONE	0886 979756
DATE OF BIRTH	751109
SEX	F
LADDER	6
CLASS	O
SUBS	

MEMBER	22
SURNAME	GRANT, T
ADDRESS	BLACK CARR FARM, BRADSHAW BR1 5XX
TELEPHONE	
DATE OF BIRTH	660215
SEX	M
LADDER	
CLASS	L
SUBS	

MEMBER	23
SURNAME	MOONEY, G
ADDRESS	4 BACK LANE, QUEENSBURY QU9 4KL
TELEPHONE	0222 598777
DATE OF BIRTH	820513
SEX	F
LADDER	
CLASS	Y
SUBS	£5.00

MEMBER	24
SURNAME	DANIELS, D
ADDRESS	12 PADIHAM RD., BURNLEY BB4 TL5
TELEPHONE	0456 344556
DATE OF BIRTH	801215
SEX	M
LADDER	
CLASS	Y
SUBS	

It is important that the secretary keeps the database up-to-date. The information on the application forms filled in by new members and the positions of current members in the competition ladders should be input on a regular basis, at least weekly. Deletions and amendments should be made promptly. If the database is not up-to-date or the data on it is corrupted, the information extracted from it will be incorrect. This is an example of Garbage In, Garbage Out (GIGO).

Processing

All the **processing** that is required is done by the database software. Processing consists of selecting some records using a search condition and sorting the selected records into a convenient order.

Setting up the search conditions

The secretary will have to set up the search conditions. Search conditions are logical statements that determine which records will be selected from the database. For example, suppose we wanted to know who was top of the competition ladder. The field called 'ladder' contains the position of the member in the competition ladder. The member who is top of the competition ladder will have the number 1 in the field called 'ladder'. The question 'who is top of the ladder' can be rewritten as the search condition 'ladder equals 1'.

If the search condition is one which will be used again, it can be saved. This enables the secretary to extract the information again at a later date without having to work out the search condition once more. It is possible that a search condition would be so complex to write that the secretary could not do it. A computer programmer might write the search condition for the secretary. In this case, it is very important that the search condition should be saved for the secretary to use when it is needed.

Carefully define the search conditions

The importance of carefully defining search conditions can be illustrated by the above example. You might expect that the search condition 'ladder equals 1' would pick out the record of the person who is top of the ladder. In fact, there will be two records selected. This is because there are two competition ladders; one for males and one for females. If you want to select only the top of the men's ladder (or only the top of the women's ladder) you will need to modify the search condition. The search condition for the top of the men's ladder is 'ladder equals 1 AND sex is male'; the search condition for the top of the women's ladder is 'ladder equals 1 AND sex is female'.

Search conditions are very important when using any database as they control what information is selected from it. The usefulness of a database depends on writing search conditions that will provide the information required.

Output

Control of the **output** from a database is restricted to choosing which fields will be displayed, the format of the output and the output medium to be used, i.e. printout, screen display or disk file.

At most, you can only display all the fields in a member's record, but you could decide to display just a few fields. For example, if the secretary was printing a list of members to telephone to invite to a surprise tournament to be held that evening, only the member's name and telephone number would be needed. The membership number might be included to be sure the identity of the member was absolutely correct.

The different output formats that can be selected depend on those that are available in the database. Some databases allow you to vary the format as you wish; however, many restrict you to only a few different layouts.

Some of the tasks the secretary of the Squash Club can do using the database are described below. There are many others.

SECRETARY'S TASK: SUBSCRIPTION REMINDERS

One of the most important jobs that the secretary has to do is to make sure all the members **pay their subscriptions**. Some members are nearly always late in paying their subscriptions and the secretary has to constantly remind them. The secretary finds it more effective to telephone members than to send written reminders, however some members are not on the telephone and these will have to be sent a reminder through the post.

Using the data base to remind members to pay their subscriptions

To do this job the secretary would find it helpful to have a printed list showing the membership number, name, address and telephone number of those members who still owe the club subscriptions. This list should be in alphabetical order.

A printed list is particularly useful for this job as it allows the secretary to work away from the computer, so that the job can be done in a variety of locations at a time to suit the secretary. It is unlikely that a squash club would have a full time secretary so that the job of reminding members that their subscriptions have not been paid may have to be done when the secretary has a few minutes free time, for example, in the lunch hour at work, in a telephone kiosk while waiting for a train, at home during the evening, etc. If a printed list is not available, the job may be much more difficult to fit conveniently into the time the secretary has access to the computer and may not be done regularly. This could seriously affect the income of the squash club.

To provide the information needed, the secretary has to decide on the search conditions, field selection and output format to be used. Members who have not paid their subscriptions will have a number greater than zero in the 'subs' field. One way of selecting those members who still have subscriptions to pay is to use the search condition 'subs is greater than zero'.

Only those fields that will be used need to be printed, that is, the membership number, name, address, telephone number and the amount unpaid for the member's concerned.

The secretary finds it convenient to have the extracted records sorted into alphabetic order on the name field before printing. This helps in finding a member's details given the name of the member.

The list of members with overdue subscriptions is shown in Fig. 10.6.

Fig 10.6 A list of members with overdue subscriptions

NAME	FARR, M	AMOUNT UNPAID	£10.00
TELEPHONE	0435 777656	MEMBERSHIP NO.	19
ADDRESS	FLAT 4, HIGHVIEW, QUEENSBURY QU4 8TH		

NAME	FORD, T	AMOUNT UNPAID	£20.00
TELEPHONE	0473 964213	MEMBERSHIP NO.	12
ADDRESS	34 LOW FOLD, ALLERTON AL3 5CX		

NAME	GOWER, N	AMOUNT UNPAID	£20.00
TELEPHONE	0234 563987	MEMBERSHIP NO.	5
ADDRESS	6 STATION RD., STEETON ST4 6TY		

NAME	HILL, J	AMOUNT UNPAID	£10.00
TELEPHONE	0788 777454	MEMBERSHIP NO.	13
ADDRESS	22 GREEN LANE, THORNTON TH5 7UY		

NAME	JONES, F	AMOUNT UNPAID	£10.00
TELEPHONE	0923 456321	MEMBERSHIP NO.	4
ADDRESS	34 RODIN AV., BRIERLEY BR5 3RT		

NAME	JONES, M	AMOUNT UNPAID	£5.00
TELEPHONE	0923 456321	MEMBERSHIP NO.	2
ADDRESS	34 RODIN AV., BRIERLEY, BR5 3RT		

NAME	MASON, T	AMOUNT UNPAID	£20.00
TELEPHONE	0234 453322	MEMBERSHIP NO.	1
ADDRESS	56 HILL VIEW, APPLEBY, AP12 3DU		

NAME	MOONEY, G	AMOUNT UNPAID	£5.00
TELEPHONE	0222 598777	MEMBERSHIP NO.	23
ADDRESS	4 BACK LANE, QUEENSBURY QU9 4KL		

NAME	SCHACK, R	AMOUNT UNPAID	£20.00
TELEPHONE		MEMBERSHIP NO.	8
ADDRESS	3 WALTON RD., ALLERTON AL12 6BN		

NAME	SMITH, J	AMOUNT UNPAID	£5.00
TELEPHONE	0121 987980	MEMBERSHIP NO.	7
ADDRESS	13 CROSSLEY RD., APPLEBY AP2 4FG		

NAME	TODD, B	AMOUNT UNPAID	£5.00
TELEPHONE	0344 343434	MEMBERSHIP NO.	14
ADDRESS	16 MALT LANE, QUEENSBURY QU11 6MN		

NAME	WORTH, A	AMOUNT UNPAID	£10.00
TELEPHONE	0223 454344	MEMBERSHIP NO.	9
ADDRESS	45 REDMOND AV., THORNTON TH5 4ED		

NAME	WORTH, N	AMOUNT UNPAID	£20.00
TELEPHONE	0223 454344	MEMBERSHIP NO.	10
ADDRESS	45 REDMOND AV., THORNTON TH5 4ED		

SECRETARY'S TASK: TOURNAMENT INVITATIONS

66 Using the data base to issue invitations to a tournament 66

Occasionally the secretary receives an invitation to enter teams from the club in inter-club knockout competitions. Often these invitations arrive too late to allow invitations to individual members to be sent by mail. Usually there are separate competitions for male and female players.

The secretary has been asked to send a team of three female players and a team of three male players to a local knockout competition. The secretary receives the invitation at very short notice. To do the job the secretary sits down at the computer with the telephone at hand.

The secretary wants to send the best players the club has, in this case the top three male and female players. These will be those players with positions 1 to 3 in the club's competition ladder. One possible search condition is 'ladder is greater than zero' AND 'ladder is less than 4'. However, as the secretary is in a hurry and members must be contacted by telephone, those members who are not on the telephone will not be invited. The search condition will need some alteration. One solution would be to change the search condition to exclude members with no telephone. Alternatively, the top five or six members could be displayed, which would allow the secretary some flexibility in deciding who to contact.

Since the secretary will need the name of the member and their telephone number, these fields should be displayed. The sex and position in the club's competition ladder should also be displayed as this is relevant to the job the secretary is doing. The membership number might also be useful for identification purposes.

The secretary might find the extracted information easier to understand if it is displayed in some order that emphasises the job being done. The data relating to male and female players will need to be separate and should be printed in the order of the player's position in the club's competition ladder. That is, the output should be displayed in order of sex, females followed by males, and within this in order of position in the club's competition ladder, with the higher positions first.

The information extracted can be neatly displayed in table form on the monitor screen (see Fig. 10.7).

Fig 10.7 The top players in both competition ladders

NAME	MEMBER NO.	TELEPHONE NO.	LADDER POSITION	SEX
PEARSON, L	18	0434 899775	1	F
JONES, F	4	0923 456321	2	F
DOWNS, S	6	0222 457342	3	F
MASON, T	1	0234 453322	4	F
WORTH, A	9	0223 454344	5	F
GOWER, N	5	0234 563987	1	M
JONES, M	2	0923 456321	2	M
SCHACK, R	8		3	M
SMITH, J	7	0121 987980	4	M
WORTH, N	10	0223 454344	5	M

SECRETARY'S TASK: VETERANS' PRESENTATION CUP

At the annual general meeting held each year, the veterans' presentation cup is given to the oldest life member or honorary member of the squash club.

Members should be over thirty five and life members or honorary members. This is expressed as the search condition 'age is greater than 35 AND (membership class is life OR membership class is honorary)'

The fields selected identify the members, confirm the search condition and allow the members to be contacted. The membership number, membership class, age, name, address and telephone number of each member are displayed.

The output displayed is shown in Fig. 10.8.

Fig 10.8 The veteran's cup award

NAME	PATEL, R	DATE OF BIRTH	540302
ADDRESS	34 SUNBRIDGE RD.. STEETON ST8 4AS	MEMBER NO.	15
TELEPHONE	0145 567788	MEMBERCLASS	L

SECRETARY'S TASK: BACKUP DATABASE

The secretary will need to do some tasks that are useful in maintaining the computer system but that are not useful in providing information the squash club needs. One of the most important of these tasks is backing up the database. Copies of the database must be made on a regular basis, at least weekly. The ancestral method of organising file backups should be used.

EVALUATION OF THE EXAMPLE DATABASE

One task that the squash club database might be used for is to print address labels for sticking on letters to be sent to club members. As the database is set up at present this would not be possible as there is only one address line. Addresses are currently printed as, for example:

FLAT 4, HIGHVIEW HOUSE, QUEENSBURY QU4 8TH

This is not the usual format for addressing letters. We would expect the address on a letter to look like:

FLAT 4
HIGHVIEW HOUSE
QUEENSBURY
QU4 8TH

To print the address in this format, the database should have been set up with at least four fields for the address, i.e. one field for each line of the address. Had this been done originally, address labels could have been printed. To make this change once the database has been created you may have to re-enter the address of every member. If this use had been planned for originally, there would be no extra time spent on it, but if an existing database has to be changed this could be extremely time consuming.

●● Planning is important ●●

The secretary of the squash club, will probably want to use the computer to print out personalised letters to members. This requires the use of a wordprocessor with a mail merge facility. A standard letter is set up with personal details omitted. These are obtained from the database when the letters are printed. Not all wordprocessors will allow you to do mail merge and many of those that do are not integrated with a database. If it is important to use the information on the database in a mail merge, a database that is integrated with a wordprocessor should be used. Claris Works is a good example of integrated software, including a wordprocessor and database. It is available for both Apple and IBM compatible computers.

Some databases will allow you to display graphs, pie diagrams or bar charts to illustrate or summarise data stored on the file. For example, you might want to look at the age distribution of members. This information could be effectively displayed in a bar chart where the height of each bar was proportional to the number of members in a given age range (see Fig. 10.9).

Fig 10.9 The age distribution of members

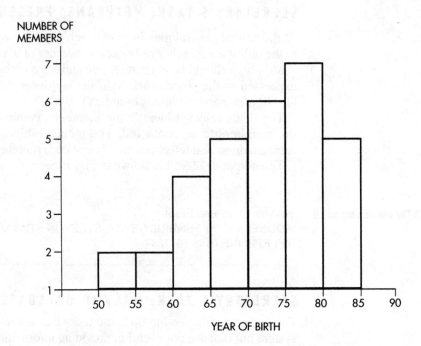

NUMBER OF MEMBERS

YEAR OF BIRTH

3 > EXAMPLE 2: A TELEPHONE ENQUIRY SERVICE

Uses of databases

Databases are useful when it is necessary to extract information very quickly from large volumes of data. For example, an Electricity Board has a very large number of customers. A record containing the details for each customer will be stored in a file. The details stored for each customer will include the name, address, customer number, details of previous electricity meter readings, method of payment and credit status.

The customer file will be used when calculating bills and mailing them to customers. Some of the bills will be calculated from new meter readings and some will be estimates based on previous meter readings. For various reasons, customers may wish to query their bills. They may also contact the Electricity Board to arrange for the supply to be connected or disconnected. Many customers will use the telephone to make their enquiries (see Fig. 10.10). Telephone enquiries demand the fast response times provided by a database.

A customer who telephones the Electricity Board will speak to a telephone operator wearing a headset that allows the hands to be free to use the keyboard of one of the terminals connected to the mainframe computer that is running the database. Ideally, the customer will tell the operator their customer number, so that this can be used as a search condition to locate their record. Unfortunately, many customers will not know their number. In these cases the operator will ask the customer their name and make a search of the database, extracting all those customers with that name. Next, the customer will be asked their address to confirm that the correct record has been found. Customer enquiries over the telephone are only practical because of the search facilities and fast response available using the database.

Fig. 10.10 A telephone enquiry
service

4 ⟩ VIDEOTEXT **Videotext** is a page-based information retrieval system (see Fig. 10.11). When displayed on the screen, one page occupies the whole screen. Each page has a number and can be accessed using it. There is usually some form of index that directs the user to the page containing the information required. For example, a page may contain a weather report; other pages may contain stock market reports, etc.

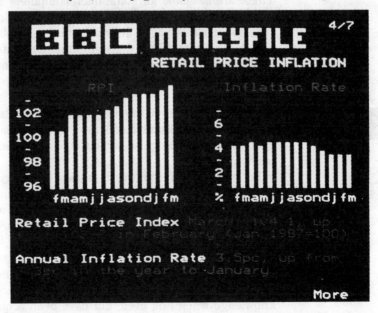

Fig. 10.11 A page of videotext

TELETEXT

Teletext is a form of videotext broadcast by television and received on a modified domestic TV or using a teletext receiver connected to a microcomputer. Ceefax (broadcast by the BBC) and Oracle (from ITV) are teletext systems. Teletext pages are broadcast interleaved with the television signal in a repeated cycle of page numbers. Pages are broadcast constantly whether they have been selected or not. When a page number has been selected, the user must wait until that page is broadcast in the cycle before it will be displayed. Once displayed, the page is updated every time it is rebroadcast.

Fastext

A type of teletext

Fastext is teletext received using a TV with built-in memory. When a page is selected it is displayed on the TV screen and stored in memory. At the same time several pages adjacent to it are also stored in memory. When the user moves from one page to the next page in sequence, the page is already in memory and is displayed immediately. You can move one or two pages backwards as well as forwards with Fastext. If you select a page outside of the range of pages stored in memory, you will have to wait as long as you would wait on a teletext TV without Fastext.

Advantage of receiving via a computer

The advantages in receiving teletext using a computer rather than a TV are that the computer can store pages on disc for later use and can print pages if requested. Often, computer software can be downloaded from teletext, saved on disc and run when needed.

VIEWDATA

Viewdata is another form of videotext. It is like teletext in that it is also a page-based system and its appearance on the screen is similar. However, viewdata is a two-way system; data can be both received and transmitted. Teletext is one way, pages can only be received. To access a viewdata system, a microcomputer and modem are preferable, although very basic hardware involving a simple numeric keypad can be used. The viewdata software is run on a mainframe computer and is accessed by using the microcomputer. Pages are only transmitted when requested. Access to some pages may be charged for by the information provider and access may be restricted in some cases by requiring a password. The information stored on viewdata systems and the services provided are more extensive than those transmitted by a teletext system. For example, goods can be bought by mail order by providing a credit card number and money can be transferred between bank accounts. Campus 2000, run by British Telecom, is a typical viewdata system.

VIEWDATA OR TELETEXT EMULATORS

These are available for some microcomputers and allow users to set up their own videotext system. Typically, they provide indexes and can be made to display a repeated cycle of pages. It is sometimes possible to download pages from Ceefax, Oracle or Prestel into the emulator. Emulators are useful for providing local information in libraries and other information centres.

5 EXPERT SYSTEMS

An **expert system** or Intelligent Knowledge-Based System (IKBS) allows users to benefit from the accumulated knowledge of human experts. It consists of software that enables users to recognise particular situations and advise on the appropriate action to take.

For example, an expert system used in medicine for diagnosis of diseases will ask the doctors who use it a variety of questions concerning the symptoms of the patient. Using the answers given, the expert system will identify the specific disease or provide a list of possible illnesses. It will then suggest appropriate action to be taken to cure the disease.

The knowledge built into an IKBS is only as good as the knowledge of the experts who set up the system. As experience grows, or new knowledge is discovered, the IKBS will need to be changed to include this. Some IKBSs do not incorporate any knowledge when first used, but have been acquired by experts to help them build their own methods and ways of working into a coherent system.

The full potential of expert systems has not yet been exploited. They have the potential to give everyone access to the most advanced human thinking, but due to the difficulties in setting up such systems this is still only a possibility.

EXAMINATION QUESTIONS

Q1. A video-film club hires films to members. The club uses separate database files to store details about:

films,
members,
films hired.

The screen below shows part of the **FILMS** database file.

Film number	Film name	Film category	Rating	Hire charge
0123	Mermaids	Comedy	15	£2.00
0124	JFK	Drama	15	£2.50
0254	Star Wars	Adventure	U	£1.50
0361	Mad Max 2	Adventure	18	£2.00
0422	City Slickers	Comedy	15	£125
0744	Die Hard 2	Adventure	18	£1.50
0813	Blackadder	Comady	15	£1.50

(a) If you look at the information in the table about the film Blackadder you will spot a mistake. Comady should be Comedy.

Put three of the following steps in the best order to correct the mistake.

A Print the whole database.
B Save the changes.
C Correct the mistake.
D Delete the whole database.
E Select the Blackadder record.

Step 1 ....

Step 2 ....

Step 3 ....

(b) Look again at the information in the table. Which other piece of information is probably a mistake?

(NEAB/WJEC, 1993)

Q2. When you start school you are asked, with your parents, to complete a data sheet. (See sample below)

Name	Address
Tel No.	Contact in Emergency
Tutor Group	Contact's Tel No.
Any Special Medications	
Doctor's Name	Doctor's Address
Doctor's Tel No.	

(a) Why does the school need this information?

(b) Explain two circumstances when this information may be important to you or your family.

(c) As well as the school needing to keep information on you, name one other person or place that may want to keep these sort of details about you and explain why.

(NDTEF, 1993)

Q3. QUESTION DATA:

SURNAME	FIRST NAME	SEX	DATE OF BIRTH
Acland	Simon	M	11–09–78
Addis	Joy	Y	26–05–80
Anders	Jane	F	03–01–80
Archer	Sandra		22–07–77
Basey	Michael	M	17–04–79
Bates	Faith	F	28–11–75
Boyer	Peter	M	21–07–79
Brodie	Carole	F	09–02–77
Davis	Jean	F	10–01–79
Dawkins	John	M	19–01–78
Dawkins	Peter	M	29–12–80
Dawkins	Peter	M	15–04–77
Dawkins	Simon	M	29–12–80

(a) St Saviour's School has recently decided to computerise their information systems. The first step has been to create a database file of pupil data. Using the extract from this database file given above:

(i) Write down two of the field names.

(ii) Write down one complete record.

(b) The school secretary asks you how you get a list of all female pupils. Write down the query command to display the surnames and first names of all female pupils.

(City and Guilds, 1993)

Q4. A hospital radio station has been given a collection of old records, unfortunately they are all mixed up. The producer needs to be able to find a record with a particular title, singer, composer, band or released in a particular year. They decide to use a computer database to help them.

(a) Give an example of one advantage and one disadvantage of inputting this information on a computer.

(b) Draw up the format for this database.

(c) State which are files, fields and records in your format.

(d) The hospital wanted to add some other information about the tapes and CDs that they have to the database. Describe how they can alter the database (using a method that you have used).

(NDTEF, 1993)

Q5. A company uses a computer to put buyers of second-hand cars in touch with people who are selling cars. It collects information from sellers by getting the sellers to complete a form. Buyers can then ring up and ask for a list of people who have the sort of car they want.

(a) Design a form for the input of information for a SELLER.

(b) Describe clearly the processes required to get a list (in price order) of all Ford Escort cars less than 5 years old in the price range £3000 to £4000.

(c) Explain why a manual card index might be better than a computer for a second-hand car dealer who usually has between 8 and 10 cars for sale.

(SEG, 1993)

Q6. A large shop sells bicycles. The information about each bicycle in stock is held in a database on a computer. Part of the information is shown below:

Maker	Model	Type	Colour	Price
Peugeot	Elite	Racing	Blue	200.00
Butler	Junior	Racing	Green	175.00
Holdsworth	Espada	Mountain	Red	220.00
Molton	Mini	Folding	Green	109.50
Muddy Fox	Shappell	Mountain	Blue	0.225
Butler	Norfolk	Touring	Red	180.00

(a) Explain why it is important to check carefully all information put into a computer.

(b) (i) There is an obvious error in the data above. Put a ring round the error.

(ii) The correct data should be:...

(iii) Describe a check that could be carried out automatically to find errors like this.

(iv) Give an example of a likely error in this column that could NOT be found out by the checking method you have described.

(c) A customer is only interested in mountain bikes. List the steps you would go through to get a printout list of all mountain bikes from the computer.

(d) An advertisement is being designed for one of the bicycles. The first draft is shown below.

> Peugeot Racing Bike
> Elite Model
> Blue
> Only £200
> Credit terms available

Give three improvements that could be made to make the advertisement more effective.

(e) The shop also sells second-hand bikes. Give two other items of information that might be useful to have in the database for the second-hand bikes.

(SEG, 1993)

Q7. A school uses a computer system to help with administration.

(a) The computer has a database which stores data about the teachers, pupils and rooms. Describe **THREE** different ways of presenting the output from the database.

(b) A new pupil joins the school. How could the computer system be used to help to fit the pupil into suitable classes?

(c) The computer system stores personal information about the new pupil. State **ONE** way that the school office staff can use the personal information stored about pupils on the computer.

(MEG, 1993)

Q8. A company of estate agents, with a main branch in one town and several branches in nearby towns, is planning to change from a manual system to a computerised one.

(a) The company plans to set-up a computer file with details of houses that are for sale. This file will store the name of the owner, the address, the 'phone number and type for each house.

Suggest four other fields that might be included on file.

(b) Explain why some of the data in the fields in this file is stored in a coded form.

(c) The file will store details of several thousand houses. People interested in buying any house should be able to obtain a print-out of the details by simply calling in at a branch of the company. What type of store would be needed for the file? Give two reasons for your choice.

(d) Some of the fields in this file are of fixed length others are of variable length.

(i) Give one advantage of using fixed length fields.

(ii) Give one disadvantage of using fixed length fields.

(e) Describe the hardware the company will need to install in each of its branches and in the main office for the new computerized system.

(NEAB/WJEC, 1993)

Q9. Study the extract from the FRUGRO database given below. The full database holds records on over 20,000 different fruits and vegetables and also contains more information on each item such as growing conditions, fertilisation etc.

Fruit	Name	Cropping	Size	Virus Resis-tant	Yield	Quality	Producer
S	Genghis Khan	Late	2–4	y	high	excellent flavour	Pearson Brother
S	Glentham Delight	Main	2–4	y	high	excellent flavour	Porter Produce
R	Frenchay Runner	Main	1–2.5	y	medium/high	superb	Frenchay Brothers
R	Frenchay Early	Early	1–2.5	n	high	excellent	Frenchay Brothers
S	Pilgrim's Progress	Late	2–5	y	medium	superb	Kent Billham
S	Pershings Pleasure	Late	2–6	y	medium	excellent	Pearson Brothers
R	Ladbrook Largesse	V Late	2–4	n	medium	superb	Kent Billham

(a) Explain why some items on the database have been coded. What is the purpose of the coding?

(b) In what way might using the database be of more use to Chris than another way of storing the data?

(c) There may be other specialist 'on-line' databases available to Chris. Explain with the use of diagrams what the term 'on-line' means in this context. How would these be of use to Chris compared to another way of accessing the data he needs?

(d) Give a way in which an 'on-line' database could be accessed by Chris. What is the main difference between an 'on-line' database and one held on CDROM at the area Agricultural College?

(RSA, 1993)

Q10. A dentist wishes to set up a simple computer system to provide information about her patients' teeth; their appointments; the treatment they have; and the money they owe her. She can afford a desktop computer with a hard disk, a monochrome monitor, a keyboard, a mouse and a dot-matrix printer.

(a) State the type or types of application software that you would recommend. Explain your choice.

(b) Describe how the system might handle the information, including the results it could produce for the dentist, the regular entry of data, the structure of the stored data and the processing carried out.

(c) Explain the benefits of using a generic application package rather than a specially programmed system, and state any likely limitations in its ease of use and efficiency of operation.

(d) Suggest possible improvements to the system if the dentist could afford different peripherals and specially programmed software.

(e) State a potential advantage of the computer system to each of the following:
the dentist
the nurse
the receptionist
the customer.

(f) State a disadvantage that might be there for any two of these people.

(RSA, 1993)

ANSWERS TO EXAMINATION QUESTIONS

A1. (a) E, C, B

(b) The hire charge of £125 for City Slickers.

A2. (a) Some of the reasons the school needs this information are:

- to know who to contact in emergencies.

- to know what medicines a pupil uses.

(b) Some of the reasons why this information may be important to you are:

- you could have an accident and the school would need to contact your family.

- the school will need your address to send letters to your parents.

(c) Some of the others needing this information are:

- your doctor - to keep a record of patients.

- the library - to keep a record of members.

A3. (a) (i) Fieldnames are: surname, first name, sex and Date of Birth.

(ii) Any single line of the table is a complete record, e.g. 'Dawkins; Simon; M; 29–12–80.

(b) Query command: An example would be:

IF SEX IS F
THEN DISPLAY SURNAME, FIRST NAME.

This command would not display the details for Joy Addis and Sandra Archer as their sex has been entered incorrectly.

A4. (a) Some advantages are:

- Fast, easy access to the information.

- Easy to edit.

Some disadvantages are:

- To access the information, you have to know how to use a computer.

- A computer must be available to use.

(b) These are some of the fields that would be in each record:

field name	*type*	*length*	*example*
title	character	25	12 Gold Bars
artist(s)	character	25	Status Quo
year	number	4	1984

(c) There are 3 fields in (b). These make up one record. There is one record for each old record. All the records make up a file.

(d) These are some of the ways in which you can alter a database:

- add more fields to a record.

- add records to the file.

A5. (a) The form asks for the seller's name and 'phone number and details about the car for sale, such as, maker, model, year, mileage, colour, etc. The form should use the following techniques where appropriate:

- boxes to fill in, e.g.

A		J	O	N	E	S		

- tick lists, e.g.

Mileage: up to 10,000   ☐
10,000–20,000   ☐
20,000–30,000   ☐
30,000–40,000   ☐
40,000–50,000   ☐
over 50,000   ☐

The form should explain simply and clearly why the information is being collected and should be signed and dated by the person filling it in. There should be simple examples of how to fill in the form where these are needed. The design should look like a form.

(b) Assuming the database is running on the computer, you would:

- query the file using a search condition, such as:
CAR IS FORD AND MODEL IS ESCORT
AND AGE IS LESS THAN 5
AND PRICE IS MORE THAN £3000
AND PRICE IS LESS THAN £4000

- sort those records selected by the query into some sensible order, such as, descending order on price.

- print or display on the screen the details required from the selected records, e.g. model, year, mileage, price, seller's name and 'phone numbers.

(c) If only 8 to 10 cars are for sale it would be better to record their details on cards because:

- You don't need a computer to access them.

- You could carry them with you all the time.

- It might be faster to find the information you want.

A6. (a) The accuracy of the information output depends on the accuracy of the information input (see GIGO).

(b) (i) Ring the cell containing 0.225.

(ii) Probably 225.00.

(iii) A validation check, specifying the range of acceptable prices, would detect this error.

(iv) A price error within acceptable limits would not be detected, e.g. £185.00 instead of £180.00.

(c) You would use the query:

'Type is Mountain'

to select the mountain bikes, then print a report showing the details of those records selected.

(d) You could enhance the appearance of the advert by using different text styles and fonts, including graphics; using colour and emphasising the more desirable aspects of the advert.

(e) Name; address and 'phone number of the previous owner.

A7. (a) Three from:

Form lists for teachers
Teacher lists
Classroom timetables
Subject options lists
Pupil timetables
Any other suitable list

(b) Using a timetabling program to produce a timetable for the pupil

Try out various patterns to see which fit
See where there are spaces in classes

(c) One from:

Storing contact names in case of illness
Storing doctor's name in case of illness
Correct spelling of name and address to check whether the pupil has brothers/sisters in the school.
Any other suitable record

(MEG, 1993)

A8. (a) Any four of:

Number of bedrooms.

Fields showing if the house has:

■ central heating

■ double glazing

■ a garage

■ a garden

(b) Information about the garage facilities could be coded, e.g.:

N - no garage

S - single garage

D - double garage

Coded fields take up less space on backing storage and are typed in faster when the data is being entered into the computer.

(c) The file would be stored on a hard disc. It is faster to read/write data from/to a hard disc than other types of backing storage. Files on hard disc can be direct access files. A record in a direct access file can be found faster than records in other types of file.

(d) (i) A fixed length field has the same length in every record. For example, a date is a fixed length in every record when it is written in DDYYMM form. As the computer knows it's length, it can be processed faster.

(ii) If fixed length fields are used for fields such as names and addresses, storage space is wasted if the data is shorter than the field length. If the data is longer than the field length, all the data cannot be stored.

(e) The company will need this hardware in each of its branches:

■ Computer(s) (monitor, processor, floppy disc drive, hard disc drive, keyboard, mouse).

■ Local printers.

■ MODEM.

■ Scanner.

■ Hardware to do backups.

The company will need this hardware at the main office:

■ Mainframe computers (processor, hard disc drives, magnetic tape drives, operator's console, line printers, local terminals).

■ Communications front end.

A9. (a) Coded fields take up less storage space on backing storage and are typed in faster when the data is being entered into the computer.

(b) The data could be stored on a card file. Using a database enables Chris to:

■ search for and find one record faster.

■ search for and find a group of records faster, e.g. Late cropping vegetables with a high yield.

■ sort the information into a different order very quickly.

■ print out selected information from the database, e.g., the producers and names of late cropping vegetables with a high yield.

(c) 'On-line' means connected to and in communication with (usually) a mainframe computer.

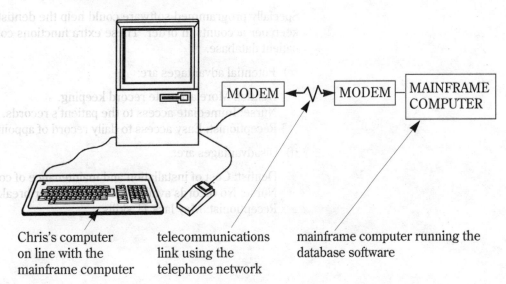

Chris's computer on line with the mainframe computer

telecommunications link using the telephone network

mainframe computer running the database software

An on-line database should be relatively up-to-date compared to a database on CD-ROM. The speed of access should be faster using an on-line database compared with teletext. A variety of on-line databases are available all over the world. You only pay for the time you are connected to them and the information used.

(d) Chris would have to use a MODEM and the telephone network to access an on-line database. An on-line database should be relatively up-to-date compared with CD-ROM.

A10. (a) Database.

The dentist can find information about a patient quickly, select various categories of patient and print appropriate reports.

(b) Description covering:

- record specification
- editing records and fields
- searching
- sorting
- reporting

(c) Benefits:

- immediately available
- very little re-programming needed
- guarantee it will work
- skills transferable to other information handling applications

Limitations:

- If it does not meet your needs you may not be able to adapt it.
- The facilities available could be too simple or too complex and consequently obstruct you in using the database.

(d) The dentist could purchase:

- A colour monitor - colour is often used to make software easier to use.
- A laser printer - this would save time as it prints faster than a dot matrix printer. It also produces better quality output.

Specially programmed software could help the dentist record appointments and keep her accounts in order. These extra functions could be integrated with the patient database.

(e) Potential advantages are:

Dentist: More accurate record keeping.
Nurse: Immediate access to the patient's records.
Receptionist: Easy access to daily record of appointments.

(f) Disadvantages are:

Dentist: Cost of installation and maintenance of computer system.
Nurse: No records available if the computer breaks down.
Receptionist: May lack IT skills.

STUDENT'S ANSWER WITH EXAMINER'S COMMENTS

Question

A company sells general hardware. It stores details of stock in a database.

For each item the database stores the following:

Stock-no
Description
Location-code (aisle number)
Supplier-code
Recorder-quantity
Minimum-stock-level
Current-stock-level
Lead-time (days)
Date-of-last-delivery

(a) The database can be accessed using a special query language.

(i) Describe the output which would be produced by the following query:

List stock-no, Description, FOR Current-stock-level less than 50

(ii) Small electrical goods are stored in aisle 10 in the warehouse. Write down the query command which would print out the stock number and date of last delivery of all small electrical goods.

(iii) Write down a query command which would print out the description, for all items that the company has more than 100 of in stock, with a lead time of less than 14 days.

(b) The company cannot function without the database. What backup procedures should be used for the database files?

(c) The database file is very large. What method can be used to minimise storage requirements when archive copies are made?

(d) To be able to produce orders to be sent to suppliers, an additional database file is used.

(i) What file would this be?

(ii) What type of information would it contain?

(NEAB/WJEC, 1993)

Student's answer

(a) (i) A list of the stock number and description if the current stock level is less than 50.

(ii) List stock-no, Date-of-last-delivery FOR Location-code equals 10.

(iii) List Description, FOR Current-stock-level greater than 100 AND Load-time less than 14.

(b) Make a copy of the files every day.

(c) Copy the files onto microfiche.

(d) (i) The supplier's database.

(ii) The supplier's name, address and 'phone number.

Examiner's comments

(a) (i) Correct, but the answer is very close to simply repeating the question. This answer would be better:

'Print the stock number and description of all products where there are less than 50 of them in stock'

(ii) Correct

(iii) Correct

(b) This is too brief and lacks detail.

The database data files should be regularly copied. All transactions should be copied during the day and a full backup made at the end of the day. Transactions and full backups should be kept for at least 3 days. The most recent backup will be on-site in a fire proof safe; other backups may be located elsewhere in the same town or a greater distance away.

(c) This is incorrect. You can minimise the storage requirements for the database file (or any other file) by compressing it using data compression software.

(d) (i) Correct

(ii) Correct. Another essential item of information about a supplier would be the supplier's code. This is a key field and identifies the supplier.

REVIEW SHEET

1. A school keeps a file of information about the pupils who attend the school. There is one record for each pupil.

   Make a list of all the fields that should be in each pupil's record.

   For each field: give a brief description of it
                        state what type of data will be stored in it
                        write down its length

2. (a) Write down the name of a database you use. _____

   (b) Which computers does it run on? _____

   (c) Describe a task you have done using it. _____

   _____

   _____

   _____

   _____

3. The data stored in a database is often coded.

   (a) Which of the following statements are true?

   ■ data is coded so that spies cannot understand it_____

   ■ if you were coding the names of towns, '10/2P' would be a better code for Leeds than 'LS' _____

   ■ data is coded to save storage space _____

   ■ you should always code peoples' names _____

   ■ dates are coded in DDMMYY form because it is easier to sort them into chronological order _____

4. Look at the records in fig. 10.5. Which records would these search conditions select?

   (a) SURNAME begins with 'G'_____

   (b) TELEPHONE contains '573'_____

   (c) LADDER is more than 9 _____

   (d) ADDRESS contains 'QUEENSBURY' or ADDRESS contains 'THORNTON'

   _____

   (e) CLASS is not 'O' and CLASS is not 'U' _____

5. (a) What information can you access on Ceefax? _____

   (b) Describe how you access the information.

   _____

   _____

   (c) What are the disadvantages in finding information in this way?

   _____

   _____

   (d) What improvements would you like to be made?

   _____

   _____

   (e) What is fastext? Is it always faster? Explain your answer.

   _____

   _____

   (f) What are the advantages in using a computer to access teletext instead of a TV?

   _____

   _____

   (g) What are the differences between teletext and viewdata?

   _____

   (h) What are the similarities between teletext and viewdata?

   _____

6. You have been asked to set up an information system that will be used in a small library. Describe an information system to control the lending of books to borrowers. You should make sure you have described any forms to be filled in, the library membership card and the record structure of the database. You should describe the reports to be printed for the librarian and say why the information in the reports is needed. Draw a diagram showing the flow of information through the system.

   _____

   _____

   _____

   _____

   _____

   _____

   _____

   _____

   _____

SPREADSHEETS AND MODELLING

MODELS

SPREADSHEETS

AN INFORMATION SYSTEM BASED ON A SPREADSHEET

MODELLING

GETTING STARTED

Spreadsheets are used for the wide variety of tasks that involve calculations laid out in columns and rows. They are especially useful for financial applications.

A **spreadsheet cell** is used to hold data. It is located at the intersection of a column and a row. You can put numbers, text and formulae in a cell.

Spreadsheet software includes cell references; movement around the spreadsheet; re-calculation of formulae; protection of cells; changing the display format of a cell; altering the width of columns; copying, moving, deleting and inserting rows and columns; looking at the spreadsheet through one or more windows; sorting rows and columns; displaying graphs; printing the results.

A simple **information system** is described. The information system is used for stock control in a small electrical appliance shop.

Models are representations of the real world. The models described in this chapter are based on a spreadsheet. There are models for price forecasting, a supermarket queue, break even analysis and a predator/prey relationship.

It is essential to remember that a model is only a representation of the real world. It is *not* the real world. The better the model, the more exactly it copies reality. Models allow us to experiment with reality. We can try out strategies and forecast what will happen. Models are based on our experience of the past. The future may not mimic the past. Consequently, we must treat forecasts based on models with care.

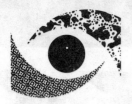

ESSENTIAL PRINCIPLES

1 MODELS

Models are representations of the real world. Our earliest introduction to modelling is likely to be moulding plasticine or clay to make representations of people or animals. You can buy toy soldiers and model cars; dolls and dolls houses. They are all models, that is, representations of the real world.

Models in some form are used throughout commerce and industry. You can build a physical model of a shopping centre or other building project to demonstrate the architectural style and layout of the planned development. Models of such developments can also be built using computer software. Computer models of large scale developments are relatively complex and expensive to build, though it is not uncommon for an architect to use Computer Aided Design (CAD) software to plan in detail the design and construction of a new building.

Models *you* can set up are our main interest here

The computer models you may encounter are likely to fall into two distinctive groups. There will be models that you set up and manipulate yourself. These models will be constructed using a spreadsheet. It is this type of model that is the focus of this chapter. Spreadsheets are widely used in many different types of activity, especially in recording and organising financial models. They provide a well structured layout and facilities for storing text and numerical data and doing calculations. Spreadsheets can vary considerably in complexity and size.

You may also encounter models that are *set up for you*, providing you with a simulation of a real situation. For example, you may use a computer based simulation of an oil spill in the North Sea. The computer will give you control over factors that limit the spread of the oil slick such as the number of workers tackling it, the quantity of detergent available, the placement of floating booms, etc. You could have a limited budget to spend to get the oil slick cleared up. The computer will simulate the effects of the weather and the tide. Using such a model will help your understanding of the constraints and difficulties that arise in such a situation. This model could also be used for training people to tackle real oil slicks.

Computer games can be realistic

Computer games are like models. Some games present you with realistic situations but many do not. Computer games often present fantasy in a context that is apparently real. It is important to distinguish between a model which tries to represent the real world as exactly as it is possible and a computer game which may make no attempt to do so.

It is essential to remember that a model is a *representation* of the real world. It is *not* the real world. You cannot expect reality to be exactly like a model of it. The better the model, the more exactly it copies reality. The advantage of using models is that they allow us to experiment. We can try out strategies and forecast what will happen. However, a forecast is based on experience of the past. The future may not mimic the past. Consequently, we must treat forecasts based on models with care.

2 SPREADSHEETS

When you are doing calculations using a sheet of paper and a pen or pencil, you will find that it is often easier to understand what you are doing if you work in *rows* and *columns*. Columns are up and down the page; rows are across the page.

Spreadsheets are used where rows and columns are involved

For example, you may layout the calculations you do in maths at school in columns. Maths teachers often insist on this! If you have studied Accounting or Commerce, you will have come across situations where you have amounts of money in columns with a description of what each sum is besides it. A supermarket receipt is a good example of this type of layout (see fig.11.1). There is a description of the items bought, the unit price, the quantity and the amount paid for the items. At the bottom of the receipt, the total to be paid for all the items bought is printed. This style of layout is widely used throughout industry and commerce for a variety of calculations.

Morrisons Supermarkets

	unit price	quantity	price
baked beans	0.30	2	0.60
rice	0.56	4	2.24
ice cream	1.47	1	1.47
meat	4.52	1	4.52
magazine	0.65	1	0.65
biscuits	0.25	5	1.25
			10.73

21.02.94

THANK YOU FOR YOUR CUSTOM

Fig 11.1 A supermarket receipt

A **spreadsheet** is the computerised equivalent of a piece of paper divided into rows and columns. A typical screen display from a Spreadsheet is shown in Fig. 11.2. Notice that the rows are numbered from 1 to 20 down the left hand side of the screen and the columns are numbered from A to G along the top of the screen. There are actually many more rows and columns in the spreadsheet. What is seen on the screen is just part of the spreadsheet. We are looking through a 'window' in which we can see only some of the rows and columns available. All spreadsheets have similar rows and columns.

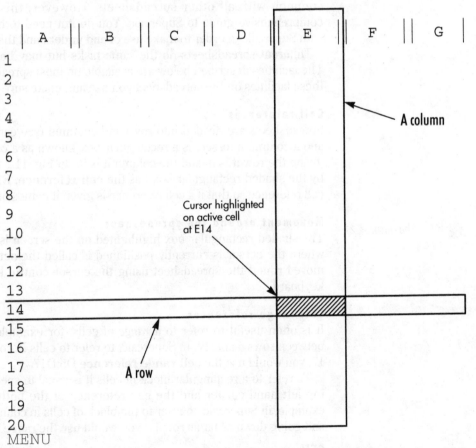

A column

Cursor highlighted on active cell at E14

A row

MENU
Arrange Blank Copy Delete Edit Format global Insert Justify Load Move Name Output Protect Quit Save Title Unprot Window Zap 1-2-3

Fig 11.2 The screen display from a spreadsheet

As this particular layout is so useful there are very many different spreadsheets available. For example, there are Supercalc and Lotus 1–2–3 for IBM compatibles, Multiplan for the RM Nimbus; Viewsheet for the BBC Master; VIP Professional for the Atari ST; Claris Works for Apple computers.

The spreadsheet used for the examples in this chapter is *Supercalc* from Computer

Types of spreadsheet

Associates. You don't need to know how to use Supercalc to understand this chapter as the examples can easily be changed to work on other spreadsheets.

WHAT A SPREADSHEET CAN BE USED FOR

Spreadsheets can be used for the wide variety of tasks where the division of the screen into rows and columns is useful. They can be used to do any calculations that may be needed. They are especially useful for doing accounts and forecasting expenditure. These are some of the many tasks where spreadsheets are used:

66 Uses of spreadsheets 99

- stock keeping in a shop
- organising milk deliveries
- company, sports club, etc. accounts
- school tuck shop income, expenses and profits
- payroll, sales information and forecasting
- models of supermarket queues
- models of predator/prey relationships

WHAT SPREADSHEETS DO

Spreadsheets are the computerised equivalent of a piece of paper divided into rows and columns. The layouts available and the calculations you can do on a piece of paper can also be represented on a spreadsheet. However, as you might anticipate, a spreadsheet is more flexible and extends what you can do.

Supercalc will be used as an example spreadsheet, as it has many features in common with all other spreadsheets. However, this section is not a detailed, comprehensive guide to Supercalc. You do not need to have access to or be familiar with Supercalc in order to make use of and understand this section.

Different spreadsheets do the same tasks but may be operated in different ways. The facilities described below are available on most spreadsheets. You should look for these facilities on the spreadsheet you use and make sure you can use them:

Cell references

Spreadsheets are divided into rows and columns (see earlier Fig. 11.2). Where a row and a column intersect is a rectangular box known as a *cell*. The cell is referred to by giving the row it is in and the column it is in. In Fig. 11.2 the cell which is highlighted by the shaded rectangular box has the **cell reference**, E14. Every cell has a different cell reference so that if a cell reference is given it names only one unique cell.

66 The cursor 99

Movement around the spreadsheet

The shaded rectangular box highlighted on the screen is called the **cursor**. The cell where the cursor is currently positioned is called the **active cell**. The cursor can be moved round the spreadsheet using the cursor control keys or 'arrow' keys, on the keyboard.

Cell range references

It is often useful to refer to a *range* of cells, for example, all the cells in column D between rows 5 and 17. In Supercalc, to refer to cells in column D between rows 5 and 17, you would use the **cell range reference** D5:D17.

To refer to a rectangular block of cells it is usual to specify the cell reference of the top left hand corner and the cell reference of the bottom right hand corner. For example, in Supercalc, to refer to the block of cells in columns A to D, starting at row 5 and going down as far as row 17, you would use the range reference A5:D17.

Cell contents

Cells can contain character strings, numbers or formulae:

66 Contents of cells 99

Character strings may be used for column and row headings that say what is in that particular column or row, eg. 'item price'.

Numbers may be amounts of money or other quantities. Numbers can be integers, eg. 4, -1, 0, 45, or real numbers, eg. 2.354, -34.6.

Formulae can be programmed into a cell allowing the contents of the cell to be calculated from the contents of other cells. For example, if in column D, rows 5 to 17 there are money values, these could be added together and their total displayed in the cell at column D, row 20 by entering an appropriate formula in that cell. In Supercalc, the formula SUM(D5:D17) is used to add the contents of cells D5 to D17. The formula itself will not be displayed on the screen in the cell at D20 but the total value calculated will be displayed.

Formulae may be arithmetic calculations, sums or more complex functions to work out averages and square roots, generate random numbers, etc. You may also be able to use programming statements, such as IF/THEN, and logical functions, such as, AND, OR and NOT. The variety of functions you can use will vary depending on the spreadsheet you are using.

66 Types of formulae 99

Automatic re-calculation

The value of a formula will be **automatically re-calculated** when the contents of one or more cells that the formula refers to are altered. Automatic re-calculation is one of the most important features of a spreadsheet that extends it beyond being merely an electronic sheet of paper.

Protecting cells

66 You can protect cells 99

Setting up a spreadsheet can be a time consuming task. You may want to **protect** some of the cell contents you have entered from accidental corruption. In particular, if you are setting up the spreadsheet for someone else to use, you will not want them to change column headings and formula. Cells can be protected to prevent their contents being changed. The contents of a protected cell cannot be altered until the protection is removed.

Cell display formats

You may want to **display** the data in a cell in various **formats**. The following are some common display formats:

66 Different data formats 99

- Right and Left justify: All cell contents are lined up with the right or left hand edge of the column, respectively.
- Centre: All cell contents are positioned mid way between the right hand edge of the column and the left hand edge.
- Dates can be displayed in various forms, for example, YYMMDD, 12 Jun 1993, etc.
- Numbers can be displayed rounded to a fixed number of decimal places with a £ sign or a minus sign, as required.

Column width

When the spreadsheet is first displayed on the screen, all the **columns** will probably be the same number of characters **wide**. You may want to alter this arrangement so that some columns are wider and some are narrower. You should be able to do this at any time without affecting the contents of any of the cells in the column adjusted. For example, if a column is twelve characters wide and you want it to contain numbers that will be at most three digits, eg. age in years, then you can reduce the width of the column.

Copying and moving cells

You may find that you want to **move** cells to a different position in the spreadsheet or **copy** cells so that they contain the same as other cells.

A spreadsheet will allow you to move a single cell or a range of cells. You can copy a single cell to another cell or a range of cells to another range of cells. You can also copy a single cell to a range of cells.

Where a cell contains a formula, the formula will also be copied across. There are these possibilities:

66 Absolute cell references 99

- The formula will be copied with the cell references unchanged. For example, if the formula SUM(D5:D17) in cell D20 is copied to cell D23 with the formula unchanged, it would remain as SUM(D5:D17) in cell D23. In this case, D5 and D17 have been specified as **absolute cell references** so that they do not change when they are moved or copied.

- The structure of the formula will remain unaltered but the cells it refers to are **changed**. For example, if the formula SUM(D5:D17) in cell D20 is copied to cell

Relative cell references ??

E20, we might want the formula to change so that it adds up E5 to E17. The formula could be changed to SUM(E5:E17) during the move or copy. In this case, D5 and D17 have been specified as **relative cell references** so that they change when they are moved or copied.

This may sound somewhat complicated! Unfortunately, different spreadsheets have different ways of dealing with moving and copying formula. Some spreadsheets default to absolute cell references and others default to relative cell references. You should carefully check formulae after doing a move or a copy.

Delete and insert rows and columns

You can **insert** rows and columns, that is, you can put in an additional row between existing rows or an extra column between existing columns. You can also **delete**, ie. remove, rows and columns.

Blanking cells

Blanking has the effect of clearing the contents of a cell. However, protected cells are not blanked. You can blank a cell or a range of cells. You can blank all the spreadsheet so that it is ready for completely new data to be entered.

When you have set up a spreadsheet, you may want to use it as a basis for several similar spreadsheets. In this case you may want to keep the headings and the formula you have programmed into the spreadsheet but blank all the other cells. If you protect the cells that you want to keep, this will prevent them from being blanked. You can then blank the entire spreadsheet to clear the unprotected cells.

Windows

A **window** is a rectangular area of the screen that is used to display part of the spreadsheet. Many spreadsheets have only one window. If this is the case and you want to see another part of the spreadsheet, you will have to move the window. Most spreadsheets have only one window at the start but will allow you to open more than one window. This can be very useful if you want to view different parts of the spreadsheet on the screen at the same time. When you want to remove a window from the screen display, you close the window.

Sorting cells

A spreadsheet should allow you to **sort** the rows into some order depending on the contents of the cells in a particular column. You should also be able to sort the columns depending on the contents of the cells in a particular row.

For example, suppose you were setting up a spreadsheet where each row contained details referring to a particular person. Column A might contain their name, column B, their rate of pay, and so on. Your aim is to end up with a list of personal details with the names in alphabetic order. You might find it easier to enter all the details in whatever order they occur, then sort the rows into alphabetic order on the names. A spreadsheet will allow you to do this.

Graphs

Many spreadsheets will allow you to construct a variety of graphs. Bar charts, pie diagrams and line graphs are often available.

Printing

A spreadsheet will allow you to *print* all of the spreadsheet or only part of the spreadsheet. You should be able to print the values of the cells as displayed on the screen or the underlying formula. You can also print graphs.

Printing the spreadsheet ??

Printers used with microcomputers usually print 80 characters on a line. If your spreadsheet has more than 80 characters on a row it cannot be printed without some adjustment. If the spreadsheet is printed out without adjustment, it may be printed in blocks 80 characters wide and 60 rows deep one under the other, working across the spreadsheet from left to right and from top to bottom.

If condensed print is possible on your printer, you might find this facility useful, as you can print 160 characters on a line that would normally be only 80 characters wide. You could also consider using a wide carriage printer. You should be able to adjust the width of the print line from within the spreadsheet to suit the print style or printer you are using.

3 AN INFORMATION SYSTEM BASED ON A SPREADSHEET

We are now going to look at an **information system** based on a spreadsheet. As an example, we will look at *stock control* in a small electrical appliance shop. There are many other similar applications that a spreadsheet can be used for.

A shopkeeper uses a spreadsheet to keep a record of sales from a small electrical appliance shop. The income from the shop does not yet justify the cost of full-scale computerisation including on-line Point of Sale terminals. The spreadsheet is used to speed up calculations, providing reliable results and additional sales information.

When goods are sold, the shopkeeper gives the customer a receipt (see Fig. 11.3). The receipt is written on a two part carbonised pad so that both the customer and the shopkeeper have a record of the transaction. At the end of the day the shopkeeper works out the quantity of each item sold from the receipts. The shopkeeper uses the form in Fig. 11.4 to help accumulate the quantity of each item sold. These are entered into a spreadsheet. The spreadsheet multiplies the quantity sold by the price to work out the value of sales of the item. The total value of sales of all goods sold that day is also calculated.

66 Stock control in a small shop **99**

ELECTRICAL
APPLIANCES LTD

NAME OF CUSTOMER _Mr Baines_   DATE _8th Sea. 1994_

Description of Goods Sold	Quantity	Unit Cost	Sales Value
AMPLIFIER	1	209.99	209.99
CD PLAYER	1	150.45	150.45
CASSETTE PLAYER	2	86.56	173.12

Total Sales 533.56

Thank you please call again

Fig 11.3 The receipt used in data capture

ELECTRICAL
APPLIANCES LTD

Description of Goods sold	Quantity Sold														Total
	Individual														
AMPLIFIER	1														1
CASSETTE PLAYER	2														2
CD PLAYER	1	1	1												3
ELECTRIC COOKERS	1	2	1	1											5
FREEZER	1	1													2
FRIDGE	1	1	1	1											4

Fig 11.4 The form used to accumulate the quantity of each item sold

At the end of the day, the shopkeeper adds up the total takings from the tills. This should be equal to the total sales value calculated by the spreadsheet. If these are not equal, there is some error in the data collection process or there has been a theft from the tills. The shopkeeper must repeat the entire process, beginning with the receipts, to be sure that the error is due to theft. This check helps indentify and prevent theft from the tills.

The system also helps the shopkeeper identify which goods have a high turn-over, which should be carefully managed because of their high price and which contribute most to profitability. Whilst the daily process of data collection is time consuming, this additional information is easily extracted.

A diagram illustrating the essentials of this simple information system is shown in Fig. 11.5

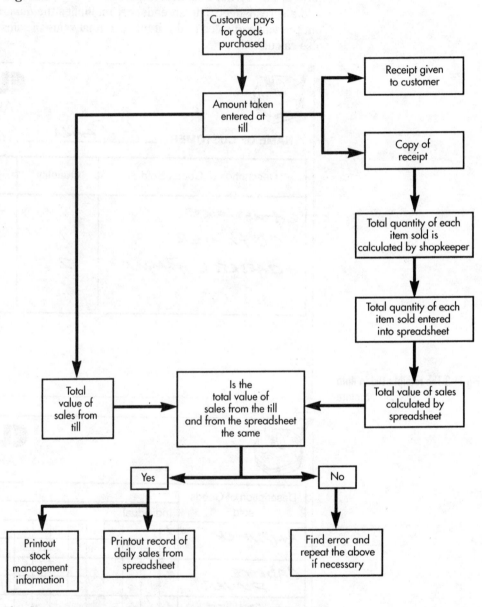

Fig 11.5 An information system for stock control in a small shop

The limitations of the spreadsheet example used

There are only a few items for sale listed in the example spreadsheet as there is not space in this book to include several printouts of a very large spreadsheet. In practice, a small electrical appliance shop might stock several hundred different items.

The spreadsheet that has been set up in the example uses only a small proportion of the rows and columns available. The spreadsheet could be set up to cover an entire week or a month. The quantity sold, sales values and profits could be worked out on a weekly or a monthly basis.

Setting up the spreadsheet

A spreadsheet is initially **set up** containing all the data which does not change very frequently (see Fig. 11.6). The variable data which changes each time the spreadsheet is used is not entered when the spreadsheet is first set up.

	A	B	C	D	E	F
1	Item	Unit	Quantity	Sales	% Profit	Profit on
2	Name	Price	Sold	Value	on Sales	Sales
3						
4	Amplifier	209.99		.00	25	.00
5	Cassette player	86.56		.00	25	.00
6	CD player	150.45		.00	25	.00
7	Electric cooker	367.99		.00	30	.00
8	Freezer	199.95		.00	30	.00
9	Fridge	149.09		.00	30	.00
10	Gas cooker	287.55		.00	30	.00
11	Gas hob	101.01		.00	30	.00
12	Radio	34.67		.00	20	.00
13	Radio alarm	35.99		.00	20	.00
14	Record player	119.95		.00	25	.00
15	Tuner	149.95		.00	25	.00
16	TV	345.99		.00	25	.00
17						
18			Total		Total	
19			Sales	.00	Profit	.00
20						

Fig 11.6(a) The spreadsheet as it was set up, showing *values* displayed

	A	B	C	D	E	F
1	Item	Unit	Quantity	Sales	% Profit	Profit on
2	Name	Price	Sold	Value	on Sales	Sales
3						
4	Amplifier	209.99		B4*C4	25	D4*E4/100
5	Cassette player	86.56		B5*C5	25	D5*E5/100
6	CD player	150.45		B6*C6	25	D6*E6/100
7	Electric cooker	367.99		B7*C7	30	D7*E7/100
8	Freezer	199.95		B8*C8	30	D8*E8/100
9	Fridge	149.09		B9*C9	30	D9*E9/100
10	Gas cooker	287.55		B10*C10	30	D10*E10/100
11	Gas hob	101.01		B11*C11	30	D11*E11/100
12	Radio	34.67		B12*C12	20	D12*E12/100
13	Radio alarm	35.99		B13*C13	20	D13*E13/100
14	Record player	119.95		B14*C14	25	D14*E14/100
15	Tuner	149.95		B15*C15	25	D15*E15/100
16	TV	345.99		B16*C16	25	D16*E16/100
17						
18			Total		Total	
19			Sales	SUM(D4:D16)	Profit	SUM(F4:F16)
20						

Fig 11.6(b) The spreadsheet, showing underlying formulae

Setting up the spreadsheet in the stock control example

For each item sold, the spreadsheet will eventually contain its name or description, unit price, the quantity sold, the value of sales, the percentage profit and the overall contribution to profits. There will be column headings, etc. The data which does not change very frequently is the column headings, item names or descriptions, unit prices, percentage profit and any formulae. These must be set up before the spreadsheet can be used by the shopkeeper. The variable data that may change each time the spreadsheet is used is the quantity sold. This is not entered at all when the spreadsheet is first set up, as the shopkeeper will enter the quantity sold at the end of each day when using the spreadsheet.

The shopkeeper does not worry about the order in which the items are entered when setting up the spreadsheet. When the spreadsheet is in use, it will be most convenient for the shopkeeper to have the list of items with their names in alphabetical order, however, the items can be sorted into this order later. Similarly, when the system has been in use for some time and the shopkeeper wishes to add extra items to the spreadsheet, these can be added at the bottom and the spreadsheet sorted.

When the shopkeeper has set up the spreadsheet, the cells containing the formulae and the row and column headings are protected so that they cannot be altered accidentally. The spreadsheet is then saved on backing storage and a backup copy made. This secures the basic spreadsheet that will be used each day to calculate the total value of sales and to provide other useful sales information. The shopkeeper will always start to use the spreadsheet, at the end of the day, by loading it as it is now set up.

Data capture

Data capture takes place when the shopkeeper fills in a receipt for a customer who is buying something from the shop. The shopkeeper fills in the receipt when goods are sold. The receipt is written on a two part carbonised pad so that both the customer and the shopkeeper have copies of the receipt.

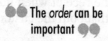

Data capture is important

The shopkeeper collects the copies of all the receipts written during the day. At the end of the day the shopkeeper goes through these receipts making a note of the total quantity sold of each item. These are accumulated on the form shown in fig.11.4.

Input and Processing

Fig. 11.7 shows the spreadsheet *after* the shopkeeper has entered the quantity sold for each item at the end of a day. It is important to note that the shopkeeper has only **input** the quantity sold for each item. The value of sales of each item, the profit on sales, the total value of sales and the total profit were automatically calculated using the formulae stored in these cells when the spreadsheet was set up. The **processing** done by the spreadsheet is the automatic calculation of the actual values from formulae already programmed into the cells. This is done automatically when numeric values are input into the appropriate cells.

	A	B	C	D	E	F
1	Item	Unit	Quantity	Sales	% Profit	Profit on
2	Name	Price	Sold	Value	on Sales	Sales
3						
4	Amplifier	209.99	1	209.99	25	52.50
5	Cassette player	86.56	2	173.12	25	43.28
6	CD player	150.45	3	451.35	25	112.84
7	Electric cooker	367.99	5	1839.95	30	551.99
8	Freezer	199.95	2	399.90	30	119.97
9	Fridge	149.09	4	596.36	30	178.91
10	Gas cooker	287.55	6	1725.30	30	517.59
11	Gas hob	101.01	6	606.06	30	181.82
12	Radio	34.67	6	208.02	20	41.60
13	Radio alarm	35.99	5	179.95	20	35.99
14	Record player	119.95	2	239.90	25	59.98
15	Tuner	149.95	1	149.95	25	37.49
16	TV	345.99	1	345.99	25	86.50
17						
18			Total		Total	
19			Sales	7125.84	Profit	2020.44
20						

Fig 11.7 The spreadsheet after the shopkeeper has entered quantities sold

Output

Output from a spreadsheet is simply a screen display or printout of the whole of the spreadsheet, a part of it or a graph generated from it. The output can be sorted or ordered according to its use.

A list of goods sold in the shop and their prices

The shopkeeper may want a list of items sold in the shop and their prices for the shop assistants to refer to. This can be printed from the spreadsheet while it is displayed with the items sorted into alphabetic order. However, the shopkeeper does not want the assistants to see the sales information. Consequently, only part of the spreadsheet is printed (see Fig. 11.8).

Lists can help the shopkeeper

	A	B
1	Item	Unit
2	Name	Price
3		
4	Amplifier	209.99
5	Cassette player	86.56
6	CD player	150.45
7	Electric cooker	367.99
8	Freezer	199.95
9	Fridge	149.09
10	Gas cooker	287.55
11	Gas hob	101.01
12	Radio	34.67
13	Radio alarm	35.99
14	Record player	119.95
15	Tuner	149.95
16	TV	345.99
17		

Fig 11.8 A list of items sold in the shop, and their prices

Output with the goods that sell the most first

The spreadsheet can be sorted so that those items which *sell the most* will be displayed first. This is achieved by sorting the rows in descending numeric order on the quantity sold (see Fig. 11.9). Sorting the spreadsheet into this order will be useful to the shopkeeper in finding out which are the best selling items. The shopkeeper will find this information useful when ordering goods. It will be necessary to order more of the items with high sales volumes, more frequently, than those that sell in lower quantities. It may also be necessary to keep higher stocks of the better selling items.

The *order* can be important

	A	B	C	D	E	F
1	Item	Unit	Quantity	Sales	% Profit	Profit on
2	Name	Price	Sold	Value	on Sales	Sales
3						
4	Gas cooker	287.55	6	1725.30	30	517.59
5	Gas hob	101.01	6	606.06	30	181.82
6	Radio	34.67	6	208.02	20	41.60
7	Electric cooker	367.99	5	1839.95	30	551.99
8	Radio alarm	35.99	5	179.95	20	35.99
9	Fridge	149.09	4	596.36	30	178.91
10	CD player	150.45	3	451.35	25	112.84
11	Cassette player	86.56	2	173.12	25	43.28
12	Freezer	199.95	2	399.90	30	119.97
13	Record player	119.95	2	239.90	25	59.98
14	Amplifier	209.99	1	209.99	25	52.50
15	Tuner	149.95	1	149.95	25	37.49
16	TV	345.99	1	345.99	25	86.50
17						
18			Total		Total	
19			Sales	7125.84	Profit	2020.44

Fig 11.9 The spreadsheet with data rearranged in order of sales quantity

Output with the goods with the highest price first

The spreadsheet can be sorted so that the *highest priced items* appear first. That is, the spreadsheet is displayed after being sorted into descending numeric order on the unit price (see Fig. 11.10). A display in this order identifies those items which are highly priced. These tie up the shopkeeper's capital to a greater extent than low priced items. These items may be withdrawn from stock and no longer sold in the shop.

	A	B	C	D	E	F
1	Item	Unit	Quantity	Sales	% Profit	Profit on
2	Name	Price	Sold	Value	on Sales	Sales
3						
4	Electric cooker	367.99	5	1839.95	30	551.99
5	TV	345.99	1	345.99	25	86.50
6	Gas cooker	287.55	6	1725.30	30	517.59
7	Amplifier	209.99	1	209.99	25	52.50
8	Freezer	199.95	2	399.90	30	119.97
9	CD player	150.45	3	451.35	25	112.84
10	Tuner	149.95	1	149.95	25	37.49
11	Fridge	149.09	4	596.36	30	178.91
12	Record player	119.95	2	239.90	25	59.98
13	Gas hob	101.01	6	606.06	30	181.82
14	Cassette player	86.56	2	173.12	25	43.28
15	Radio alarm	35.99	5	179.95	20	35.99
16	Radio	34.67	6	208.02	20	41.60
17						
18			Total		Total	
19			Sales	7125.84	Profit	2020.44

Fig 11.10 The spreadsheet with data rearranged in order of unit price

Output with the goods that make the least profit first.

A listing of the spreadsheet with the goods that *make the least profit* first (see Fig. 11.11) helps the shopkeeper identify goods that are not profitable. These may not be re-ordered. At the bottom of the list will be the most profitable goods. These should be re-ordered as stocks are sold. The shopkeeper can maximise profits by reducing the stock of goods that make low profits and increasing the stock of goods that make high profits.

	A	B	C	D	E	F
1	Item	Unit	Quantity	Sales	% Profit	Profit on
2	Name	Price	Sold	Value	on Sales	Sales
3						
4	Radio alarm	35.99	5	179.95	20	35.99
5	Tuner	149.95	1	149.95	25	37.49
6	Radio	34.67	6	208.02	20	41.60
7	Cassette player	86.56	2	173.12	25	43.28
8	Amplifier	209.99	1	209.99	25	52.50
9	Record player	119.95	2	239.90	25	59.98
10	TV	345.99	1	345.99	25	86.50
11	CD player	150.45	3	451.35	25	112.84
12	Freezer	199.95	2	399.90	30	119.97
13	Fridge	149.09	4	596.36	30	178.91
14	Gas hob	101.01	6	606.06	30	181.82
15	Gas cooker	287.55	6	1725.30	30	517.59
16	Electric cooker	367.99	5	1839.95	30	551.99
17						
18			Total		Total	
19			Sales	7125.84	Profit	2020.44

Fig 11.11 The spreadsheet with data rearranged in inverse order of profitability

Graphs

A *bar chart* showing total value of sales and profits (see Fig. 11.12) will provide further help to the shop keeper in identifying which items should be stocked.

> A visual display can help

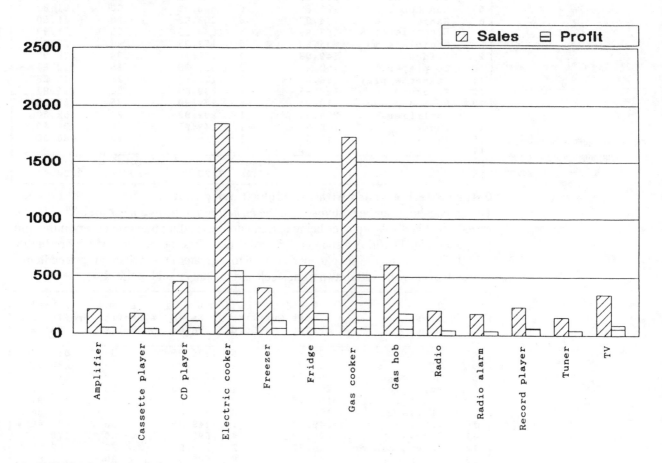

Fig 11.12 A bar chart showing total sales and profits

Evaluation

> Item codes can avoid confusion

Various essential items of information, such as Value Added Tax (VAT), have been left out. VAT is added to all sales of electrical goods. The VAT payable should be shown for each item and as a total for the shop.

As the number of items sold in the shop increases, confusion may arise between items with similar names. This should be avoided by giving each item stocked a *unique* item code.

This spreadsheet based information system is of limited effectiveness. It will make useful stock control and sales data available more easily, however, the task of working out the quantity of each item sold each day will still need to be done by the shopkeeper. This is likely to be a very time consuming task. The system might not function effectively if it had to deal with a large number of customers. The need to do this task manually can be avoided by purchasing new checkout tills that print a receipt for the customer and at the same time save a record of the sale on a magnetic tape or disc connected to the till. At the end of the day the sales records for all the tills, recorded on magnetic tape or disc, can be read into the computer where the quantity sold of each item will be calculated for use in the spreadsheet.

4 ▷ MODELLING

> Models are all around us

Models are representations of the real world. We are all familiar with some form of model. Our earliest introduction to **modelling** is likely to be moulding plasticine or clay to make representations of people or animals. You can buy toy soldiers and model cars; dolls and dolls houses. They are all models, that is, representations of the real world. Models in some form are used throughout commerce and industry. You can build a physical model of a shopping centre or other building project to demonstrate the architectural style and layout of the planned development. Models of such developments can also be built using computer software.

It is essential to remember that a model is a *representation* of the real world. It is *not* the real world. You cannot expect reality to be exactly like a model of it. The better the model, the more exactly it copies reality. The advantage of using models is that they allow us to experiment with reality. We can try out strategies and forecast what will happen. However, a forecast is based on experience of the past. The future may not mimic the past. Consequently, we must treat forecasts based on models with care.

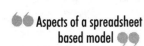
You can try out strategies on models

This ability to try out strategies is an important use of models. Models are safe. Managers do not have to bankrupt their employers when trying out new commercial strategies; farmers have no need to devastate their crops by blindly trying new methods of pest control. Whilst exploring a model is unlikely to lead us to the perfect solution to our problems, we may well improve our understanding of them and discover a range of useful strategies to tackle them.

SPREADSHEET MODELS

Spreadsheets can be used for a variety of tasks. We can use spreadsheets to record information from day-to-day and to do simple calculations. However, when a model is constructed using a spreadsheet, there is usually an intention to use it to improve our understanding of a real system, for problem solving or for prediction.

The **stock control information system** described earlier in this chapter is mainly used to record what is sold and to do simple addition and multiplication. It could be used to predict sales, but its main focus is not prediction. Whilst, to some extent we can consider all spreadsheets to be models, we would construct a model based on a spreadsheet with the intention to use it mainly to improve our understanding of a real system, for problem solving or for prediction.

A spreadsheet based model will:

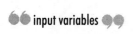
Aspects of a spreadsheet based model

- allow a range of input variables to be set
- use formulae to define the rules on which the model is based
- output information using the input variables and the rules

Typically, a spreadsheet based model will have a limited number of input variables. These variables will be processed using the rules defined by the structure of the spreadsheet and the underlying formulae. These rules will reflect the assumptions made by the author about the relationships evident in the real world. These relationships will be built into the model. However, the author may have simplified these relationships or otherwise modified them. The rules built into a model when it is constructed do not always exactly reflect the real world.

The models described below are constructed using a spreadsheet. You may be expected to set up such models yourself. Alternatively, your teacher may set them up for you and you would be expected to explore the extent to which they represent the real world and to adjust the underlying rules so that they more closely mimic reality.

PRICE FORECAST MODEL

The **price forecast model** is shown in Fig. 11.13. The model is used to predict the price of a commodity over a span of ten years.

input variables

The *input variables* are the initial price, the base year and the rate of inflation. These are changed when the model is used.

Rules

The *rules* are the formulae in the cells A13 to A22 and B13 to B22 (see Fig. 11.13(c)). For example, the effect of the formula in B13 is to increase the initial price copied into B12 by the percentage input in C5. This is done using the formula:

B12*(1+C5/100)

In Fig. 11.13(a), this gives:

£100.00*(1+7.5/100)
= £100.00*1.075

Multiplying by 1.075 increases £100.00 by 7.5% to £107.50 as required.

```
     !    A    !!       B     !!   C   !!   D   !
 1   Price forecasting
 2
 3
 4   Initial price                Rate of inflation
 5       £100.00                        7.5 percent
 6
 7       Base year
 8        1994
 9
10
11            Year         Price
12            1994         100.00
13            1995         107.50
14            1996         115.56
15            1997         124.23
16            1998         133.55
17            1999         143.56
18            2000         154.33
19            2001         165.90
20            2002         178.35
21            2003         191.72
22            2004         206.10
23
```

Fig 11.13(a) The price forecast model with 1994 as the base year

```
     !    A    !!        B      !!   C   !!   D   !
 1   Price forecasting
 2
 3
 4   Initial price                 Rate of inflation
 5       £74.80                          3.5 percent
 6
 7        Base year
 8         1985
 9
10
11            Year               Price
12            1985                74.80
13            1986                77.42
14            1987                80.13
15            1988                82.93
16            1989                85.83
17            1990                88.84
18            1991                91.95
19            1992                95.17
20            1993                98.50
21            1994               101.94
22            1995               105.51
```

Fig 11.13(b) The model with 1985 as the base year

```
     !    A    !!:      B       !!   C   !!   D   !
 1   Price forecasting
 2
 3
 4   Initial price                 Rate of inflation
 5    74.80                             3.5 percent
 6
 7       Base year
 8    1985
 9
10
11       Year                Price
12   A8                          A5
13   A12+1          B12*(1+$C$5/100)
14   A13+1          B13*(1+$C$5/100)
15   A14+1          B14*(1+$C$5/100)
16   A15+1          B15*(1+$C$5/100)
17   A16+1          B16*(1+$C$5/100)
18   A17+1          B17*(1+$C$5/100)
19   A18+1          B18*(1+$C$5/100)
20   A19+1          B19*(1+$C$5/100)
21   A20+1          B20*(1+$C$5/100)
22   A21+1          B21*(1+$C$5/100)
```

Fig 11.13(c) The formulae used in the model

It is worth noting that $C$5 refers to the same cell as C5. Supercalc defaults to relative cell references which change when cells are copied. $C$5 is an absolute cell reference which does not change when the cell is copied. This is an important distinction when setting up a model. In setting up the Price forecast model, B13 was copied into cells B14 to B22. As this was done, the relative cell references changed. B12 changed to B13 as the formula was copied from B13 into B14; B13 changed to B14 as the formula was copied from B14 into B15; and so on. This pattern of changes was repeated as B13 was copied to cells B14 to B22. However, to prevent C5 from being changed, it was set up as an absolute cell reference by using $C$5. Although spreadsheets differ in the way they define relative and absolute cell references, they will all have some method of showing which is which. Setting up models is much easier if formulae can be copied from one cell to another with appropriate adjustment.

The *information output* from the model is the price adjusted for inflation over a ten year span. This can be used, for example, to predict the price of goods worth £100 in 1994 in up to ten years time (see Fig. 11.13(a)). It can also be used to work out the likely price of goods today if the price in a previous year is known (see Fig. 11.13(b)).

The model uses the average inflation figure over a ten year period. This is reasonable providing you do not assume that inflation will be constant over the ten year period. Inflation will rise and fall. The actual price each year may fluctuate considerably from the model. However, over a ten year period, the model adequately represents the overall trend in price inflation.

SUPERMARKET QUEUE MODEL

The **supermarket queue model** is shown in Fig. 11.14. The model can be used to regulate the time a customer spends in the queue at a checkout.

```
   |      A     ||      B     ||      C      |
1  Shopping queue model
2
3        INPUTS:
4
5     Number of         Number       Time to get a
6      people             of       person through a
7      waiting         checkouts    checkout (mins)
8        50               10             2.00
9
10       OUTPUTS:
11
12   Average number       Last
13    of people          person
14    queuing per       wait time
15     checkout          (mins)
16        5               10.00
```

Fig 11.14(a) The model of a supermarket shopping queue, showing a waiting time of ten minutes

```
   |      A     ||      B     ||      C      |
1  Shopping queue model
2
3        INPUTS:
4
5     Number of         Number       Time to get a
6      people             of       person through a
7      waiting         checkouts    checkout (mins)
8        50               20             2.00
9
10       OUTPUTS:
11
12   Average number       Last
13    of people          person
14    queuing per       wait time
15     checkout          (mins)
16        3                5.00
```

Fig 11.14(b) The model showing the waiting time reduced to 5 minutes by increasing the number of checkouts

```
|        A        ||      B      ||         C          |
1   Shopping queue model
2  ─────────────────────────────────────────────────────
3            INPUTS:
4
5         Number of          Number       Time to get a
6          people              of      person through a
7         waiting          checkouts    checkout (mins)
8            50                 10                 1.00
9  ─────────────────────────────────────────────────────
10          OUTPUTS:
11
12     Average number          Last
13       of people           person
14     queuing per         wait time
15       checkout            (mins)
16          5                5.00
```

Fig 11.14(c) The waiting time reduced to 5 minutes by reducing the time taken to pass through checkout

```
|        A        ||      B      ||         C          |
1   Shopping queue model
2  ─────────────────────────────────────────────────────
3            INPUTS:
4
5         Number of          Number       Time to get a
6          people              of      person through a
7         waiting          checkouts    checkout (mins)
8            50                 10                 2.00
9  ─────────────────────────────────────────────────────
10          OUTPUTS:
11
12     Average number          Last
13       of people           person
14     queuing per         wait time
15       checkout            (mins)
16         A8/B8             A16*C8
```

Fig 11.14(d) The formulae used

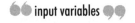
input variables

The input variables are the number of people waiting, the number of checkouts and the time it takes to get a person through a checkout, that is, the time taken to serve a customer at a checkout. These are changed when the model is used.

The rules are the formulae in cells A16 and B16 (see Fig. 11.14(d)). The formula in A16 is:

A8/B8

This represents the relationship:

$$\text{the average number of people queueing per checkout} = \frac{\text{The number of people waiting}}{\text{The number of checkouts}}$$

The formula in B16 is:

A16*C8

This represents the relationship:

$$\text{The time the last person in a queue has to wait} = \left(\begin{array}{l}\text{The number} \\ \text{of people} \\ \text{waiting per} \\ \text{checkout}\end{array}\right) \times \left(\begin{array}{l}\text{The time to get} \\ \text{a person through} \\ \text{a checkout}\end{array}\right)$$

The information output from the model is the average number of people in a checkout queue and the length of time the last person in the queue will have to wait. A supermarket manager could use the model to quickly see the effect of adjusting the number of checkouts and the time taken to get a person through a checkout. For example, Fig. 11.14(a) shows the last person wait time to be 10 minutes. If the manager considers this unacceptable, the model can be used to explore alternatives. Suppose the manager wished to reduce the last person wait time to 5 minutes. The input variables could be adjusted to show how this can be done. In Fig. 11.14(b), a

5 minute wait time is achieved by increasing the number of checkouts to 20. This would double the costs involved, for example, the wages paid to checkout operators. In Fig. 11.14(c), a 5 minute wait time is achieved by reducing the time to get a person through a checkout to 1 minute. This might involve training staff, introducing a productivity scheme or buying more up-to-date checkout technology. Other solutions could be found by both increasing the number of checkouts and reducing the time to get a person through a checkout.

The model assumes that there will be a steady flow of customers to the checkouts, that they will distribute themselves equally across all the checkouts, that every checkout operator works at the same speed and that people will not get tired of waiting and simply leave. These assumptions are needed so that a simple, understandable model can be constructed.

BREAK EVEN MODEL

The **break even model** is shown in Fig. 11.15. A model can be used to find the break even point. This is the point at which the total value of sales equals the total cost of production. Above the break even point companies can expect to make a profit; below the break even point they will make a loss.

To illustrate what is meant by the 'break even point' and to show why it is most important to find it, the example of a company making up T-shirts is used. The company buys in cloth and makes the cloth into T-shirts.

	A	B	C	D	E
1	Break even model				
3	Fixed	Quantity	Variable Cost		Selling Price
4	Cost	Base	per unit		per unit
5	£400.00	100	£5.00		£6.50
7		Quantity			
8		Increment			
9		50			
11	Fixed	Quantity	Variable	Total	Value of
12	Cost	Sold	Cost	Cost	Sales
13	400.00	100	500.00	900.00	650.00
14	400.00	150	750.00	1150.00	975.00
15	400.00	200	1000.00	1400.00	1300.00
16	400.00	250	1250.00	1650.00	1625.00
17	400.00	300	1500.00	1900.00	1950.00
18	400.00	350	1750.00	2150.00	2275.00
19	400.00	400	2000.00	2400.00	2600.00
20	400.00	450	2250.00	2650.00	2925.00
21	400.00	500	2500.00	2900.00	3250.00
22	400.00	550	2750.00	3150.00	3575.00
23	400.00	600	3000.00	3400.00	3900.00
24	400.00	650	3250.00	3650.00	4225.00

Fig 11.15(a) The break-even model: first attempt, with base 100 and increment 50

	A	B	C	D	E
1	Break even model				
3	Fixed	Quantity	Variable Cost		Selling Price
4	Cost	Base	per unit		per unit
5	£400.00	250	£5.00		£6.50
7		Quantity			
8		Increment			
9		5			
11	Fixed	Quantity	Variable	Total	Value of
12	Cost	Sold	Cost	Cost	Sales
13	400.00	250	1250.00	1650.00	1625.00
14	400.00	255	1275.00	1675.00	1657.50
15	400.00	260	1300.00	1700.00	1690.00
16	400.00	265	1325.00	1725.00	1722.50
17	400.00	270	1350.00	1750.00	1755.00
18	400.00	275	1375.00	1775.00	1787.50
19	400.00	280	1400.00	1800.00	1820.00
20	400.00	285	1425.00	1825.00	1852.50
21	400.00	290	1450.00	1850.00	1885.00
22	400.00	295	1475.00	1875.00	1917.50
23	400.00	300	1500.00	1900.00	1950.00
24	400.00	305	1525.00	1925.00	1982.50

Fig 11.15(b) Second attempt, with base 250 and increment 5

	A	B	C	D	E
1	Break even model				
2					
3	Fixed	Quantity	Variable Cost		Selling Price
4	Cost	Base	per unit		per unit
5	£400.00	265	£5.00		£6.50
6					
7		Quantity			
8		Increment			
9		1			
10					
11	Fixed	Quantity	Variable	Total	Value of
12	Cost	Sold	Cost	Cost	Sales
13	400.00	265	1325.00	1725.00	1722.50
14	400.00	266	1330.00	1730.00	1729.00
15	400.00	267	1335.00	1735.00	1735.50
16	400.00	268	1340.00	1740.00	1742.00
17	400.00	269	1345.00	1745.00	1748.50
18	400.00	270	1350.00	1750.00	1755.00
19	400.00	271	1355.00	1755.00	1761.50
20	400.00	272	1360.00	1760.00	1768.00
21	400.00	273	1365.00	1765.00	1774.50
22	400.00	274	1370.00	1770.00	1781.00
23	400.00	275	1375.00	1775.00	1787.50
24	400.00	276	1380.00	1780.00	1794.00

Fig 11.15(c) Third attempt, with base 265 and increment 1

Line graph showing the Break Even point.

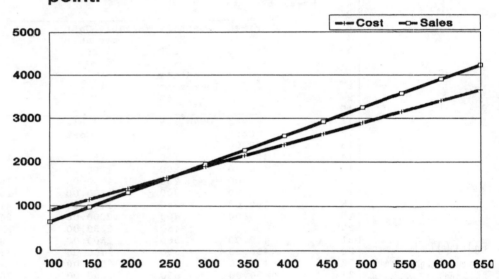

Fig 11.15(d) A line graph indicating the break even point

	A	B	C	D	E
1	Break even model				
2					
3	Fixed	Quantity	Variable Cost		Selling Price
4	Cost	Base	per unit		per unit
5	£400.00	100	£5.00		£6.50
6					
7		Quantity			
8		Increment			
9		50			
10					
11	Fixed	Quantity	Variable	Total	Value of
12	Cost	Sold	Cost	Cost	Sales
13	A5	B5	B13*$C$5	A13+C13	B13*$E$5
14	A13	B13+$B$9	B14*$C$5	A14+C14	B14*$E$5
15	A14	B14+$B$9	B15*$C$5	A15+C15	B15*$E$5
16	A15	B15+$B$9	B16*$C$5	A16+C16	B16*$E$5
17	A16	B16+$B$9	B17*$C$5	A17+C17	B17*$E$5
18	A17	B17+$B$9	B18*$C$5	A18+C18	B18*$E$5
19	A18	B18+$B$9	B19*$C$5	A19+C19	B19*$E$5
20	A19	B19+$B$9	B20*$C$5	A20+C20	B20*$E$5
21	A20	B20+$B$9	B21*$C$5	A21+C21	B21*$E$5
22	A21	B21+$B$9	B22*$C$5	A22+C22	B22*$E$5
23	A22	B22+$B$9	B23*$C$5	A23+C23	B23*$E$5
24	A23	B23+$B$9	B24*$C$5	A24+C24	B24*$E$5

Fig 11.15(e) The formulae used

The spreadsheet in Fig. 11.15(a), shows that the T-shirts are sold for £6.50 each. The cost to the company of making up the T-shirts is made up of fixed costs and variable costs. The fixed costs are expenses such as the rent that must be paid for the buildings and equipment the company uses. These do not vary with the quantity of T-shirts sold and must be paid regularly and promptly. The variable costs are those that depend on the number of T-shirts sold, for example, the amount of cloth used.

The company needs to know when it is making a profit. The profit made depends on the number of T-shirts sold. If the company sells a large quantity of T-shirts, it can expect to make a profit. However, the company needs to know exactly how many T-shirts it has to sell to make a profit. The break even point is the sales quantity at which the value of sales equals the total cost of producing the T-shirts. When the company sells more T-shirts than the break even point, it makes a profit; when it sells less than the break even point, it makes a loss.

The input variables to be entered in the spreadsheet are the fixed costs, the variable costs, the selling price per T-shirt, the quantity base and the quantity increment. The quantity base and the quantity increment are used to adjust the range of sales quantities the spreadsheet covers. To find the break even point, you would first enter the fixed cost, the variable cost and the selling price. You would then adjust the quantity base and the quantity increment to help you find the break even point.

The formulae used are shown in Fig. 11.15(e).

The formulae in cells A13 to A24 copy the value of fixed costs entered in A5.

In cell B13, the value entered for the quantity base is copied. The formulae in cells B14 to B24 add the quantity increment in C5 to the contents of the cell immediately above them. This ensures that the quantity sold increases by the quantity increment starting at the quantity base. For example, in Fig. 11.15(a), the quantity base is 100 and the quantity increment is 50. This ensures the quantities sold start at 100 and go up 50 at a time to give 100, 150, 200, 250, etc.

The formulae in C13 to C24 calculate the variable costs for the relevant quantity sold, using the formula:

variable cost　　=　　quantity sold　　　　　*　　　　variable cost per unit

The total cost is calculated in D13 to D24 by adding the corresponding fixed and variable costs.

The value of sales in E13 to E24, is worked out using this formula:

value of sales　　=　　selling price per unit　　*　　　quantity sold

The model can be used to find the break even point by adjusting the quantity base and the quantity increment. Suppose the T- shirts are selling for £6.50 each, fixed costs are £400 and variable costs per unit sold are £5.00.(see Fig. 11.15(a)). Setting the quantity base at 100 and the increment at 50 generates a table of total costs and the corresponding value of sales. The break even point is where the total cost is equal to the value of sales. Fig. 11.15(a) shows that the break even point must lie between the sales quantities of 250 and 300 because between these quantities the value of sales moves from being less than total cost to being more than total cost. Using 250 as the quantity base and an increment of 5 (see Fig. 11.15(b)), indicates that the break even point lies between 265 and 270. This suggests a quantity base of 265 and an increment of 1 (see Fig. 11.15(c)). At a quantity sold of 267 the total cost equals the value of sales. This is the break even point.

The break even model can be used to explore the options available to the company as it seeks to remain profitable in a competitive market. For example, it can be used to find solutions to operating problems such as those that arise due to price competition. If it is necessary to lower prices due to competition, what can be done and what are the likely effects? The company could seek to reduce fixed and variable costs or try to sell more. The break even model can be used to indicate the different impact of these strategies.

The model assumes that fixed costs do not increase as sales quantities increase. This is reasonable for relatively small changes in sales quantities. However, if sales quantities increase significantly so that, for example, larger premises are required, fixed costs may well go up. This consideration could be built into a more complex model.

It is also assumed that variable costs remain the same per T-shirt. This is unlikely to be the case. For example, as sales quantities increase, the company will use more cloth in making the T-shirts. Purchasing larger quantities will usually attract more discount than buying smaller quantities. This reduces the variable cost per T-shirt. The company can either make more profit or pass on the discount in price reductions in the hope of attracting even more sales. Again, a more complex model might have this consideration built into it so that it more exactly represents the company's operating environment.

The company is unlikely to make only one product, that is, a T-shirt selling for a single price. It is likely to sell a range of differently price T-shirts or other similar products such as shirts, skirts, etc. These affect the overall break even point for the company. It will need to look at all its products and their cost of production when trying to find the overall break even point. The break even model shown here could be adapted to include more than one product.

Despite its limitations, an understanding of the break even model is essential in predicting when profits will be made and forecasting the effect of changes in costs and market price on the profitability of a company.

PREDATOR/PREY MODEL

Predator/prey models can be used to explore the relationship between predators and their prey. The particular example used here looks at the relationship between birds and the grubs they eat. Understanding these relationships is increasingly important as farming becomes more organic and less dependant on the use of pesticides, etc.

Imagine that a crop of cabbages is being attacked by grubs. These will destroy the whole crop if they are not controlled. The farmer uses pesticides to control the grubs. When pesticides are used, the whole population of grubs is killed. The birds that eat the grubs die off too. The following year, the crop attracts more grubs. The grubs breed rapidly un-checked by the birds. The farmer now has no choice but to use pesticides as the birds that ate the grubs have died off. Having once used pesticides, the farmer must use them every year.

The farmer could use the birds to control the grubs, instead of using pesticides. In this case the farmer would not wipe out the grubs but would try to regulate them. The ideal is an equilibrium state where the bird population and the grub population are both stable. The equilibrium should be established at a level where the grub population is a minimum so that little damage is done to the crop.

The spreadsheet in Fig. 11.16, illustrates this predator/prey relationship. The numbers have been kept small for simplicity. It is assumed that the birds breed in May and die off in October; the grub population increases every month; the grubs breed at a different rate from April to September than during the rest of the year; the birds eat a fixed number of grubs each month and die if they do not get them.

	A	B	C	D	E
1	Predator/prey model: birds vs grubs				
2					
3	BIRDS:				
4		breeding	death		Birds
5	Number	rate	rate		eat
6	at start	in May	in Oct		4
7	10	2	.5		grubs
8					
9	GRUBS:	breeding	breeding		
10		rate in	rate in		
11	at start	Oct-Mar	Apr-Sept		
12	40	2	3		
13					
14					
15		Number of	Number of		
16	Start of	birds	grubs		
17	Jan	10	40		
18	Feb	10	40		
19	March	10	40		
20	April	20	40		
21	May	20	40		
22	June	20	40		
23	July	20	40		
24	Aug	20	40		
25	Sept	20	40		
26	Oct	10	40		
27	Nov	10	40		
28	Dec	10	40		
29	Jan	10	40		

Fig 11.16(a) The predator/prey model: birds vs grubs, the equilibrium state

	A	B	C	D	E
1	Predator/prey model: birds vs grubs				
2					
3	BIRDS:				
4		breeding	death		Birds
5	Number	rate	rate		eat
6	at start	in May	in Oct		4
7	10	2	.75		grubs
8					
9	GRUBS:	breeding	breeding		
10		rate in	rate in		
11	at start	Oct-Mar	Apr-Sept		
12	40	2	3		
13					
14					
15		Number of	Number of		
16	Start of	birds	grubs		
17	Jan	10	40		
18	Feb	10	40		
19	March	10	40		
20	April	20	40		
21	May	20	40		
22	June	20	40		
23	July	20	40		
24	Aug	20	40		
25	Sept	20	40		
26	Oct	5	60		
27	Nov	5	100		
28	Dec	5	180		
29	Jan	5	340		

Fig 11.16(b) More birds die in October: the grub population increases out of control

	A	B	C	D	E
1	Predator/prey model: birds vs grubs				
2					
3	BIRDS:				
4		breeding	death		Birds
5	Number	rate	rate		eat
6	at start	in May	in Oct		4
7	10	2	.25		grubs
8					
9	GRUBS:	breeding	breeding		
10		rate in	rate in		
11	at start	Oct-Mar	Apr-Sept		
12	40	2	3		
13					
14					
15		Number of	Number of		
16	Start of	birds	grubs		
17	Jan	10	40		
18	Feb	10	40		
19	March	10	40		
20	April	20	40		
21	May	20	40		
22	June	20	40		
23	July	20	40		
24	Aug	20	40		
25	Sept	20	40		
26	Oct	15	20		
27	Nov	10	0		
28	Dec	0	0		
29	Jan	0	0		

Fig 11.16(c) Fewer birds die in October: grubs and birds die off

	A	B	C	D	E
1	Predator/prey model: birds vs grubs				
14					
15		Number of	Number of		
16	Start of	birds	grubs		
17	Jan	A7	A12		
18	Feb	IF(C18>0,B17,INT(C17/4))	IF(C17*$B$12-B17*$E$6>0,C17*$B$12-B17*$E$6,0)		
19	March	IF(C19>0,B18,INT(C18/4))	IF(C18*$B$12-B18*$E$6>0,C18*$B$12-B18*$E$6,0)		
20	April	IF(C20>0,B19*$B$7,INT(C19/4))	IF(C19*$C$12-B19*$E$6*B7>0,C19*$C$12-B19*$E$6*B7,0)		
21	May	IF(C21>0,B20,INT(C20/4))	IF(C20*$C$12-B20*$E$6>0,C20*$C$12-B20*$E$6,0)		
22	June	IF(C22>0,B21,INT(C21/4))	IF(C21*$C$12-B21*$E$6>0,C21*$C$12-B21*$E$6,0)		
23	July	IF(C23>0,B22,INT(C22/4))	IF(C22*$C$12-B22*$E$6>0,C22*$C$12-B22*$E$6,0)		
24	Aug	IF(C24>0,B23,INT(C23/4))	IF(C23*$C$12-B23*$E$6>0,C23*$C$12-B23*$E$6,0)		
25	Sept	IF(C25>0,B24,INT(C24/4))	IF(C24*$C$12-B24*$E$6>0,C24*$C$12-B24*$E$6,0)		
26	Oct	IF(C26>0,B25*(1-$C$7),INT(C25/4))	IF(C25*$B$12-B25*$E$6*(1-$C$7)>0,C25*$B$12-B25*$E$6*(1-		
27	Nov	IF(C27>0,B26,INT(C25/4))	IF(C26*$B$12-B26*$E$6>0,C26*$B$12-B26*$E$6,0)		
28	Dec	IF(C28>0,B27,INT(C27/4))	IF(C27*$B$12-B27*$E$6>0,C27*$B$12-B27*$E$6,0)		
29	Jan	IF(C29>0,B28,INT(C28/4))	IF(C28*$B$12-B28*$E$6>0,C28*$B$12-B28*$E$6,0)		
30					

Fig 11.16(d) The formulae used in the predator/prey model

The input variables to be entered in the spreadsheet are the number of birds and their breeding rate and death rate; the number of grubs the birds eat each month; the number of grubs and their breeding rate from October to March and from April to September. The number of birds and the number of grubs at the start of the year are also entered.

The formulae used are shown in Fig. 11.16(d).

The formula in cell C17 copies the number of grubs at the start from A12 and that in B17 copies the number of birds at the start from A7.

The formulae in C18 to C29 can be expressed in pseudo code, as follows:

> IF the number of grubs that remain IS MORE THAN zero
> THEN the value of the cell is the number of grubs that remain
> ELSE the value of the cell is zero

The number of grubs that remain is calculated using the formula:

$$\begin{pmatrix} \text{the number} \\ \text{of grubs} \\ \text{that} \\ \text{remain} \end{pmatrix} = \begin{pmatrix} \text{the number} \\ \text{of grubs} \\ \text{in the} \\ \text{previous} \\ \text{month} \end{pmatrix} \times \begin{pmatrix} \text{the} \\ \text{breeding} \\ \text{rate} \end{pmatrix} - \begin{pmatrix} \text{the number} \\ \text{of birds} \end{pmatrix} \times \begin{pmatrix} \text{the number} \\ \text{of grubs} \\ \text{one bird} \\ \text{eats} \end{pmatrix}$$

The formulae in B18 to B29 can be expressed in pseudo code as follows:

> IF there are sufficient grubs to eat
> THEN all the birds survive
> ELSE only those birds that can be fed survive

The formula in B20, C20, B26 and C26 take into account the birds' breeding rate in May and their death rate in April.

Fig. 11.16(a) shows the equilibrium state for the model. This shows a situation where there are sufficient grubs to feed a stable bird population. The bird population in turn stabilizes the size of the grub population. The equilibrium state can be recognised by comparing the figures for the first January with the following January. These should be the same, ie. we should have B17 = B29 and C17 = C29 for equilibrium. If the same rules hold every year, then if we end the year as we start it, we must once again start and end with the same values. This equilibrium state is not unique. There will a large number of different settings of the input variables that will lead to an equilibrium state.

In practice, models such as this are likely to be used to find a suitable equilibrium state. The farmer would start with the input variables set to the values estimated by observation. By changing these variables the farmer would try to control the grub population. This might suggest a suitable equilibrium state could be established by increasing the 'breeding rate' for the birds in May by releasing more birds. Other possibilities are to increase the 'death rate' by culling the birds in October (see Fig. 11.16(b)) or to decrease the 'death rate' by feeding the birds alternative foods (see Fig. 11.16(c)). A range of possible actions can be explored and their outcomes investigated without taking risks with the actual crop.

This predatory prey model is not a very good representation of the real world. It assumes that there is a self contained environment in which the populations of birds and grubs change according to fixed rules. This is unlikely to be the case. There are likely to be other influences on the size of the populations, such as, the weather, the availability of alternative food for the birds, etc. However, despite its limitations, this model is useful in helping us understand the relationships between the bird population and the grub population.

EXAMINATION QUESTIONS

Q1. EWE AND WOOL is a small business making woollen items of clothing. The owner has created a spreadsheet to help him calculate the cost of making each item. The spreadsheet display is shown below:

	A	B	C	D	E	F	G	H
1	Type	Cost of wool	Time taken to	Pay per hour	Total Pay	Total Cost		
2		(£)	make 1 (hrs)	(£)	(£)	for 1 (£)		
3	Cardigan	5.00	3	3.00	9.00	14.00		
4	Sweater	5.00	2	2.50	5.00	10.00		
5	Gloves	1.50	2	3.00	6.00	7.50		
6	Scarf	3.00	1	2.00	2.00	5.00		
7	Hat	2.00	1	2.00	2.00	4.00		
8								
9								

(a) How is the Total Pay calculated by the spreadsheet?
  A Cost of wool × Pay per hour
  B Cost of wool × Time taken to make 1
  C Time taken to make 1 × Total Cost for 1
  D Time taken to make 1 × Pay per hour

(b) Which other values does the spreadsheet work out for you?

(c) The workers who knit the sweaters are unhappy about their pay and you decide to increase their pay to £2.75. You need to see the effect on the Total Cost for 1.

Which cell or box on the spreadsheet would you have to change?

(d) (i) The design of the cardigan changes and it will now take longer to make one.

Which cell or box would you have to change?

(ii) Which other cells would change as a result?

(NEAB/WJEC, 1993)

Q2. The spreadsheet below shows data on agriculture in the British Isles.

	A	B	C	D	E
1	Country	Agriculture	%	%	%
2	Name	Area	Grass	Arable	Fruit & Veg
3	England				
4	Wales				
5	Scotland				
6	Ireland				
7					
8					

(a) Which cell would you use to put the total Agriculture Area?

(b) What formula would you put in that cell?

(c) The spreadsheet has the ability to produce the following types of graph:

Bar   Line   Pie   Scatter

Which one would be the most suitable for showing:

(i) The proportions of Grass, Arable and Fruit & Veg for England?

(ii) To compare the Agricultural Areas for the four countries?

(d) If you want to add similar data for other countries where could you find that data?

(SEG, 1993)

Q3. The spreadsheet shown below is designed to give the price of a number of items in three different currencies.

	A	B	C	D
1				
2	Item	British	Australian	French
3		Pounds	Dollars	Francs
4				
5	Litre of Milk	0.40	0.20	
6				
7	Bar of Soap	0.36	0.18	
8				
9	Kilo of Sugar	0.48	0.24	
10				
11	Litre of Petrol	0.44	0.22	
12				
13	Newspaper	0.26	0.13	
14		───	───	
15	Total Cost	1.94	0.97	

(a) How many Australian Dollars made one British Pound when the spreadsheet was created?

(b) When cell B11 is altered to 0.40 it is noticed that the display of cell B15 immediately changes to 1.90.

(i) Describe the contents of cell B15.

(ii) If the spreadsheet was well designed state what other cells should have changed and give their value.

(c) If there are 9 French Francs to one British Pound describe what must be put in the cells in column D so that the prices in French Francs will displayed automatically.

(d) Assume that you have set up the spreadsheet using a microcomputer system.

   (i) If you want to use the same spreadsheet tomorrow, describe in detail what you should do before you switch off the computer.

   (ii) When you come back to the computer tomorrow and want to use the same spreadsheet, describe in detail what you will do to get the spreadsheet back on to the screen.

(ULEAC, 1993)

Q4. Below is the information which was given to you to enter into a spreadsheet.

Monday	28.60	Shopping
Tuesday	5.60	Went to cinema
Tuesday	10.20	Received cheque to pay into bank
Wednesday	2.50	Bread and cakes
Thursday	108.00	Wages paid into bank
Friday	18.50	Went out with friends
Saturday	11.99	Bought CD
Sunday	6.25	Paid for newspapers

You enter this data into a spreadsheet as follows:

Items	Mon	Tue	Wed	Thu	Fri	Sat	Sun	Total
Income								
Wages				108				
Sub-Total				108				108
Expenditure								
Shopping	2.86							
Cinema		5.60						
Bread & Cake			2.50					
Cheque		10.20						
Out - friends					18.50			
Bought CD						11.99		
Newspapers							6.25	
Sub-Total	2.86	15.80	2.50		18.50	11.99	6.25	57.90

(a) Circle the errors on the spreadsheet, and explain what difference this makes to the final field total.

   Explain what this could mean to the family.

(b) Give an example of an organisation which uses spreadsheets in real life, and state the advantages of using them.

(NDTEF, 1993)

Q5. You use a spreadsheet package to analyse the cost of a holiday in Australia.

(a) Write down ONE item of information which you want output.

(b) Write down TWO items of data you enter on the spreadsheet.

(c) Give TWO items of data which you should use to test if the results are reasonable.

(MEG, 1993)

Q6. The owner of a cafe has decided to offer customers a new range of vegetarian dishes. She needs to work out the price to charge for the dishes. She knows how many she expects to sell each week, and is going to make 20 of each at once. She knows the cost of the ingredients, how long it takes to make a batch, and what the cost of cooking them is.

(a) State what software she would use to help her decide what to charge. Give a reason for your answer.

(b) Explain why this method is better than using a simple calculator.

(c) State another advantage for the IT method compared with setting out her plans on paper and calculating manually.

(RSA, 1993)

Q7. Describe, using the diagram, how a model of a pupil's weekly finances could be constructed.

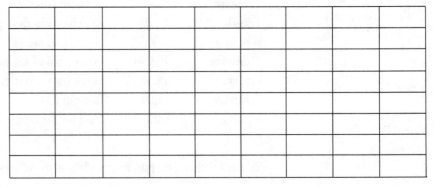

(MEG, 1993)

Q8. A Milkman orders milk of various types (e.g. Full cream, Skimmed, Semi-skimmed) and other produce from a dairy and delivers to many customers. The milkman wishes to use a spreadsheet to manage the ordering and billing system for the daily deliveries to customers' homes.

Use the grid below to show the main elements of a suitable spreadsheet design. Indicate the formulae that would allow you to show each customer's weekly bill and the total weekly ordering requirements for each type of milk and other dairy products to be obtained from the dairy.

	A	B	C	D	E	F	G	H	I	J
1										
2										
3										
4										
5										
6										
7										
8										
9										
10										
11										
12										

(NEAB/WJEC, 1993)

Q9. (a) Give one advantage of using a computer model to study the relationship between hunting animals and their prey?

(b) Give two reasons why your teacher may prefer to use a simulation rather than a school trip to an African jungle.

(c) What software package would you use to display the data collected.

(City and Guilds, 1993)

Q10. You can use spreadsheet software to make a computer model.

(a) Give an example of an investigation for which you would use a spreadsheet package to make a computer model.

(b) Describe how you would set up the model on the spreadsheet.

(c) Explain why you would use the computer model instead of creating the real thing.

(MEG, 1993)

ANSWERS TO EXAMINATION QUESTIONS

A1.
(a) D
(b) total cost
(c) D4
(d) C3
(e) E3 and F3

A2. (a) B7 or B8

(b) SUM(B3 to B6)

(c) (i) pie chart

(ii) bar chart

(d) Encyclopaedia or Geography book

A3. (a) 0.50

(b) (i) Cell B15 contains a formula that adds up cells B5, B7, B9, B11 and B13.

(ii) C11 = 0.20
C15 = 0.95
(D11 and D15 would also change in the completed spreadsheet).

(c) D5 = B5*9
D7 = B7*9
D9 = B9*9
D11 = B11*9
D13 = B13*9

(d) (i) Give the spreadsheet a file name. Save the file on backing storage, e.g. floppy disc.

(ii) Load and run the spreadsheet software. Load the spreadsheet file from backing storage, e.g. floppy disc.

A4. (a) 2.86 entered instead of 28.60 for Monday, shopping. The cheque paid into the bank has been entered as Expenditure.

The family is £5.34 worse off than they think. They could overspend by mistake.

(b) Shops use spreadsheets.
Some of the advantages are:
■ No human error in the calculations

- You can set up a spreadsheet once and use it repeatedly for similar tasks.
- Easy to edit.
- Multiple printed copies can be made.

A5. (a) One of:

The cost of the holiday for different numbers of people
The cost of the holiday for different seasons

(b) Two from:

Number of people going on holiday
Cost of one person going on holiday
Different prices for different times of year
Different lengths of time

(c) Produce zero cost if the number of people are zero
Enter simple numbers (e.g. 1 person) and calculate by hand

(MEG, 1993)

A6. (a) She should use a spreadsheet. The spreadsheet will help her do the original calculations. Once it is set up, she can use it again for different dishes or to re-assess the cost of the same dish.

(b) A calculator does not store the structure of the model or the formulae used. If you change one value in a spreadsheet, the whole spreadsheet recalculates automatically. With a calculator you would have to do all the calculations again yourself.

(c) A spreadsheet is more effective than a calculator because:

- You can store the structure of the model and the formulae
- A spreadsheet recalculates automatically
- The results are always accurate
- The results are produced much quicker
- You can quickly do 'what if' calculations.

A7. Diagram or description should include:
Days of the week
Items in the left column
Values in boxes
Formulae for row totals
Formulae for column totals
Formatting in columns (in £ and justification)

(MEG, 1993)

A8.

	A	B	C	D	E	F	G	H	I	J
1	Prices	Full=	0.57							
2		Semi=	0.51							
3		Skimmed=	0.48							
4										
5	NAME	TYPE	M	T	W	T	F	S	S	Total
6	Jones	Full	1	1	1	1	1	2	2	Sum(C6 to I6)
7		Semi	2	1	2	2	1	2	2	Sum (C7 to I7)
8		Skimmed	0	1	0	0	1	2	2	Sum (C8 to I8)
9			Customer's weekly bill (J6*C1)+(J7*C2)+(J8*C3)
10	Rows 6 to 9 are repeated for every customer
11	At the end of the spreadsheet we have:
12	Total Sales = Sum(All the customer totals)

The weekly total for Full Cream milk is obtained using the formula J6+ . .

Similarly, a weekly total for Semi Skimmed uses the formula J7+ . . . and for Skimmed, J8+ . . .

Note that the prices are stored only once in cells C1, C2 and C3. Elsewhere they are inserted as cell references. This means that when prices change at most 3 cells have to be changed.

A9. (a) Some advantages are:

- The relationship in the model can be studied without the observer travelling to the area the animal lives.

- The observer does not interfere with the relationship or the animals' habitat.

- The observer is not in danger from the animals.

(b) See above in (a). Cost and danger to pupils are avoided.

(c) You could use a spreadsheet or a dedicated, pre-programmed model.

A10. (a) One from:

- Capacitor decay
- Radioactive decay
- Economic model
- Any suitable answer

(b) Description of model given in part (a)
Should include:

- numerical data
- formulae
- replication of formulae
- tabular display
- results

(c) One from:

- Too costly to build a physical model
- Too time consuming to build a physical model
- Variables can be changed easily to see the effects of any change in input
- Any suitable answer

(MEG, 1993)

STUDENT'S ANSWER WITH EXAMINER'S COMMENTS

Question Data:

snack	cost of ingredients per item	preparation cost per item in p	possible sales	selling price per item in p	total profit in £
apples	.10	.00	50	.12	1.00
muesli bar	.07	.02	55	.10	0.55
fruit salad	.15	.01	20	.20	0.80
fruit and nut	.09	.01	30	.15	1.50

This spreadsheet is a model of the possible costs and profits for the business.

(a) What would be the overall effect on profits if you were to increase the selling price of muesli bars to 15p each?

(b) Identify the main advantage of storing these costs in a spreadsheet.

(c) Give two other examples of the use of spreadsheets.

(C&G, 1993)

Student's answer

(a) <u>You would make more profits.</u>

(b) <u>You will not lose them and they will be safe in the computer.</u>

(c) <u>Drawing graphs and modelling.</u>

Examiner's comments

(a) This answer lacks detail.
The overall effect would be to increase total profits by £2.75

(b) This answer may well be true. However, information can be stored safely and securely without using IT. You should give an advantage which is true for a spreadsheet but not true for other methods.

For example:
• The totals are recalculated quickly and automatically when the values are changed.
• Calculations are accurate.

(c) You can draw graphs and do modelling with a spreadsheet. However, the context of the question suggests that it is *applications* of a spreadsheet that should be given.

Better answers are:
• An orders and billing system for a newsagent.
• Modelling the costs involved in planning a school trip.

REVIEW SHEET

1. Which of these statements is true or false? Why?

(a) You can do everything that can be done on a spreadsheet using a piece of paper and a pen.

_____

_____

(b) A column goes across the page and a row goes down the page.

_____

_____

(c) When you save a spreadsheet on a floppy disc, you do not lose it when you switch off the computer. You can load the same spreadsheet into the computer at a later date.

_____

_____

(d) A model used for weather forecasting can tell us exactly what the weather will be like in 2 weeks time.

_____

_____

(e) The design of an information system must always take into account the flow of information through the human system as well as the use of information technology.

_____

_____

2. Using these words, complete the sentences. You can use the words more than once, if you need to:

active cell   column   cursor   re-calculated   row

(a) The _____ is the cell where the _____ is.

(b) The cell at E14 is where _____ E and _____ 14 cross.

(c) You can move around a spreadsheet using the _____ control keys.

(d) When you change a number in a cell, all the formulae that use that cell will be _____.

3. A small shopkeeper intends to use a spreadsheet for stock control.

(a) Describe the hardware needed so that the shopkeeper can use spreadsheet software. Justify your choice.

_____

_____

_____

_____

(b) Describe some of the information that the shopkeeper could obtain using the spreadsheet.

_____

_____

_____

(c) What other software could be used that would be useful to the shopkeeper? Describe how the shopkeeper could use the software.

_____

_____

_____

_____

4. Spreadsheets can generate graphs. Describe a situation in which each of the following graphs might be more useful than looking at the spreadsheet itself.

(a) bar chart_____

_____

(b) line graph_____

_____

(c) pie chart_____

_____

5. Which of these statements describes a situation in which a computer based model could be used?

(a) Deciding which colour will be fashionable next year. _____

(b) Training pilots to fly. _____

(c) Forecasting inflation in 5 years' time._____

(d) Deciding how many petrol pumps will be needed when building a petrol station. _____

(e) Designing a new car. _____

6. What are the advantages and disadvantages of using computer based models?

_____

_____

_____

_____

7. Which of these formulae gives the number in cell B3 as a percentage of the number in cell C4?

B3*C3*100 _____

B3/(C3*100) _____

B3/100*C3 _____

(B3/C3)*100 _____

B3/C3*100 _____

CHAPTER 12

MEASUREMENT AND CONTROL SYSTEMS

**LOGIC GATES:
(AND, OR, NOT,)**

LOGIC CIRCUITS

**LOGIC GATES
(NAND, NOR, XOR)**

**COMPUTER CONTROL
SYSTEMS**

ROBOTS

FLIGHT SIMULATOR

**COMPUTER PROGRAMS AND
LANGUAGES**

GETTING STARTED

Measurement and control systems may be dedicated or computer controlled. Dedicated systems are designed using electronic components, including **logic gates**. AND, OR, NOT, NAND, NOR AND XOR logic gates are explained and their use illustrated.

Computer control systems have *sensors* so that they can measure environmental variables, such as the temperature. The computer will look at the environmental variables and try to adjust them by activating a range of **control devices**, such as heaters and motors.

Measurement and control systems often involve *feedback loops*. These are cycles of sensing, processing and reaction. Some computer control systems are described. These are a system to control the operation of a lift in a building; a system to control the temperature and humidity in a greenhouse; robotic arms; a flight simulator.

Programs control computers. Computers only understand machine code but programs can be written in a variety of languages, such as Assembly language, Logo, BASIC, Pascal and COBOL. All computer languages must be converted to machine code so that the computer can understand them. An assembler, an interpreter or a compiler are used to convert other computer languages to machine code. You may not write the program that controls the computer but you will be expected to be aware of some of the more common programming languages.

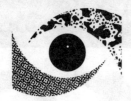

ESSENTIAL PRINCIPLES

Dedicated systems

Measurement and control systems may be dedicated or computer controlled. *Dedicated systems* are designed using electronic components, including logic gates. AND, OR, NOT, NAND, NOR AND XOR logic gates are explained and their use in some dedicated control systems is illustrated.

Computer control systems have sensors so that they can measure the environmental variables, such as the temperature. The computer will look at the environmental variables and try to adjust them by activating a range of control devices, such as heaters and motors to open the windows.

Feedback loops

Measurement and control systems often involve *feedback loops*. These are cycles of sensing, processing and reaction. For example, the cycle of finding out the room temperature, deciding if it is at the right level and taking action to get the temperature to the right level is a feedback loop. Feedback loops are important in constructing systems that control their environment. Some computer systems with feedback loops are described. These are a system to control the operation of a lift in a building; a system to control the temperature and humidity in a greenhouse; robotic arms; a flight simulator.

Types of language

Programs control computers. Computers only understand machine code but programs can be written in a variety of **languages**. Machine code is difficult for people to use and understand as it consists of a list of ones and zeros. Assembly language is easier for us to understand but it is still too similar to machine code for general use. High level languages, such as Logo, BASIC, Pascal and COBOL are much easier to use and understand.

All computer languages must be converted to machine code so that the computer can understand them. An assembler, an interpreter or a compiler is used to convert other computer languages to machine code. You may or may not write the program that controls the computer but you will be expected to be aware of some of the more common programming languages. Examples of programs written in Logo, BASIC, Pascal and COBOL are shown.

1> LOGIC GATES AND, OR, NOT

Although the electronic components used in computers are very complex, they are made up of very simple basic elements. The complexity lies in the ways in which these basic elements are combined together. The basic elements used in the design of computer systems are **logic gates**.

You are not going to make a computer for GCSE, though a program to monitor a heat or light sensor is a possibility. However, you are expected to know how logic gates and some logic circuits work.

TRUTH TABLES

Truth Tables are a convenient way of expressing the possible input conditions affecting a decision based on well defined rules and the results of it. Look at Figure 12.1. There are two inputs, 'On holiday' and 'A weekday' that are combined to give four different input conditions. 'False' means Paul is *not* 'On holiday' and 'true' means he *is* 'On holiday'. Each input condition has a result defined by the rule given.

Fig. 12.1 A rule defining a Truth Table

Rule: Paul has decided that he will go fishing if he is on holiday OR if it is NOT a weekday.

Inputs		Output
A weekday	On holiday	Goes fishing
FALSE	FALSE	TRUE
FALSE	TRUE	TRUE
TRUE	FALSE	FALSE
TRUE	TRUE	TRUE

SWITCH CIRCUITS

Truth tables can be used to describe how electrical circuits containing switches work. Look at Figure 12.2. This shows a **switch circuit** and the corresponding truth table. There are three switches labelled, A B and C, in the circuit. Since there are three switches, these combine to make eight different input conditions. In order for the light bulb to come on, either switch C must be on or switches A and B must both be on.

Fig. 12.2 A switch circuit and the corresponding truth table

Inputs			Output
A	B	C	Light bulb
OFF	OFF	OFF	OFF
OFF	OFF	ON	ON
OFF	ON	OFF	OFF
OFF	ON	ON	ON
ON	OFF	OFF	OFF
ON	OFF	ON	ON
ON	ON	OFF	ON
ON	ON	ON	ON

Rule: The light comes on if either switch C is on OR switches A AND B are both on.

BINARY LOGIC

In both of the above examples we see **binary logic** being used. If we consider '1', 'true' and 'on' to be equivalent and similarly with '0', 'false' and 'off j218
j223
', we get the truth tables shown in Figure 12.3 (a) and (b). These are binary logic truth tables, because only *two* possible states are possible for each individual condition. These states are represented using a '1' or a '0'. In electronic binary logic circuits '1' is represented by a voltage level of 5 volts, '0' is represented by 0 volts. Notice that the different input conditions shown in the truth tables could be generated by counting in binary starting at zero.

(a)

Inputs		Output
a weekday	on holiday	goes fishing
0	0	1
0	1	1
1	0	0
1	1	1

(b)

Inputs			Output
A	B	C	Light bulb
0	0	0	0
0	0	1	1
0	1	0	0
0	1	1	1
1	0	0	0
1	0	1	1
1	1	0	1
1	1	1	1

Fig. 12.3 Binary logic truth tables

LOGIC GATES

Logic Gates and Truth Tables

In both of the above examples, the rule expressing the relationship between the inputs and the output uses the terms AND, OR and NOT. These are basic logical relationships. **Logic gates** are electronic components whose function can be described using the logical AND, OR or NOT terms. The operation of each of these logic gates can be fully described in a truth table (see Fig. 12.4).

AND gate

Inputs		Output
0	0	0
0	1	0
1	0	0
1	1	1

The output is 1 only if both inputs are 1

OR gate

Inputs		Output
0	0	0
0	1	1
1	0	1
1	1	1

The output is 1 if either input is 1

NOT gate

Input	Output
0	1
1	0

The output is 1 if the input is 0
The output is 0 if the input is 1

Fig. 12.4 AND, OR and NOT logic
gates

2 ⟩ LOGIC CIRCUITS

Logic gates can be combined to make **logic circuits**. They can be built into machine tools, washing machines, etc. to perform the simple logic required for some monitoring and control tasks. These are dedicated control systems. A computer is also built up from many different logic circuits.

HOW A LOGIC CIRCUIT WORKS

❝❝ Logic Circuits and Truth
Tables ❞❞

The example shown in Figure 12.5 is not a useful circuit. It is an example to show how the output from a logic circuit can be worked out from the inputs. In the example, A, B and C are the inputs; E and F are intermediate processing states; X is the output.

The truth table is worked out by first entering all the different input conditions. Since there are three inputs, there will be eight different input conditions. These can be listed by counting in three bit binary from zero to seven. The intermediate processing state, E, is the result of A AND B; F is the result of NOT C. The output, X, is given by E OR F.

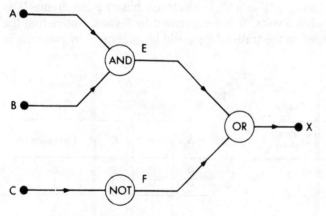

Inputs			Processing		Output
A	B	C	E	F	X
0	0	0	0	1	1
0	0	1	0	0	0
0	1	0	0	1	1
0	1	1	0	0	0
1	0	0	0	1	1
1	0	1	0	0	0
1	1	0	1	1	1
1	1	1	1	0	1

Fig. 12.5 A logic circuit and the
corresponding truth table

A DECODER

A **decoder** is used to select a single output from a range of possible outputs in response to the binary code input. A two bit decoder is shown in Figure 12.6. Notice that only one of the four outputs is selected, i.e. has a value of 1, depending on the input binary code. For example, if 01 is input then B is the only output that has a value of 1, that is, an input of 01 selects output B.

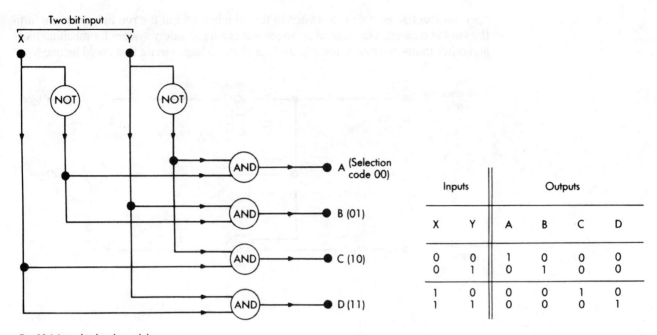

Fig. 12.6 A two bit decoder and the corresponding truth table

A CONTROL SWITCH

A **control switch** is used to allow or prevent data from passing down a data bus. A **data bus** is a set of parallel wires that carry binary data. In Figure 12.7 a control switch is being used on a four bit data bus. If the control switch is set at 0, the switch is off and the output from all data lines is 0; if the control switch is set at 1, the switch is on and whatever is input is output, i.e. if 0 is input then 0 is output, if 1 is input then 1 is output.

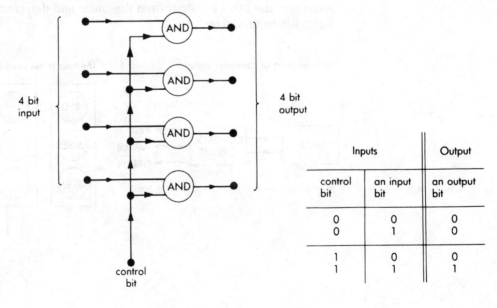

Fig 12.7 A control switch and the truth table showing the effect on a single input bit

A FAULT DETECTION SYSTEM

All industrial machines should have automatic systems for monitoring their performance. This is essential for good quality manufacture and safety. Logic circuits can be designed to detect breakdowns, etc. as they occur. The following describes a typical arrangement.

An industrial machine has its own monitoring system which sets a 'fault detect' signal when the machine breaks down. When a breakdown happens, a green light which is normally *on* is turned *off*, a *red light* comes on and a *bell* rings. The machine operator can use an over-ride switch to turn the bell off but the red light stays on until the fault is cleared. This type of arrangement is a basic safety system for machine tools and other industrial machines. Figure 12.8 shows a logic circuit that could be used.

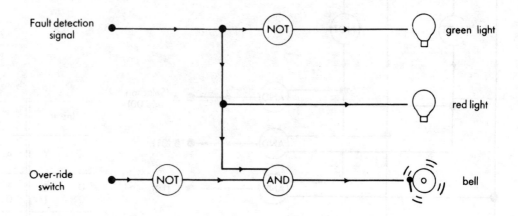

Inputs		Outputs		
over-ride switch	fault detection signal	Green light	Red light	Bell
0	0	1	0	0
0	1	0	1	1
1	0	1	0	0
1	1	0	1	0

Fig. 12.8 A safety system for industrial machines

A TRAFFIC LIGHT CONTROLLER

Logic circuits can be used to control traffic lights (see fig. 12.9). The control circuit interprets the two bit output from the timer and determines which combination of lights will be turned on.

Block diagram of controller circuit:

The four states used in a basic traffic light system:

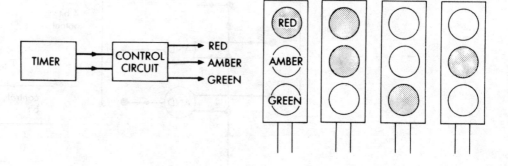

Outputs from Timer, input to Control Circuit		Outputs (lights)		
A	B	Red	Amber	Green
0	0	0	0	1
0	1	0	1	0
1	0	1	0	0
1	1	1	1	0

Fig. 12.9 A traffic light control

The AND, OR and NOT logic gates are designed to work in the same way that we use language. However, there are other logic gates. The NAND, NOR and XOR logic gates are shown in Fig. 12.10.

NAND gate		
Inputs		Output
0	0	1
0	1	1
1	0	1
1	1	0

The output is 1 if one or both inputs are not 1.

NOR gate		
Inputs		Output
0	0	1
0	1	0
1	0	0
1	1	0

The output is 1 if both inputs are 0 .

XOR gate		
Inputs		Output
0	0	0
0	1	1
1	0	1
1	1	0

The output is 1 if one but not both of the inputs are 1.

Fig. 12.10

NAND LOGIC

All these logic gates must be constructed on a microchip if they are to be a part of an electronic circuit. You can buy microchips with the different logic gates built into them. However, microchips are cheaper and more reliable if they are made in very large quantities. You can make all of the other logic gates using a NAND gate (see Fig. 12.11). For these reasons, NAND gates are produced in very large quantities and are often used to replace all the other logic gates. The fault detection system from fig. 12.8 is shown in fig. 12.12 as a NAND logic circuit.

❝❝ NAND, NOR and XOR Logic gates ❞❞

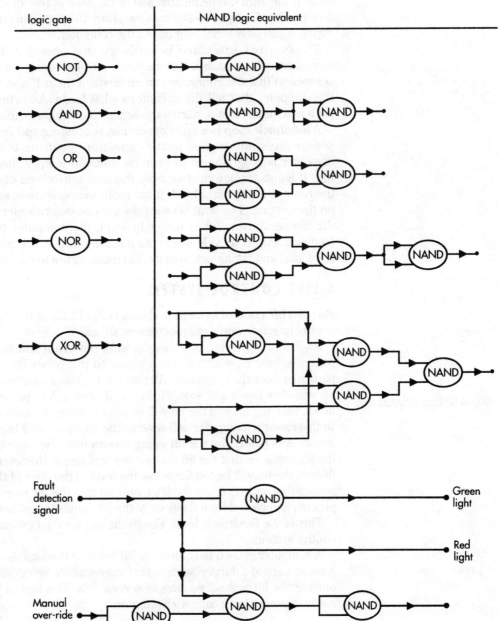

logic gate	NAND logic equivalent

Figs 12.11 NAND logic equivalents of NOT, AND, OR, NOR and XOR

Fig. 12.12 The safety system for industrial machines (from fig. 12.8) in NAND logic

66 Uses of Computer Control Systems 99

Computers may replace dedicated logic circuits in larger and more complex control applications as they are more flexible. Computers can be re-programmed so that the environmental variables and the logic controlling the system can be changed. For example, at a road junction controlled by traffic lights, you might want to vary the time the lights are on green throughout the day, on different days and for special occasions, such as, when the local football match ends. It would be easier to make adjustments if the traffic lights were computer controlled. If all the traffic lights on the same road were connected to the same computer, it could coordinate them so that you could drive through all lights, on green, without having to stop. The computer could regulate the speed of the traffic by regulating all the traffic lights. The speed would usually be the same from day-to-day, but might change if there were road works, etc. The computer could easily be reprogrammed to make these changes.

Computer control systems may have:

- sensors
- a control interface
- actuators
- feedback loops.

A **sensor** is a device which responds to a particular environmental condition by outputting a voltage in proportion to the magnitude of the condition sensed. In the case of the lift control system (see below), sensors A and B will normally output 0 volts. If the infra red beam attached to the base of the lift shines on them, they output 5 volts. The *Analogue to Digital Convertors* (ADCs) convert the analogue voltage to a digital signal which can be input by the computer.

The **control interface** is hardware that provides the interface between the computer and the control system. The control interface translates the signals from the sensors so that the computer can understand them It also translates the signals from the computer that tell the **actuators** what to do. An actuator is a hardware device, such as a motor, that performs the actions the computer tells it to do.

A **feedback loop** is a cycle of sensing, processing and reaction. For example, a heat sensor gives information to the computer about the temperature in a room. The computer is programmed to maintain different temperatures at different times of the day. It inputs the information from the heat sensor and decides if the temperature in the room is at the right level. If the room temperature is too low, the computer turns on the heating. The heat sensor tells the computer the temperature is higher. When the temperature reaches the right level, the computer turns off the heating. The feedback loop is a cycle of finding out the room temperature, deciding if it is at the right level and taking action to get the temperature to the right level.

A LIFT CONTROL SYSTEM

Part of a **lift control system** is shown in fig. 12.13. In this case, sensors, an actuator, a control interface and a microcomputer are used.

66 A lift Control System 99

As the lift is moving upwards the infra red beam attached to the bottom of the lift passes sensor B, which sends a signal to the computer. If the lift has to stop at a particular floor the computer will signal the control interface to stop the motor and the lift will slow down and stop. However, if sensor A is passed while the lift is slowing down, then the floor of the lift will be too far above the level of the floor of the building. In this case the computer will reverse the lift motor and the lift moves downwards. As sensor A is passed by the lift going downwards, the computer detects this and stops the lift motor so that the lift slows down and stops. However, if sensor B is passed the floor of the lift will be too far below the level of the floor of the building! The computer senses this and reverses the lift motor so that the lift is moving upwards again. This process is repeated until the floor of the lift comes to rest between sensors A and B.

This is the **feedback loop**. Feedback loops are an essential part of most computer control systems.

A computer is used to control the lift because the logic is complex. This may be only a small part of a larger system that may involve selection of floors from inside or outside the lift and scheduling of several lifts. The logical decisions involved can be easily expressed in a computer program.

Fig. 12.13 Part of a computer control system for a lift

A COMPUTER CONTROLLED GREENHOUSE

Figure 12.14 is an illustration of a computer control system for a greenhouse. The aim of such a system is to regulate temperature and humidity, so that optimum plant growth is achieved. The temperature and humidity sensors monitor the environmental conditions in the greenhouse and the heater, window motor and overhead spray actuators are used to control it.

The humidity sensor generates a voltage that is proportional to the amount of water vapour in the air. Voltage is an analogue signal. This signal is input to the ADC which converts it to a binary number. If the humidity is low, the voltage is low and the binary number is also low. The size of the binary number output from the ADC and input to the computer is proportional to the humidity in the greenhouse.

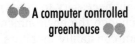
A computer controlled greenhouse

The computer is programmed to respond to low humidity by turning on the overhead spray and closing the windows. This is done by sending control signals to the window motor actuator and the overhead spray actuator. These turn on the overhead spray and the motor to close the windows. This has the effect of increasing the humidity. As the humidity increases, the sensors sense this and the system responds until an *equilibrium state* is reached. This is another example of a **feedback loop.**

If necessary, temperature and humidity data can be recorded at regular intervals so that a record of the environmental conditions in the greenhouse is kept. This data would be saved on backing storage, in this case floppy discs. The process of collecting and saving environmental data is known as **data logging**. Data logging is done so that we can analyse the recorded data at a later date.

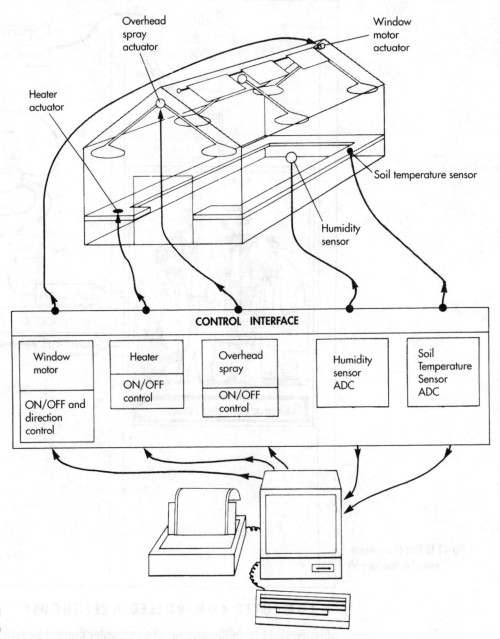

**Fig. 12.14 A computer control
system for a greenhouse**

A computer control system for a greenhouse is only justified if the business is large enough for the improved quality and quantity of produce grown to pay for the computer system. In practice, one computer would control several greenhouses.

In a large business with several greenhouses the advantages of a computer control system lie in its ability to *precisely* control temperature and humidity in all the greenhouses at all times. Each greenhouse will have its own program of temperature and humidity settings stored in the computer. These can be set at different levels depending on the time of day. To alter the settings it is only necessary to enter new values at the keyboard. The computer will automatically change the environment in the greenhouse to these new settings. The control system constantly monitors the environment day and night. It responds immediately to any variation from the required settings. The entire system can be controlled from the computer. Other sensors and activators could be fitted to control lighting, shade and other factors if needed.

5 ▷   ROBOTS

Robots are hardware devices that perform mechanical tasks. These tasks may be complex industrial or manufacturing tasks. Robots are used for welding, paint spraying, assembling products, packaging and handling molten metals, etc. They have many different shapes and sizes, however, they all work in broadly similar ways.

A common example of a robot is the robotic arm (see fig. 12.15). The robotic arm

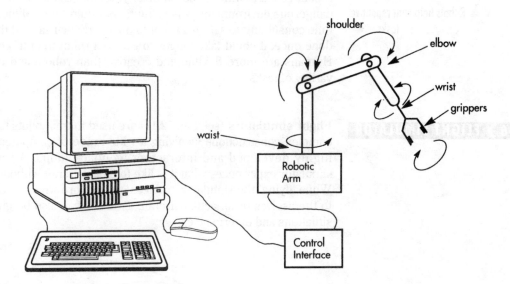

Fig. 12.15 A Computer controlled
robotic arm

illustrated is typical of this type of robot. The arm can rotate horizontally at the waist
and vertically at the shoulder, elbow and wrist. The gripper can turn its jaws so that
the object to be lifted can be placed between them. The grippers could be replaced
with any useful tool, for example, a hook, a scoop, a magnet, a vacuum cup, a welding
torch, etc.

The way robots are controlled is determined by the complexity of the task that is to
be done and the purchase cost. Robots with simple control systems that do simple
tasks cost less than those with more complex control systems. A simple robot may be
programmed directly using a numeric keypad built into it. More complex robots may

Control of robots

be controlled by a computer. Such robots can be told what to do by programming the
computer. The computer is programmed using a language similar to the Logo
language (see later in this chapter) that is adapted to the particular robot to be
controlled. For example, a simple robot may be instructed to pick up an object by a
program like this:

```
START
OPEN GRIPPERS
DOWN 5
CLOSE GRIPPERS
UP 5
STOP
```

**Teach and learn
methods**

Robots can also be programmed to do tasks using a variety of 'teach and learn'
methods. You can program the robot under direct control of the computer, one
instruction at a time. You watch what the robot does as it performs the instruction. If it
is what you want the robot to do, you can save the instruction. In this way you can
build up a complete program to control the robot. You can also program a robot by
physically moving it through the actions you want it to do. The computer converts
these actions into a program and saves it.

**It helps if the robot does
have a feedback system**

Computer controlled robots may *not* have a *feedback system* built into them. In this
case, it is difficult to know exactly what the robot is doing. These robots cannot
respond to their environment. It may be dangerous for humans to work with this type
of robot. As the robot cannot sense the presence of a person, it may continue doing its
task, for example, welding, when a human is in the way or when there is no panel to
weld. More intelligent robots have built-in feedback systems that tell the computer
what the robot is doing. These help the robot detect and avoid humans and alert them
to unusual situations, such as the absence of a panel to weld.

If humans are asked to do the same task over and over again, they may become bored or lose concentration. This could affect the quality of their work. Robots can do repetitive tasks with no loss of quality. Robots can also work in dirty, hot, radioactive, dangerous environments where humans would find it difficult to work. However, it is time consuming to set up a robot to do a particular task. If this task is only going to be done once, it could take longer to set up a robot than to get a human to do the task. Humans are more flexible and creative than robots and can do a wider range and variety of tasks.

❝ Robots help with repetitive tasks ❞

6 ⟩ FLIGHT SIMULATOR

Flight simulators (see Fig. 12.16) are used to train pilots to fly aircraft. They are very complex constructions involving a wide range of computer control sub-systems with highly developed and interacting feedback loops. A trainee pilot using a flight simulator experiences what it is like to fly an aircraft without actually having to fly one. While 'flying' the simulator, trainees can explore what the aircraft can do without risk to themselves or an actual aircraft. Trainees can also be given experience of unusual situations and emergencies.

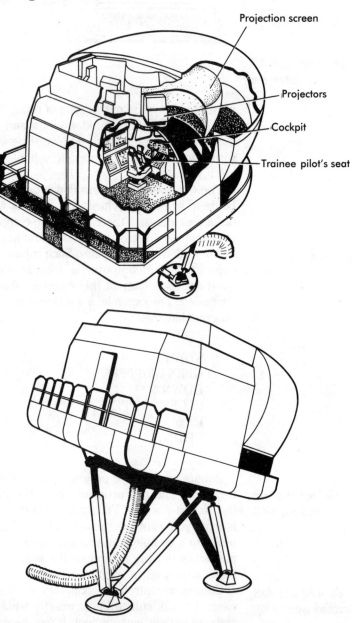

Projection screen

Projectors

Cockpit

Trainee pilot's seat

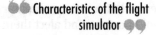

Fig. 12.16 A flight simulator

❝ Characteristics of the flight simulator ❞

A flight simulator will have a cockpit of the same size and shape and with the same controls, seats, etc. as those in the real aircraft. A computer controls the view the trainee pilot sees through the cockpit windows and gives the trainee a realistic feeling of how the real aircraft would move. The view through the cockpit windows is a projected video image. It is controlled by the computer and changes as the pilot 'flies' the simulator. The simulator is mounted on mobile legs which are used to alter the position of the cockpit. The computer moves the legs when the pilot moves the simulator's controls. The trainee pilot feels the simulator move in the way the real aircraft would move.

Unusual situations and emergencies can be simulated. Fire can be simulated by the introduction of smoke into the simulator's cockpit and the programming of the pilot's displays to mimic their reaction on a real aircraft that is on fire. Similarly, the displays and the reaction of the simulator to the pilot's controls can be modified to represent bad weather conditions, engine failure, etc.

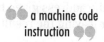

COMPUTER PROGRAMS AND LANGUAGES

WHAT IS A PROGRAM?

A **program** is a list of instructions to the computer. Programs control the computer and any devices connected to the computer. A program will be written in a computer language. The computer always starts at the beginning of the program and executes, or runs, the instructions one at a time. It begins at the top of the list and works down the list, one instruction at a time, unless told otherwise.

When a computer executes an instruction, it is always in machine code. Programs can however, be written in other languages and *converted* into machine code before running on a computer. This section looks at machine code, assembly language and high level languages, such as BASIC and LOGO.

MACHINE CODE AND ASSEMBLY LANGUAGE

Machine code is the language that computers use. Every different type of computer will have its own machine code. Machine code instructions are written as binary codes.

❝ a machine code instruction ❞

operation code	data or address
0000	0000 0101

Unless we knew that 0000 0000 0101 was a machine code instruction, we might easily mistake it for a character code or a number in binary. Even so, it is not immediately obvious what is meant! Machine code instructions are understood by computers, but are very difficult for most people to remember and use. For this reason it is very unlikely that a programmer would write a computer program in machine code.

To make programming at this level easier, **low level languages**, or **assembly languages**, have been developed. Assembly language is slightly easier to understand than machine code. Every machine code instruction has a single corresponding assembly language instruction.

This is a typical assembly language instruction:

❝ an assembly language instruction ❞

mnemonic	data or address
add	5

This is easier to understand! However, it is not clear what we are to add, or what the 5 stands for.

In a typical machine code, or the corresponding assembly language, all arithmetic is done using an **accumulator** - a special register located in the Arithmetic and Logic Unit (ALU), within the Central Processing Unit (CPU). A **register** is a small memory located outside the main memory that can do more than simply store data. In the case of the accumulator, arithmetic and logic operations are possible. All addition, subtraction, etc. is done using the accumulator. Other registers are the Program Counter and the Current Instruction Register (see below).

However, the instruction 'add 5' is not telling us to add 5 into the accumulator, as might be expected. It is instructing the computer to add the data stored in memory address 5 into the accumulator.

Every memory location in the main memory has an address. The **memory address** directs the computer to the location of the stored data. The data can then be taken from the address and added into the accumulator. The layout of the memory of a computer can be shown in a **memory map**. This is a plan of the memory, giving the addresses where programs and data will be stored.

To help understand the idea of a memory address and the data stored at it, think of a memory address as the address of a house. The data stored in the memory address are the people who live in the house. A memory map is a street plan which has the addresses of the houses on it.

An example should help to make these ideas clearer. The machine code used is simplified to illustrate the principles of machine code programming, rather than to demonstrate an actual machine code. The equivalent assembly code is also shown. Again, this is not an actual assembly language.

EXAMPLE: MACHINE CODE AND ASSEMBLER PROGRAM

Some of the program instructions available in our example machine code and assembly language are as follows:

machine code	assembly language	
operation code	mnemonic	meaning
0000	add	add the data stored at the address given to the contents of the accumulator leaving the result in the accumulator
0001	sub	subtract the data stored at the address given from the contents of the accumulator leaving the result in the accumulator
0010	mult	multiply the data stored at the address given by the contents of the accumulator leaving the result in the accumulator
0011	div	divide the data stored at the address given into the contents of the accumulator leaving the result in the accumulator
0100	lda	load the data stored at the address given into the accumulator
0101	sta	store the data in the accumulator at the address given
0110	in	input the data into the accumulator
0111	out	output the data from the accumulator
1000	halt	halt program execution

Each instruction has the following format:

Machine code		Assembly language	
operation code	address	mnemonic	address
e.g. 0010	0000 0111	e.g. mult	7

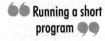

Running a short program

We now look at how a short program runs. The program is given in both assembly language and machine code. The machine code program is shown as it might appear in the memory of the computer and the address of each memory location is shown.

Several locations are shown in memory after the program has been ended by a halt instruction. These addresses contain data.

memory address	program and data stored in memory				
	machine code			assembly language	
	operation code	address		mnemonic	address
0001	0100	0000	1000	lda	8
0010	0000	0000	0111	add	7
0011	0001	0000	0110	sub	6
0100	0101	0000	1000	sta	8
0101	1000	0000	0000	halt	
0110	0000	0000	0011		
0111	0000	0101	0101		
1000	0000	0001	0010		
1001	0000	0001	0010		

Executing the program instructions

The program instructions are executed, starting at the beginning with the first instruction.

The memory address of the first instruction is held in the **Program Counter (PC)**. This instruction is *fetched* from memory and stored in the **Current Instruction Register (CIR)**. One is added to the PC so that it points to the next instruction. The instruction in the CIR is now *executed* or run. When the current instruction has been executed the next instruction is fetched from the memory address contained in the PC, and so on. This is the *fetch/execute cycle*.

When the example program instructions are executed they have the following effect:

lda 8   This loads the data stored at address 8 (1000 in binary) into the accumulator.

The accumulator now contains   0000 0001 0010

add 7   The data stored at address 7 (0111 in binary) is added to the data in the accumulator and the result is stored in the accumulator. This is shown below:

data in accumulator before 'add 7'   0000 0001 0010

data from address 7 (0111 in binary)   0000 0101 0101 −

data in accumulator after 'add 7'   0000 0110 0111

sub 6   The data stored at address 6 (0110) is subtracted from the accumulator and the result is stored in the accumulator. Subtraction is done by adding the corresponding negative number in two's complement form.

The equivalent base 10 calculation is   103 − 3

$$= 103 + (-3)$$
$$= 100$$

This is done as follows:

data in address 6   0000 0000 0011

two's complement of data in address 6   1111 1111 1101

data in accumulator before 'sub 6'   0000 0110 0111 −

result of addition   1 0000 0110 0100

Notice that we have gained an extra bit on the left hand side. This is overflow which is lost.

data in accumulator after 'sub 6'   0000 0110 0100

sta 8   The contents of the accumulator are left untouched but they are stored in address 8(1000), as follows:

data stored at address 8 before 'sta 8'   0000 0001 0010

data stored at address 8 after 'sta 8'   0000 0110 0100

halt   This instruction brings the program to an end.

The program instructions are stored in the memory starting at address 0001 and ending at address 0101 with the halt instruction. The numbers involved in the calculation are also stored in the memory, after the program, starting at address 0110. The halt instruction must be present to separate the program instructions and the data.

This is a short program to add two numbers together and subtract a third number from the result. The numbers are already stored in the memory and the result is returned to the memory. This is a rather lengthy and complex process just to do an addition and a subtraction.

Programs written in assembly language must be translated into machine code before they can be executed. **Assemblers** convert assembly languages to machine code. They work in the same way as compilers (see below) except that the source code is written in an assembly language rather than a high level language.

Assembly language and machine code programs are **machine orientated**, that is, they will not run on any computer other than the particular type they are designed for. Every computer runs a machine code, but they do not all run the *same* machine code. This means that a machine code or assembly language program cannot be run on *all* computers. When programs can be run on any computer, we say that they are **portable** from one computer to another. Assembly language and machine code programs are not portable between different types of computer.

Because machine code and assembly languages are difficult to understand and are not portable, they will not be used unless there are good reasons to do so. Assembly language is always used in preference to machine code unless it is unavoidable. Programs in assembly language or machine code are usually small compared to other languages. They will be needed if a program is likely to be too big to fit into the amount of RAM memory available. Also, machine code runs *very quickly* and is therefore used if a program must be fast.

For these reasons, games programs for home microcomputers are often in machine code, as there is a need to write fast programs to run on computers with relatively small memories. Competition between software writers to produce more varied games encourages the introduction of more and better graphics (see Fig. 12.17) which use up more memory. Similarly, they attempt to cram programs with more and more facilities in the same amount of memory. Machine code programs give software writers a

F16 Combat Pilot, by Digital Integration

Fig. 12.17 A graphics screen from a computer game

competitive edge in these circumstances.

Some industrial machine tools, robots and modern domestic appliances, such as washing machines, are microprocessor-controlled devices. A **microprocessor** is a 'computer on a chip' (see Fig. 12.18), i.e. a computer consisting of a CPU and very small amounts of RAM and ROM memory built onto a single silicon chip. A machine code program, either stored in ROM or loaded into RAM, controls the device when it is used.

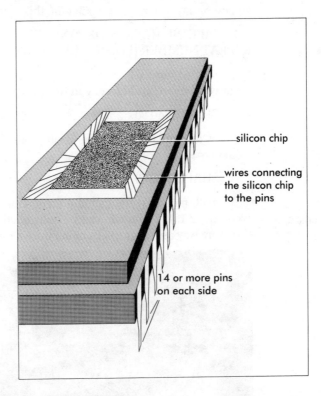

Fig. 12.18 A microprocessor

HIGH LEVEL LANGUAGES

Machine code and assembly languages are difficult to understand and write. They are machine orientated, and not portable from computer to computer. High level languages attempt to overcome these difficulties. Programs in **high level languages** are easier to understand, as the program instructions are closer to English than low level languages.

The **high level programming languages** most commonly used in schools and in the education system generally are Logo, BASIC and Pascal. COBOL is the high level language most commonly used in Business and Commerce. You may not be required to write a computer program in any of these languages for GCSE but you should be aware of them and understand why they are used. Brief examples of programs written in Logo, BASIC, Pascal and COBOL are illustrated below:

LOGO: (from the Greek word LOGOS, which means 'word')
Logo is a dialect of LISP, which is a language used in research into artificial intelligence. Logo is a simple, but powerful, language that can be used for a wide range of tasks.

Logo can be used to program screen graphics. For example, this logo program could be used to draw a square on the screen. You would type in the instructions at the keyboard and a 'pen' draws the square on the screen.

🙢🙢 A Logo program 🙢🙢

```
FD 40
LT 90
FD 40
LT 90
FD 40
LT 90
FD 40
LT 90
```

FD 40 means 'go forward 40 units'.
LT 90 means 'turn left, i.e. anticlockwise, 90 degrees'.

As a square has four sides of equal length, these instructions repeated four times draw a square.

As the FD 40 and LT 90 are repeated four times, Logo lets us abbreviate the program to one instruction:

REPEAT 4 [FD 40 LT 90]

If we wished to turn this instruction into a procedure that would allow us to draw a square or any other regular polygon, this could be extended to:

TO SHAPE 'NUMBER' 'SIDE' 'ANGLE'
REPEAT:NUMBER [FD:SIDE LT:ANGLE]
END

To draw a square, as before, you would type in:

SHAPE 4 40 90

To draw an equilateral triangle (3 sides, all of length 50 and all angles 60 degrees), you would type in:

SHAPE 3 50 60

66 A turtle 99

A small, mobile robot called a turtle can be attached to a computer running Logo (see fig. 12.19). The turtle can be controlled by the Logo program so that it moves in the same way as the graphics being drawn on the screen.

Fig. 12.19 A Valiant turtle in action
(photo courtesy of Valiant
Technology Ltd)

Logo can also be used to manipulate text, for example:

66 A LOGO program 99

```
TO FAN.CLUB
LOCAL "NAME
PR [HI, WHAT'S YOUR NAME?]
MAKE "NAME RL
TEST EQUALP :NAME JOE DAVIES
IFTRUE [PRINT [WOW, CAN I HAVE YOUR AUTOGRAPH?]]
IFFALSE [PRINT SE [OH, HELLO,] FIRST :NAME]
END
```

BASIC: Beginners All-purpose Symbolic Instruction Code

BASIC is the main language supplied and used with microcomputers. It is widely used in education and is often the first programming language learnt. BASIC is a powerful, flexible language used for a wide variety of commercial and scientific applications.

❝❝ A BASIC program ❞❞

```
10    REM *************** Sample BASIC program ***************
20    REM This is a Menu driven program to calculate areas
30    PRINT "Menu"
40    PRINT "A. Area of Rectangle"
50    PRINT "B. Area of Circle"
55    PRINT "C. Finish"
60    PRINT "Please input your option choice (A, B or C)"
70    INPUT A$
80    IF A$ = "A" THEN GOTO 110
90    IF A$ = "B" THEN GOTO 180
95    IF A$ = "C" THEN GOTO 999
100   GOTO 30
110   REM ******** Calculate the area of a Rectangle ********
120   PRINT "Input the length of the rectangle"
130   INPUT L
140   PRINT "Input the breadth"
150   INPUT B
160   PRINT "The area of the rectangle is"; L*B
170   GOTO 30
180   REM ********** Calculate the area of a Circle **********
190   PRINT "Input the radius of the circle"
200   INPUT R
210   PRINT "The area of the circle is"; 3.14*R*R
220   GOTO 30
999   END
```

PASCAL: (Named after the French mathematician Blaise Pascal)

Pascal is often the second language learnt by students of computing. It is used extensively in colleges, universities, scientific computing and commerce. Pascal is available for most microcomputers and almost all mainframes.

Pascal is a *structured* language. It was designed as a teaching language to encourage good program design and a clear structure. Procedures are used to make programs easier to write, read and understand. Any variables used must have their type declared before they are referred to. There are a range of facilities that make programming easier and more convenient.

Fig. 12.20 Blaise Pascal, the French mathematician

❝❝ A PASCAL program ❞❞

```
program swap (input, output);
(* sample pascal program: two numbers are input in order,*)
(* their order swapped and then they are printed          *)
var first, second : integer;
(* ************************************************** *)
procedure numbersin;
begin
      write ('This program inputs two integers');
      writeln ('and prints them in reverse order');
      writeln ('Input the first number');
      readln (first);
      writeln ('Input the second number');
      readln (second);
end;
(* ************************************************** *)
procedure switch;
var temporary : integer;
begin
      temporary := first;
      first := second;
      second := temporary;
end;
(* ************************************************** *)
procedure printout;
begin
      write ('In reverse order the numbers input are');
      writeln (first, 'and', second);
end;
(* ************************************************** *)
(* the main program which calls the procedures       *)
begin
      numbersin;
      switch;
      printout;
end.
```

COBOL: COmmon Business Orientated Language

Is used widely in data processing applications throughout business and commerce. It is particularly useful in data processing because files, records and fields are easily defined and manipulated. COBOL instructions read very like English in comparison with other languages.

COBOL has been the most popular commercial language for at least twenty years. It has been regularly updated with extra features, so that it can cope with the changes in computer technology that have taken place during that time. The death of COBOL is frequently predicted by the computer press. However, it has survived, probably because of its enormous popularity! COBOL is available for all mainframes and the more powerful personal microcomputers.

66 A COBOL program 99

```
IDENTIFICATION DIVISION.
PROGRAM-ID. RESULTS.
PURPOSE. PRINTS OUT GCSE RESULTS.
PROGRAMMER. A. HOULBROOKE.

ENVIRONMENT DIVISION.
INPUT-OUTPUT SECTION.
FILE-CONTROL.
SELECT RESULT-FILE
ASSIGN DK ACCESS DYNAMIC ORGANISATION INDEXED.
SELECT PRINT-FILE
ASSIGN PROUT.

DATA    DIVISION.
FILE    SECTION.
FD      RESULT-FILE
        BLOCK 12 RECORDS
        DATA RECORD RESULT-DETAILS
        LABEL RECORD STANDARD.

01      RESULT-DETAILS.
        03 ID-NO          PIC    X(5).
        03 NAME           PIC    X(50).
        03 SYLLABUS-CODE  PIC    999.
        03 EXAM-GRADE     PIC    X.

FD      PRINT-FILE
        DATA RECORD PRINT-LINE
        LABEL RECORD OMITTED
        LINAGE 60 FOOTAGE 60 TOP 3 BOTTOM 3.
01      PRINT-LINE    X(132).
WORKING STORAGE SECTION.
01      PRINT-IMAGE.
        03 DUMMY-1        PIC X(28)
            VALUE " RESULT FOR CANDIDATE, NAME ".
        03 PRINT-NAME     PIC X(50).
        03 DUMMY-2        PIC X(12)
            VALUE ", ID NUMBER ".
        03 PRINT-CODE     PIX 999.
        03 DUMMY-3        PIC X(4)
            VALUE " IS ".
        03 PRINT-GRADE    PIC X.

PROCEDURE DIVISION.
OPEN INPUT RESULT-FILE.
OPEN OUTPUT PRINT-FILE.
READ-LOOP.
        READ RESULT-FILE NEXT END GO TO END-ROUTINE.
        MOVE ID-NO TO PRINT-NAME.
        MOVE NAME TO PRINT-NAME.
        MOVE SYLLABUS-CODE TO PRINT-CODE.
        MOVE EXAM-GRADE TO PRINT-GRADE.
        MOVE PRINT-IMAGE TO PRINT-LINE.
        WRITE PRINT-FILE BEFORE ADVANCING 1 LINE.
END-ROUTINE.
        CLOSE RESULT-FILE.
        CLOSE PRINT-FILE.
        EXIT.
```

IMPORTANT FEATURES OF HIGH LEVEL LANGUAGES

High level languages are easier to understand than machine code or assembly language. You can design and write a program in a high level language more easily than in machine code or assembly language.

If your program has a 'bug', i.e. a mistake, it will be easier to find it. Most high level languages have diagnostic aids that help you find mistakes. A diagnostic aid will provide a trace of the instructions executed while the program is running. You can look at this trace to find out where the program is going wrong.

> ❝ Diagnostic aids help programmes find 'bugs' ❞

High level languages have several common features that make programming in them easier. They allow the programmer to use expressions very much like the algebra and arithmetic used in maths, e.g. A = (3 × B + C).

Key words, that is, words that define an operation, e.g. PRINT (in BASIC), are universally used. Labels are used for branching to other parts of the program. Sometimes the labels will be words or simply line numbers as in BASIC. Structures such as procedures, subroutines, functions and loops are often available. Loops are typically FOR/NEXT, WHILE/WEND or REPEAT/UNTIL. Conditional branching is possible using IF/THEN/ELSE statements and unconditional branching using GOTO.

However, before a high level language program can be run, it must be converted to machine code. Each high level language instruction will be translated to several machine code instructions.

TRANSLATING TO MACHINE CODE

All high level languages have to be *translated to machine code* before they are run. A computer can only execute machine code. It cannot execute any other language.

Interpreters

An **interpreter** converts a program written in a high level language into machine code (see Fig. 12.21). It does this one instruction at a time as the program is run. The **source code**, i.e. the high level language program, is saved on backing storage. This is loaded into the memory of the computer and run. As the program is run, the interpreter converts one instruction in the source code to machine code, then executes it.

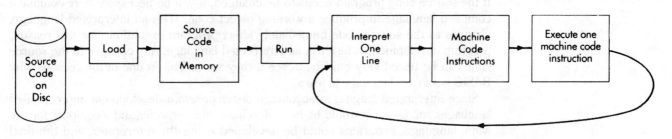

Fig. 12.21 How an Interpreter works

Before an instruction is converted to machine code, it is checked for syntax errors. **Syntax errors** are errors resulting from incorrect use of the rules governing the structure of the language, e.g. using PRONT instead of PRINT in BASIC would result in a syntax error. As the program is run, execution errors may be detected. An **execution error** is an error that occurs while the program is running, e.g. division by zero.

The interpreter does not, and cannot, check for **logic errors**. These are errors in the logic of the program. The syntax may well be correct and the program may run and produce output but because the program logic is incorrect, the required processing will not be done. Consequently the output will be faulty.

The most frequently used interpreted language is BASIC.

Compilers

A **compiler** converts a program written in a high level language into machine code (see Fig. 12.22). The source code is saved on backing storage. This is loaded into the memory of the computer and compiled. The compiler converts the whole of the source code program into machine code. This machine code program is known as the **object code**. The object code is an independent machine code program which can be saved on backing storage. A compiled language is not run from the source code. To run the program, the object code is loaded into memory and executed.

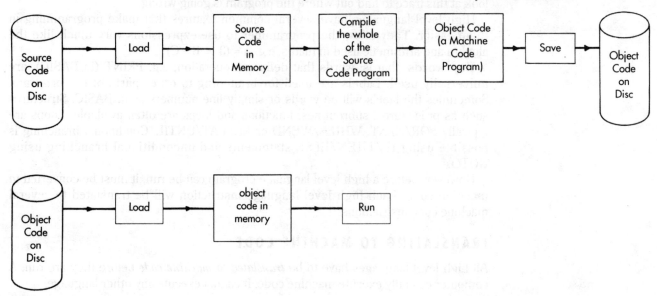

Fig. 12.22 How a compiler works

During compilation the source code is checked for syntax errors and while the object code is run, execution errors are reported. Almost all high level languages are compiled languages. PASCAL and COBOL are compiled languages.

Interpreted languages run slowly because they are converted to machine code as they run. Compiled languages run from the object code which is a machine code version of the program, output from the compiler. Consequently programs written in a compiled language run much faster than programs written in an interpreted language. If the source code program needs to be changed, it will be necessary to re-compile a compiled language to produce a working object code. With an interpreted language, changes to the source code immediately affect program execution. For this reason, program development is faster in an interpreted language. Any changes to the source code can be tested very quickly, to see if they work. This is one of the reasons why BASIC is an easy language to learn.

Since interpreted languages encourage faster program development and compiled languages run faster, it would be helpful to have an interpreter and a compiler for the same language. Programs could be developed using the interpreter, and the final version could be compiled to obtain a faster, executable version. Unfortunately, this is not often possible, as either an interpreter or a compiler is available, but not both. Some of the more recent versions of BASIC do have both an interpreter and a compiler available.

Interpreters and compilers are programs. They are somewhat different from most programs in that their input is a source code program and their output is machine code. However, as they are programs they can be saved onto disc and loaded into RAM memory when required. If there is plenty of room in RAM memory for the interpreter or compiler and the source code program, this is not a problem. Unfortunately, on microcomputers with very small RAM memory the interpreter or compiler will often be so large that it will not fit in memory with a source code program. In this case, the translation program will be supplied in a ROM microchip. This does not use any RAM memory and can be permanently installed in the microcomputer. As interpreters tend to be smaller than compilers, the translation program used is likely to be an interpreter. This is why the language used with the majority of home microcomputers is BASIC, supplied on a ROM microchip.

EXAMINATION QUESTIONS

Q1. Tick the TWO examples of computer control:

Automatic pilot	
Flight-booking system	
Producing a price list	
Robots making a car	
A model of traffic flow	

(SEG, 1993)

Q2. Many computer controlled devices are activated by sensors. Write down what type of sensor might be used to:

(a) Switch on street lights automatically when it is dusk.

(b) Activate traffic lights when cars approach a junction.

(c) Switch on a heater when the temperature falls below 50°C.

(City and Guilds, 1993)

Q3. QUESTION DATA:

INSTRUCTIONS FOR USING A DISHWASHER
Heat water   [   ]
Select program   [   ]
Start dishwasher cycle   [   ]
Fill with water   [   ]

The above instructions for running a dishwasher are incorrect. Put a number from 1 to 4 in the square brackets to show a correct sequence.

(City and Guilds, 1993)

Q4. (a) Sort the statements listed below into the right order, so you can record a programme from TV onto a video recorder.

Select time on
Turn timer on
Load tape into machine
Select time off
Turn recorder on
Select day
Select TV channel

(b) Describe one task you have done on a computer. What other way could you have done the task, and which would be the easier?

(NDTEF, 1993)

Q5. The heating of water in a tank is under the control of a microprocessor. Cold water enters the tank via Valve 1. It is heated to a set temperature and leaves the tank via Valve 2.

(a) Describe how feedback could be used in the system.

(b) (i) Where should an analogue-to-digital converter be placed in the system? Draw your answer on the diagram.

(ii) Why is the analogue-to-digital converter necessary?

(MEG, 1993)

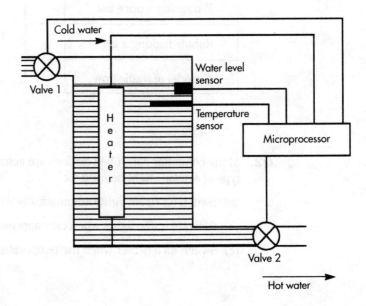

Q6. A floor turtle contains a pen and faces east. The turtle follows these instructions:

PEN UP	Lift the pen off the floor
PEN DOWN	Place the tip of the pen on the floor
FORWARD n	Move n steps forward
BACKWARD n	Move n steps backward
LEFT b	Turn left b degrees
RIGHT b	Turn right b degrees

Write instructions for the turtle to draw this triangle.

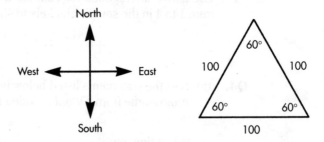

(MEG, 1993)

Q7. A robot is used to retrieve fuel rods from a nuclear reactor. To get the rod labelled from the position labelled 'X', the following instructions could be given:

FORWARD 3
TURN RIGHT
FORWARD 1
TAKE

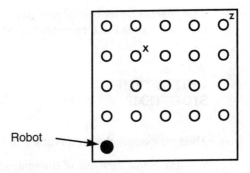

(a) Write sensible instructions to get this rod placed into position Z and bring the robot back to its starting place.

(b) Why would a robot be used for this job?

(SEG, 1993)

Q8. (a) A computer program is used to control a robot which is moving and stacking boxes in a warehouse. The program uses commands to control its movements.

FORWARD steps
BACK steps
RIGHT angle
LEFT angle
UP steps
DOWN steps

For example, FORWARD 50 moves the robot forward 50 steps in a straight line.
RIGHT 45 turns the robot 45° to the right.
UP 2 raises the forks 2 steps.
It is found to be dropping the boxes in the wrong place.

Give two different mistakes in the program that could be making this.

(b) Following a nasty accident, the robot has to be adapted to stop if it meets an unexpected obstacle in its path. What changes would need to be made to the robot design?

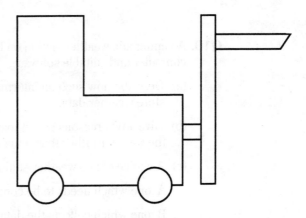

(NEAB/WJEC, 1993)

Q9. Tilda Shower is a geography teacher.

Tilda wants the school weather station to provide her class with very detailed weather data over a period of a week.

The instructions below are part of a computer program which, every 30 minutes, stores the temperature that the weather station detects.

WAIT 30
DETECT TEMP
STORE TEMP

Tilda now wants the temperature to be stored every 15 minutes.

    (a) Show how one of the instructions will have to be changed.

    (b) (i) Explain why these three instructions by themselves would not keep on storing the temperature.

        (ii) Show the extra instructions that would be needed so that the computer will store the temperature 'forever'. (You may invent your own instructions)

    (c) 50 dec. C is very very hot.
       – 50 deg. C is very very cold.

       Sometimes the weather station does not work properly so silly values of temperature are stored.

       Explain how the program could be improved to prevent the computer storing silly values for temperature.

    (d) Tilda wants the rainfall data to be recorded every hour for a whole year.

       She also wants the results to be printed in the form of a booklet.

       (i) Describe how this amount of data could have been collected without the aid of a computer.

       (ii) Explain why, in a school, it would not be practical to collect this amount of data without a computer.

       (iii) State one advantage to Tilda's pupils of having this amount of data.

                                     (ULEAC, 1993)

Q10. An automatic weather station on the roof of a house is connected to a home computer and suitable software.

    (a) Describe how such an information system might be used to collect and store weather data.

    (b) Give TWO reasons why it may be better to use a computer to help record the weather rather than a manual method.

    (c) A choice of two weather stations is available.

       A one which needs to be connected to the computer at all times

       B one which collects the data inside the station for transmission at a later date

       Discuss the relative merits of these two systems.

                                        (MEG, 1993)

ANSWERS TO EXAMINATION QUESTIONS

A1. Automatic pilot

Robots making a car

A2. (a) light sensor

(b) pressure sensor

(c) temperature sensor

A3. 1. add water

2. heat water

3. select program

4. start dishwasher cycle

A4. (a) Turn recorder on

load tape into machine

turn timer on

select time on

select time off

select day

select T.V. channel

(b) I use a database to keep records of all the cars in the school car park. I can use the database to find out who owns a particular car if I know the registration number. I can also print out a list, in alphabetical order on the owner's name, of all the cars. I can edit this information and printout a new list. I can print other lists, such as, all red Fords. It is faster than if I kept the information on a card file.

A5. (a) The sensor reads the temperature

If it is too cold the microprocessor turns on the heater

If it is too hot the microprocessor turns off the heater

The tap is only opened when the water is in the correct temperature range

(b) (i) between the temperature sensor and the microprocessor

(ii) Temperature is analogue data and must be converted to a digital signal which the computer can interpret.

(MEG, 1993)

A6.

PEN DOWN		PEN DOWN		PD
FORWARD 100		FORWARD 100		B100
LEFT 120	OR	RIGHT 60	OR	R60
FORWARD 100		FORWARD 100		B100
LEFT 120		RIGHT 60		R60
FORWARD 100		FORWARD 100		B100
PEN UP		PEN UP		PU

(MEG, 1993)

A7. (a) FORWARD 3

TURN RIGHT

FORWARD 1

TAKE

FORWARD 3

TURN LEFT

FORWARD 1

PLACE
TURN LEFT
FORWARD 4
TURN LEFT
FORWARD 5

(b) Because the inside of a nuclear reactor is not a safe place for a human.

A8. (a) The commands in the program could be in the wrong order or missing. Incorrect values could have been given for the number of steps or the angle.

(b) There would have to be sensors on the front of the robot. The program would stop the robot if there was an object in its way.

A9. (a) WAIT 30 becomes WAIT 15.

(b) (i) Because there are no instructions to repeat the three instructions given.

(ii) For example:

REPEAT
          WAIT 30
          DETECT TEMP
          STORE TEMP
UNTIL THE PROGRAM IS INTERRUPTED

(c) You would validate the temperature detected and ignore it if it was not realistic. For example, if this instruction:

IF $-5°C >$ TEMP OR $35°C <$ TEMP
THEN go to the DETECT TEMP instruction

was inserted after DETECT TEMP, the program would loop until a realistic temperature was detected.

(d) (i) If you don't use a computer, you would have to use a thermometer, read it yourself and write down the results.

(ii) You could not expect school pupils or teachers to record the temperature every hour, without fail, especially at night.

(iii) Whatever you are studying, you should collect as much data as you can. You can always discard the data you don't need. The more data you have, the more accurately you can describe what is happening.

A10. (a) Weather data is recorded using sensors for temperature, wind speed, wind direction, rainfall, pressure and humidity. The sensors translate the data into digital form and either store the data or transfer it directly to the computer. The computer stores the data in memory or on disc. Data is displayed when the user needs to see it.

(b) Two from:
Computers can automatically record the weather whereas humans have to remember to collect the data.
Computer readings are usually more accurate than readings taken by humans.
Computers can store historical data.
Computers can retrieve and display data in a variety of forms quickly.

(c) A will require the computer to be connected at all times. It would be tricky to use the computer for other functions whilst it is collecting data whereas with B, data can be viewed at the convenience of the user. With A the computer must never be switched off which could cause a problem. If it was switched off by accident data would be lost from the weather station.

(MEG, 1993)

STUDENT'S ANSWER WITH EXAMINER'S COMMENTS

QUESTION DATA

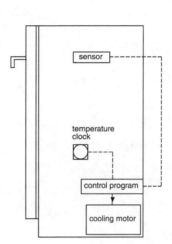

This is a diagram of a fridge. The fridge has a sensor, a control program and a cooling system motor which takes the heat out of the refrigerator.

(a) What does the sensor in the fridge do?

(b) The fridge uses feedback. What is feedback?

(c) Write down instructions to show how the control program operates the cooling system.

(City and Guilds, 1993)

Student's answer

(a) It senses the temperature in the fridge.

(b) Feedback occurs when a sensor detects a situation that causes the computer to indicate action that alters the data collected by the sensor.

(c) If the temperature is too high the cooling system is switched on.

Examiner's comments

(a) Correct.

(b) This is a text book definition of feedback. It is not incorrect but it does not relate to the context of the question. A better answer would be:

'If the temperature is too high, the sensor detects this and the control program turns on the cooling motor. The temperature in the fridge falls. When the temperature is too low, the sensor detects this and the control program turns the cooling motor off. This cycle of sensing and re-action is called feedback'.

You should always relate what you have learnt to the context of the question.

(c) This answer is correct but incomplete. The student has forgotten that the cooling motor should be turned off when the temperature is too low.

REVIEW SHEET

1. Draw a truth table for each of these situations:

   (a) Jane will go to the football match if it is at home. If it is away, she will only go if it is not raining.

   (b) A security light outside a building is turned on automatically if it is dark. The caretaker can turn the light on or off at any time.

   (c) Traffic lights at a panda crossing.

2. Draw the truth tables for each of the AND, OR, NOT, NAND, NOR and XOR logic gates.

3. Why are most logic circuits constructed using NAND logic?

_____

_____

_____

4. Complete these sentences using these words.

> actuator
> assembly code
> BASIC
> feedback loop
> machine code
> sensor

(a) A ————————————— connected to a computer can tell it the temperature.

(b) An ————————————— is used by the computer to turn motors on and off.

(c) A ————————————— is a cycle of sensing, interpretation and action.

(d) ————————————— is a high level computer language.

(e) ————————————— is the language the computer understands.

5. Data logging could be used in a school's weather station to record the amount of rain that falls every hour, every day of the year.

(a) Explain what is meant by data logging.

_____

_____

(b) Explain why a school would use data logging to record the rainfall every hour, every day of the year.

_____

_____

(c) Draw a diagram of the hardware that would be used.

(d) Is a feedback loop needed? Explain your answer.

_____

_____

_____

(e) Describe the human intervention needed to run this information system successfully.

_____

_____

_____

_____

GETTING STARTED

The information systems needs of large companies are many and varied, and very high volumes of data are captured and processed.

Batch systems are suitable when the data to be processed is all available at the start of the task and there is plenty of time to get the job done. An example is an information system for **payroll** processing.

Real time systems are used when a fast response is needed. An international **airline booking system** is an example, but real time systems are also used to control industrial and manufacturing processes and to control robots, etc.

On-line interactive systems are the most frequently used. They have fast response times but are slower than real time systems.

On-line interactive computers are flexible, general purpose systems that may be used to run a variety of different applications at the same time. An example is a supermarket stock control system.

All information systems go through the stages of the **system's life cycle**. First, new ideas are developed in the **systems investigation**. If the idea is considered useful, then a **feasibility study** is undertaken. This is a more detailed investigation.

Systems analysis and design shows how the system will work. All input and output data is fully detailed. A systems flowchart illustrates the processing done. The individual programs of the system are described. When the new system is complete, program specifications are used for **program design, coding, testing and documentation**.

The new system is then **implemented**.

The system design is recorded in the **system documentation**. Any need for improvements is identified by constant **evaluation** of the system; design errors or useful extensions to the system may be discovered. **Maintenance** of the system is vital to sustain its usefulness, but any new system will eventually become obsolete and a replacement will be needed.

Jobs in IT and IS are related to systems development and usage. The **systems analyst** is involved at all stages. They design the system and write the program specifications. Using this specification, the computer **programmer** will design programs to do the processing, and write them in a suitable language.

Data that cannot be read directly by the computer will need transferring to a computer-readable medium, such as magnetic tape or disc – this is the job of a **data preparation clerk**.

The **computer operator** looks after the computer while it is running. They change tapes, discs, printer stationery, etc. as required, and hand printed output on to the data control department.

Data control clerks regulate the flow of data through the computer system. Users send all their input data to data control, who supervise processing and return the output to the appropriate user.

Most students who are following a course in Information Systems or Information Technology expect to work with IT in the future, either as users, or as specialists. The section on jobs in IT and IS in this chapter is written with this in mind.

INFORMATION SYSTEMS AT WORK

PAYROLL

AIRLINE BOOKING SYSTEM

SUPERMARKET STOCK CONTROL

GEOGRAPHIC INFORMATION SYSTEMS

THE SYSTEM LIFE CYCLE

SYSTEMS INVESTIGATION

FEASIBILITY STUDY

SYSTEMS ANALYSIS AND DESIGN

PROGRAM DEVELOPMENT

IMPLEMENTATION

SYSTEM DOCUMENTATION

EVALUATION

MAINTENANCE

JOBS IN IT AND IS

ESSENTIAL PRINCIPLES

Large companies and businesses need to access high volumes of data every day. They need to be able to do this quickly, accurately and inexpensively. Because of the large scale of their information needs they invest in information systems that are designed to meet their own requirements. They are likely to employ their own staff to design and implement information systems that will provide solutions to their own information needs.

The applications described in this chapter have been chosen to illustrate the variety of demands placed on information systems. The systems have been characterised as **batch**, **real time**, and **on-line interactive**. These types of information systems are commonly found in commerce and industry.

Only simple outlines of the payroll, airline booking, supermarket stock control and geographical information systems described have been given. In reality, these information systems are much more complex than described. The data structures will be more extensive and detailed and the volumes of data processed much greater than can reasonably be described in a GCSE revision text.

It is also most likely that, in practice, an information system will be a *hybrid*, involving some batch and on-line interactive processing with links to a real time system where one is in use. For example, both payroll and stock control could be run by a supermarket on the same mainframe computer.

The organisation of an IT department in a large company and the life cycle of an Information System are inextricably linked. This is perhaps not surprising since the role of the IT department is to meet the needs of the company by providing appropriate information systems and staff with the skills to run the systems.

1 > PAYROLL

❝ An example of a payroll information system ❞

Every company or business has to pay its employees. Although this is a fairly straightforward task, it has to be done frequently and accurately. Employees will be annoyed if they are not paid the correct amount at the appropriate time. However, it is not a task which needs to be done instantaneously. The data to be input is readily available when required and it might be possible to do the data processing needed over a few days or longer. Provided the system is well organised and the payroll software works to our satisfaction, all should be well! In following through the description of the payroll system given below, it would be useful to refer to the systems flowchart (see Fig. 13.1).

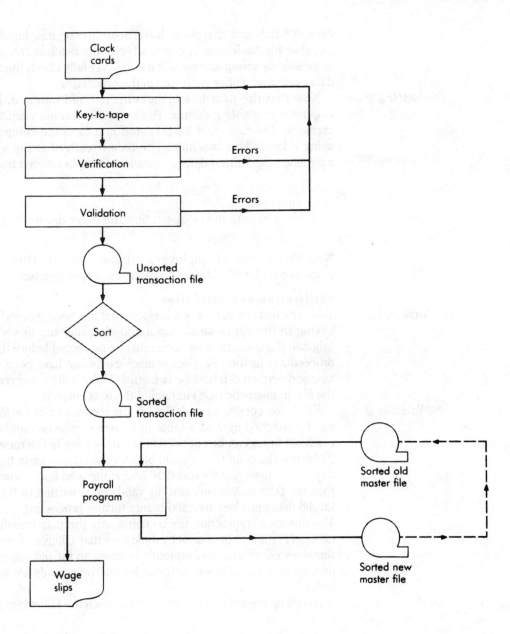

Fig. 13.1 An information system for Payroll processing

Data capture

In a warehouse, workers each have their own 'clock-card'. When they arrive at work they 'clock-in', that is they put the clock-card in a slot in a machine which prints the time onto the clock-card. When they leave work, they 'clock-out' by putting the clock-card in the slot again, so that the time they finished work is printed on the clock-card. Workers find their own clock-card by using their name which is printed on the card but there is also an 'employee number' printed on the clock-card that uniquely identifies each worker. The clock-card is used to *capture* the data needed for processing so that a wages slip can be printed for each employee.

The information about an employee on each clock-card is:
> name
> employee number
> clock-in time and clock-out time for every day worked

Workers are paid a week in arrears, that is they are paid for the week *before* the one they have just worked. If the clock-cards are collected at the end of the week there is one week to process the payroll data.

When the clock-cards have been *collected*, as there are a very large number of them, they are divided into *batches*, i.e. bundles, of 50. A hash total is calculated for each batch by adding up the employee numbers. This total is a meaningless number, but each time it is calculated it should be the same. To check that all the cards are in the correct batch and that none have been lost or misplaced, all we have to do is re-calculate the hash total. If it is unaltered, the batch is complete; if it is different, there is something wrong and we will have to carefully check the batch. This will be done by data control staff after each step in the processing.

Recording

Now that the data has been collected and batched, it must be *recorded* on a computer readable medium. The computer cannot read the printing on the clock-cards, so this data must be prepared in a form the computer *can* use. This is done using a key-to-tape machine. The data is *entered* at the keyboard and recorded on magnetic tape. During data preparation, the data entered from each clock-card is:

Entering

> employee number
> clock-in time and clock-out time, for every day worked

Note that names of employees are not entered. This is not necessary, as each employee is identified by their unique employee number.

Verification and validation

Verification

To check that the data on each clock-card has been entered accurately, it is *verified* by keying in the entire batch again and checking the newly entered data against the original. If any errors arise they must be corrected before the batch of clock-cards can proceed any further. Batches of clock-cards that have been successfully transferred to tape and verified can now be *validated*. There will be one record for each clock-card in the file on magnetic tape containing the data entered.

Validation

Validation checks on each field in the record can be performed. Employee numbers can be checked against a table of known employee numbers; the clock-in time and clock-out times can be checked to see if they are in the range between 0.00 Hours and 23.59; the clock-out time should be later than the clock-in time; the hours worked each day should usually not exceed 16 hours; the total hours worked should usually be less than 60. Data that is successfully validated is written to the unsorted transaction file; invalid data must be corrected before further processing.

The unsorted transaction file contains only the data transferred to it from the clock-cards. This is the data about employees that changes from week to week. The data that does not change so frequently is saved on the old master file. There is one record on the old master file for each employee. The records are stored in employee number order.

A record on the old master file would contain the following:

> employee number
> name
> address
> hourly rate of pay
> tax and national insurance details
> total tax paid this year
> total national insurance paid this year
> total pay this year

Sorting

Sorting

For each employee the record on the transaction file and the record on the old master file must be matched, so that all the data for an employee is available when the payroll program is run. For this reason the unsorted transaction file is next *sorted* into the same order as the old master file. Both files are sorted into ascending order on the employee number. It is important to have both files in the same order because they are recorded on magnetic tape. Magnetic tape only allows sequential access to files recorded on it, that is, records are read in order from the beginning of the file to the end. If the sorted transaction file and the master file were not in the same order, matching the corresponding records for an employee would be very slow.

Processing

Now that the data to be processed has been captured, entered, verified, validated and sorted, it can be *input* to the payroll program. In the payroll program each sorted transaction file record will be matched with the corresponding old master file record. The *hours worked* will be calculated from the clock-in and clock-out times on the sorted transaction file. The *hourly rate of pay* is found on the old master file so that *gross pay* can be calculated. Gross pay is the amount earned before deductions. Tax and national insurance details on the old master file are used to calculate deductions from the gross pay to arrive at *net pay*. Net pay is the actual amount paid to employees after deductions from the amount earned.

The *tax paid* will be added to the total tax paid this year and the *National Insurance contribution paid* will be added to the total National Insurance paid this year. These totals are changed each week, so a new master file record is created containing the updated totals.

Wage slips

A *wage slip* is printed for each employee, giving all the pay details necessary (see Fig. 13.2) and including the name of the employee, taken from the old master file. The wage slips will be printed on continuous computer stationery with perforations between each one. The stationery must be trimmed to remove the sprocket holes and separated at the perforations before distributing the wage slips to employees.

It will also be necessary to *add* records for new employees to the new master file and *remove* the records of those who have left the company. This is done by adding extra records to the transaction file containing the necessary data to indicate which records are to be inserted and deleted. When the payroll program is run, an extra record is created on the new master file for each new employee. The records of those employees that have left are not copied across from the old master file to the new master file.

File backup

Backups of files for security purposes are generated as a consequence of the need to create a new master file each time the payroll program is run. Using the ancestral backup system, the new master file is the son, while the old master file (which was the previous son) becomes the father. The previous old master file (which was the father) now becomes the grandfather. Copies of the sorted transaction file must also be kept. Such a system allows recovery from the loss of current files by regenerating them from the historical data contained in the backup files.

This payroll processing system would run effectively using either magnetic tape or magnetic disc files on a mainframe computer. Provided the files are sorted into the same order before input to the payroll program, magnetic tape is unlikely to be significantly slower than magnetic disc relative to the time available to do the job. Consequently, magnetic tape should be used in preference to disc, as it is a cheaper medium for storage of high volumes of data.

RADIO U.K. LTD.		
Name: A. Jones	Employee number: 86502	Date: 10/07/92
Hours worked: 45	Hourly rate of pay: £3.50	
Gross pay: £157.50		
Tax: £26.25	Tax paid this year: £240.75	
National insurance: £17.40	National insurance paid this year: £136.14	
Net pay: £113.85		

Fig Fig. 13.2 A wage slip printed by the Payroll information system

BATCH PROCESSING

The system described above is known as a **batch processing** system because the data captured is divided into batches before processing. It is characteristic of batch processing that *all* the data to be processed is available *before* processing begins and that there is no need to process the data immediately. The system is not interactive. The user sends the batches of data to be processed to data control who pass it on to data preparation for input, computer operators supervise the processing and then the final output is returned to the user. There is no need for additional input from users of the system while the payroll program is running.

2 > AIRLINE BOOKING SYSTEM

66 an example of an airline booking information system 99

A large airline keeps details of flight schedules and passenger bookings (see Fig. 13.3).

Finding a seat
Passengers may make enquiries at travel agents anywhere in the world to find if a seat is free on any of the flights operated by the airline. Passengers require immediate up-to-date information. The travel agent can make on-line contact with the main computer using a microcomputer and a modem connected via the telephone network. This give the agent and the customer access to the flight information and booking file held on magnetic disc on the main computer.

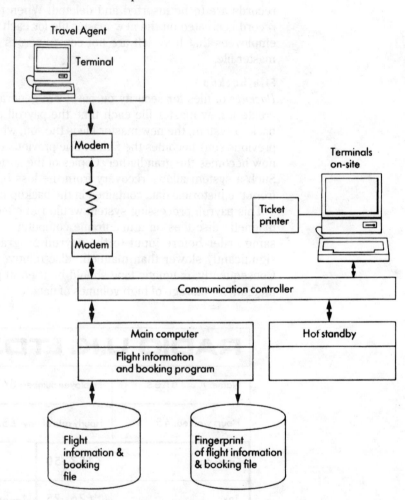

Fig. 13.3 An airline booking system

The main computer should support multiaccess, as there may be a large number of travel agents wanting to make enquiries at the same time. The flight information and booking file must be held on magnetic disc as data held on disc can be read by direct access. Access to the flight information and booking file must be made using direct access for high speed data retrieval. The information requested can be displayed instantaneously and will be kept up-to-date while displayed on the screen.

Booking a seat
66 Example of an airline booking system 99

The customer may decide to book a seat on a flight. The travel agent books the seat using the terminal. Once a seat has been booked the flight information and booking file must be updated immediately so that further enquiries, perhaps by other agents, show the seat as already booked. When the flight information and booking file is being accessed to book a flight, to avoid double booking, all other attempts to book the seat must be locked out. Tickets for booked seats may be printed out on-the-spot or may be sent to customers at a later date. Payment may also be made via the on-line link using a credit card, or customers may be sent the bill by mail some days later. If a customer pays the travel agent in cash this will be charged to the travel agent in due course. There should also be a facility for cancellation and refund of payments using the on-line link.

66 Security 99

Security of access to the system is maintained by giving agents a unique user identification and password. Since the system may be on-line twenty four hours a day, it is very important that the computer is not out of action for any time due to mechanical breakdown. This is avoided by having two identical computers, the main one in use and an additional computer available as a **hot standby** to be used if the main computer breaks down.

File backup

As the system is in constant use, file backups cannot be done in the usual way by copying all the files on disc to tape. This would mean halting the flight information and booking program while the backups are done. Instead, two discs are used, both having copies of the flight information and booking file on them. Any changes that are made to the file are made on both discs at the same time. This technique is known as **finger printing**. It ensures that if one disc becomes faulty there is an exact copy of the file immediately available on the other disc.

The computer hardware and software involved are only used for running the airline booking system. This is a dedicated information system and any other processing required must be done on other computers.

REAL TIME PROCESSING

An on-line booking system such as the one described above is an example of a **real time processing** system. It is so called because processing is in real time, i.e. as data is input it is processed, before any further input can be processed. A real time computer system must be fast enough to ensure that input data is processed immediately because the results can influence any further input. Typically, data can be input to a real time system at any time, from a variety of sources. Even so, processing must be instantaneous and immediate.

66 Example of process control 99

Real time systems are also commonly used in industry for **process control**. A manufacturer of a chemical product may use electronic sensors at various points in the production process to monitor the progress of dangerous reactions. For example, a heat sensor may be used to record the temperature. If the reaction becomes too hot, an explosion may occur. To avoid this the process must be cooled or shut down immediately if it overheats. If the heat sensor is connected to a computer control system, via an Analogue to Digital converter, the computer can be used to monitor the heat of the reaction. When the reaction overheats, the computer will take immediate action to lower the temperature or shut down the reaction if necessary. A computer control system must be a real time system as a slow or delayed response could lead to an explosion or some other disaster.

The need for the immediate response of a real time computer system is also important when computers are used to control the movements of robots. A slow reaction to a touch sensor indicating an obstruction could mean loss of life to workers or damage to the robot.

3 SUPERMARKET STOCK CONTROL

66 An example of a supermarket stock control information system 99

A large modern supermarket will have a computer system situated within the store. At the checkout, the Point of Sale (POS) terminal has attached to it a laser scanner. This is used to read the bar code printed on items sold in the supermarket (see Fig. 13.4). The POS terminal also has a keyboard for entering the product details of items that do not have bar codes printed on them. A small screen is used to display messages sent from the central computer to the POS terminal and a small dot matrix printer built into the terminal is used to print receipts. There will be several checkouts in the supermarket, each with a POS terminal. All of these are connected to the computer located in the store. This computer also has network stations in the warehouse and elsewhere. There are disc drives, a printer and a modem link to other computers via the telephone network.

Fig 13.4 Supermarket checkout

The computer system is a general purpose system and is used for all the data processing done by the supermarket, including payroll, etc. However, we are only going to look at its use for stock control (see Fig. 13.5).

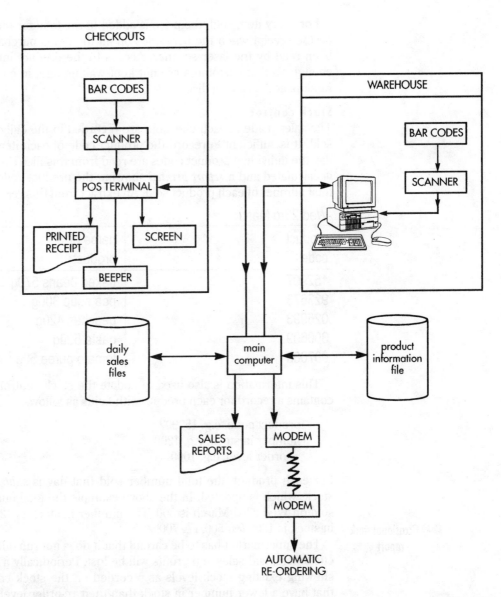

Fig 13.5 A supermarket stock control system

Using bar codes

Most products sold by the supermarket have on them a bar code. The data held on a bar code identifies the product and includes a *product code* and a *check digit*. When an item is sold, the bar code is read by the laser scanner and the data on it is transmitted to the main computer. Here the check digit is re-calculated from the product code and checked against the check digit received from the POS terminal. If these are not the same, the bar code must be re-entered. If both check digits are the same, the product code is checked against the product information file. A record on the file contains the following fields for each product:

> product code, e.g. 152907
> name of product, e.g. baked beans 570 g
> price

If the bar code received from the POS terminal is *not* on the product information file, the bar code may have been entered incorrectly. In this case the bar code must be re-entered. The entry of valid bar codes is indicated by a loud beep.

The product code is used to find the corresponding record in the product information file. The name of the product and the price contained in this record are sent to the POS terminal from the main computer. These are printed on the customer's receipt by the small dot matrix printer built into the POS terminal.

It is a very common belief that the bar code contains the name of the product and its price. This is not so. These are only kept in the product information file stored on the main computer. They are transferred to the POS terminal when required.

The price is *not* in the bar code

For every item sold, the price is added to the total for the customer. This is printed on the receipt when the bar codes on all the items purchased by the customer have been read by the laser scanner. Access to the product information file must be fast enough so that customers are not kept waiting and, in consequence, it is a direct or random access file on disc.

Stock control

The sales made at each checkout are recorded in the daily sales file as the goods are sold. It is sufficient to record the product code of each item sold. At the end of every day the individual product codes are read from this file. The quantity of each item sold is calculated and a *report printed* showing the product code, name of product and the total number of each product sold. An extract from this report follows:

Wed 23rd March

product code	name of product	total number sold
152907	baked beans 570g	500
923673	pea soup 300g	258
025993	peaches 420g	367
300609	pasta 500g	124
007085	tomato puree 50g	356

This information is also used to update the stock control file. The stock control file contains a record for each product with fields as follows:

> product code, e.g. 152907
> number in stock, e.g. 1200
> re-order level, e.g. 1000

For each product, the total number sold that day is *subtracted* from the number in stock, which is updated. In the above example the total number of baked beans 570g sold on Wed 23rd March is 500. The number in stock is 1200 so the updated number in stock is 1200 *less* 500, i.e. 700.

 Occasional stock report

The supermarket has to be careful that it does not run out of stock as this will annoy customers, and sales and profits will be lost. Periodically a *stock report* will be printed showing existing stock levels as recorded on the stock control file. Those products that have a lower number in stock than their re-order level will be emphasised in the report. The supermarket manager will go through the report and re-order those products that are needed, using the information contained in the report. In this case, the manager should re-order baked beans 570 g as 700 is less than 1000.

Automatic ordering

If the manager wishes, items can be ordered automatically when the stock control file is updated. For these products, if they have a lower number in stock than their re-order level, the manufacturer is contacted and asked to send more of the product. This is done automatically using electronic mail sent by the supermarket's computer to the manufacturer's computer using a modem and the telephone system.

When items that have been ordered arrive at the supermarket they are sent to the warehouse. At the warehouse the goods are checked as they arrive and stored until they are moved into the supermarket to be sold. As they arrive, the warehouse manager enters the quantity of each product that is delivered at the network station in the warehouse. This data is used to update the stock control file, e.g. if 800 cans of baked beans 570 g are delivered then the number in stock is updated to 700 plus 800, i.e. 1500, bringing the number in stock above the re-order level. Using this system the manager can control the flow of stock into the supermarket in response to sales of stock to customers.

Extra information

The above description focuses on one basic aspect of a stock control system. In practice, the same system would be used to do a range of *additional* tasks:

■ the *number of items sold* and the *takings at each till* could be recorded and used to monitor the performance of checkout operators;

■ the *rate of sales of each product* could be calculated and used to increase the choice of popular goods or to reduce stocks of unpopular items;

- the *pattern of sales* of every product could be recorded so that the stocks are not held at times of the year when goods are unlikely to sell;

- the *effectiveness of sales promotions* can be monitored;

- goods that have *high profit margins* can be stocked in preference to those with lower profit margins.

❝❝ Low stock = low costs ❞❞

To keep business expenses to a minimum, stocks of goods should be kept as low as possible. If a *maximum stock level* is recorded for each product on the stock control file, then the quantity re-ordered can be adjusted so that this level is *not exceeded* when new supplies arrive at the warehouse. This maximum stock level can be adjusted so that the extra costs involved in frequent re-ordering are balanced against the expense of storing larger quantities of a product in the warehouse.

Security

❝❝ Reducing the loss of stock ❞❞

The system can also be used to determine the extent of theft from the supermarket and improve security. If the actual number of each product in stock is counted and found to be less than the number in stock on the stock control file, then this difference is due to loss of stock. Loss of stock can be due to damage or theft. If damages are recorded as they occur then loss due to theft can be calculated.

❝❝ Advantages of a computer stock control system ❞❞

Computer based stock control systems allow managers to monitor stock levels very closely and to exercise greater control over the business. This allows the manager to increase the profitability of the business and improve customer service. Prices can be kept lower and customer service is quicker due to the speed of the POS terminals. The customer's receipt is itemised and fewer mistakes occur at the checkout. However, the purchase cost of the system is high and it will be necessary to train employees to use it. Because the productivity of checkout employees is increased there will be a reduced number of employees at the supermarket.

ON-LINE INTERACTIVE PROCESSING

The stock control system described above is an **on-line interactive processing** system. On-line systems use terminals connected to a computer. These terminals interact with the computer system, sending data to it and receiving data from it. A real time system is an on-line interactive system but not all such systems are real time. The stock control system described here is not real time.

Sales data is captured using the POS terminals, which must be permanently connected on-line to the computer. In order to print an itemised receipt showing the description and price of every item sold, this data must be found in the product information file, using the product code contained in the bar code input by laser scanner, i.e. interactive processing is necessary as an interchange of data takes place. However, there is no need to immediately update the stock control file as goods are sold. Stock control data does not need to be updated immediately. It is quite acceptable for recorded stock levels to be a day or two out of date, as this is unlikely to significantly affect the business. The expense of a specialised real time system cannot be justified in these circumstances.

The most important feature of **Geographic Information Systems** is that they can display maps (see Fig. 13.6). These maps are often based on aerial photographs that have been recorded in a form that computers can manipulate. The GIS can zoom in and out to display the maps at various levels of detail. For example, a local map showing the houses in a street or a district map showing only the towns could be displayed.

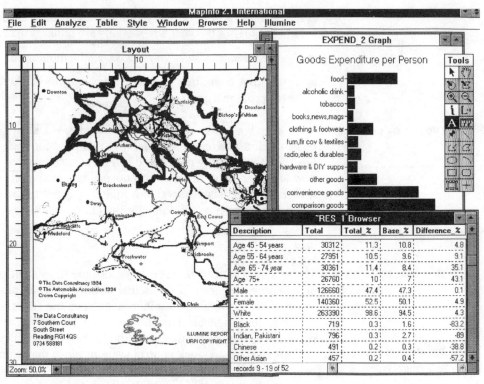

Fig. 13.6 A screen map in a GIS
(Courtesy of the Data Consultancy)

The maps could have various layers. A layer might show the location of all the schools, all the hospitals, all the roadworks, all the night clubs, etc. You could alter the map so that it displayed only the layer with the motorways and A roads. You could display only one layer on the map or several layers at the same time.

A GIS uses the maps to display data in relation to its geographic location. Most data has a geographic component, for example: an address. A GIS has a powerful database to store the information it displays. The information in the database can be provided with the GIS, for example, census data. Alternatively, users can input their own data.

Examples of the use of GIS

These are a few of the tasks you can do using a GIS:

 **Route planning**

- Transport companies can plan the route that each truck in a fleet will take to deliver its load throughout the country. The actual location of the trucks can be shown on the map as they move around the country. The position of roadworks and accidents can be shown so that the trucks can be re-routed to avoid them.

 **Marketing**

- Manufacturing companies can use GIS to market their products more effectively. The location of actual and potential customers can be shown on a map. Comparisons with census data will identify potential customers. Only those customers with particular needs can be shown. This helps companies target their advertising and other marketing activities more effectively. For example: from census data you can find out which areas have most young people living there. Young people buy the most computer games but tend not to buy furniture. An area with a large number of young people would be a good place to sell a new range of computer games but might not be such a good place to sell filing cabinets. Sales territories can be more easily allocated and the impact of sales promotions can be seen.

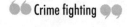 **Crime fighting**

- The police can record and analyse crime, pinpointing areas of high criminal activity. Patterns of crime can be displayed on a map. You can look at the pattern for burglaries, compare it with patterns for other crimes and with other layers of the map, to identify likely suspects. You can compare census data with a crime pattern to see if lifestyle and criminal behaviour are connected. You can use the GIS to generate bar charts showing the percentage of different crimes committed each hour, from day-to-day. GIS make crime patterns more visible and more understandable. They can also predict when, where, how much and what type of crime will happen in the future. When used to model crime in this way, the predicted results should be used with care, however, GIS do help the police record, analyse and predict crime more effectively.

GIS display data in a way which is more meaningful. Instead of lists of numbers, you can look at a map which shows you what is happening and where it is happening. GIS are essentially visual map based displays of data extracted from a database. They are interactive systems and, in some instances on-line or, more rarely, real time systems. These information systems are currently at the developmental stage. It is likely that their use will be widespread and much more important in the future.

5 > THE SYSTEM LIFE CYCLE

Every information system goes through a cycle of development and use until it becomes obsolete or is replaced by a better system (see Fig. 13.7). The stages in this cycle are described below in the sequence in which they occur.

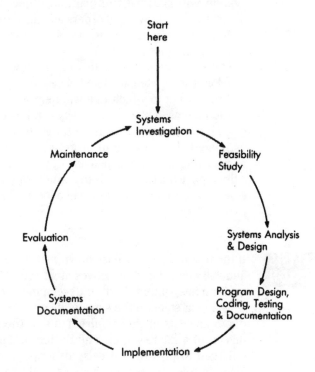

❝❝ Stages in the information systems life cycle ❞❞

Fig. 13.7 The system life cycle

6 > SYSTEMS INVESTIGATION

The realisation that it would be useful to have an information system to do a particular task may arise due to a new and completely novel idea, or to a new technological invention. However, many new information systems are created because the system currently in use is unable to handle increased volumes of data, or new demands on it.

For example, a manual system for processing orders might work quite well until the rapid growth of the company and product diversification leads to many more customer orders, with a wide variety of terms and conditions of sale. Because of the increased complexity of the task, mistakes are made and there is a general confusion over what processing is required in some cases. Customers want their orders to arrive on time, to contain the items ordered and to be charged the right price! They become angry and frustrated when this does not happen. This in turn leads to a decline in orders. Having worked hard to increase production and sales, it is disappointing to find that confusion within the department dealing with order processing is responsible for lost sales. To improve this situation a computer based system to help process customers' orders is suggested.

The **systems investigation** outlines the organisational problems identified, and recognises the *need* for improvements. A brief outline of a proposed system is made. This will identify the desired objectives, in this case the processing and delivery of the correct order, within a stated period, and charging customers the right price. A system will be described in broad outline and a rough estimate of costs will be made.

7 FEASIBILITY STUDY

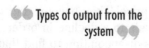 Conducting a feasibility study

If the systems investigation has uncovered a development that will be of use to the company, then a **feasibility study** is undertaken. This is a rather more detailed investigation of the proposed information system.

Firstly, the *present* system is examined in greater detail.

■ The order processing manager is asked what is done, and how it is done.

■ The staff who do the job are asked to describe what they actually do.

■ The records kept by the department, the forms they receive from customers, those filled in within the department and all correspondence are looked at.

■ Customers are asked to provide details of letters and forms received from the department and are encouraged to explain how the service might be improved.

The new system is now developed in greater detail in a written report. Where possible, the new system is based on existing practice, to minimise the eventual disruption and retraining of staff when it is introduced. It must be shown that the new system will achieve the original objectives of i) improved performance in the processing, ii) delivery of orders and iii) the accurate charging of customers.

Additional benefits of the new system will also be described, for example, improved working conditions for staff.

The software required to run the new system will be specified and the costs to develop it in-house calculated. The extra cost of additional hardware should be given and the extent to which this will help with other processing tasks estimated. Savings due to increased staff productivity can be taken into account and the cost of necessary re-training shown. The time taken to develop and introduce the system is also estimated. In the case of large, complex or expensive systems, several different designs might be developed and outlined in the report.

The report on the feasibility study is passed to senior management within the company for approval. They will allocate the resources necessary if the new system is to proceed.

8 SYSTEMS ANALYSIS AND DESIGN

If the feasibility study has shown that the proposed information system is worthwhile, and will meet stated objectives at an economic cost, then it is likely to be approved by senior management. Further development will then proceed.

The next stage in the system life cycle is **systems analysis and design**, i.e. the in-depth analysis of the requirements of the system and the preparation of a detailed design of a final system. The design outlined in the feasibility study will be further enlarged to provide a precise description of what the new system will do. At every stage in this process the systems analyst will refer back to the eventual users of the system, i.e. the order processing department and senior management, to ensure that the detailed system design meets their needs.

OUTPUT

The **output** required from the system will be specified. In the case of the order processing system this will include:

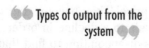 Types of output from the system

■ **Invoices** to be sent to the warehouse and to customers. An invoice is a printed confirmation of a customer's order. It lists what the customer has ordered, with the price of each item and the total cost. The invoice is first sent to the warehouse where it is used to select the items the customer has ordered. The invoice is then sent with the order to the customer. The customer uses the invoice to check that the order is correct and that the company has delivered everything that was ordered. The company will need to store the information shown on the invoice so that it knows what has been sold and how much is owed by the customer.

■ **Internal reports and statistics**. Reports and statistical summaries of performance will be needed by senior management to help them improve the performance of the company. The total sales of every item stocked can be summarised using the stored information from each invoice, either for all items stocked, in a printed report, or for a selection of items, on a monitor screen.

The layout of all printed reports and screen displays will be shown in detail. They must be presented in a way which is clear and easy to understand. An example of what each looks like will be drawn in sufficient detail to allow a programmer to write a computer program to produce the required output exactly.

The demand for specific data displays implies a need for the corresponding output peripherals. These could be simply monitor screens and printers but may also be more specialised output devices, for example, graph plotters. The way in which output is obtained from the system will also need to be examined. For example the systems analyst must consider whether reports need to be obtained immediately on request or if printouts are to be optional or the report *only* printed?

These considerations may lead us to equip the order processing department with network stations connected to local printers, so that reports can first be displayed on screen and only output if required. For reports that will always and only be printed the system line printer may be satisfactory.

INPUT

The **input** to the system is now looked at in greater detail. All the output from the system is produced from the input. It is important to be sure at an early stage that all the data needed will be *captured*. If this does not already occur in the existing system, then arrangements will have to be made to get the required data. The way in which data is input to the system should be designed in order to help data preparation staff and others to work quickly and easily.

In the case of the order processing system, it is likely that most of the input needed for the new system is already being generated by the old. It is possible that a manual system could manage without customer numbers if the orders are filed using the customer's name. However, a computer based system must have customer numbers, to be used as a key field to identify customers. If the existing order processing system does not use customer numbers, then arrangements will have to be made to generate these and persuade customers to use them.

Similarly, in a manual system the invoice containing details of the order can be identified using the date of the order. In the case of two or more orders on the same day the actual items ordered could be used to identify the invoice. This is rather cumbersome and makes reference to orders difficult. Consequently each invoice is given an invoice number which the customer and the order processing department can refer to in case of enquiries, etc. concerning the order.

The *way* in which the data is input must also be considered. Key-to-tape or key-to-disc may be satisfactory, but other methods should be considered. Customers could be sent mark sense documents, i.e. specially designed order forms that can be read directly into the computer by a mark sense reader. In some cases Kimball tags may be used to automatically re-order items that have been sold. All useful possible means of input should be looked at and the benefits of each evaluated.

FILE STRUCTURES

The **file structures** used within the system are decided on by examining the permanency of the data and whether it relates more closely to an invoice, or to a customer. Some of the data to be input could be recorded on backing storage and used several times, whereas some data will change from order to order. For example, an order from a customer will generate the following data:

        name
        address
        customer number (identifies customer)
        invoice number (identifies order)
        date of order
        for each item ordered: item code (identifies item)
                                  description
                                  quantity
                                  price per item

Types of input into the system

The customer number (to identify the customer) and the invoice number (to identify the order) are both generated by the order processing department.

Invoice files

The customer's name, address and customer number do not change from order to order, whereas the other data relating to the items ordered will almost certainly change. The transient data relating to the order rather than to the customer will be kept on the **invoice file**. The invoice file contains a record for each invoice as follows:

An invoice file

> invoice number (identifies order)
> customer number (identifies customer)
> date of order
> for each item ordered: item code (identifies item)
>   description
>   quantity
>   price per item

When an invoice is paid it is deleted from the invoice file. This file contains only those invoices that have not yet been completely processed.

Customer files

The name, address and customer number are kept on the **customer file**. This file has a record for each customer containing information that relates more directly to the customer rather than to an actual order. The customer file records include the following fields:

A customer file

> customer number (identifies customer)
> name
> address
> credit limit
> discount rate

Records on the invoice file can be matched with the corresponding record on the customer file, using the customer number. Invoices can be printed and sent to the warehouse. The warehouse packs the items ordered and sends them to the customer with the invoice. The total amount owed by each customer can be calculated by adding up the amounts owed on individual invoices still to be paid.

At this point it is perhaps worth noting that an order processing system is unlikely to be designed in isolation. It is likely to be integrated with, at least, a stock control system and possibly with wider financial reporting and control systems. The system described in the example is the basis of the more complex systems that are used in practice.

Following through the above discussion we can see that the output requirements of the system suggest what input is needed. The file structure is decided upon by analysing the input data and the processing needed to be done to produce the necessary output. Inevitably, the file structures, the processing to be done and the style of output chosen, influence the choice of backing storage. Sequential access files on magnetic tape will be used for economy if only printed output is needed and the slower turnaround time is acceptable. Otherwise, direct access files on magnetic disc will be used to give immediate access to up-to-date date for screen displays and printed reports. An order processing system could be designed using either batch processing or on-line interactive processing.

Choice of backing storage

TELEPHONE ENQUIRY SERVICE

In the example of the order processing system, a telephone enquiry service may be offered (see Fig. 10.10 in an earlier chapter). In this case, immediate access to customer and invoice files would be needed in order to answer enquiries on-the-spot. This would necessitate the use of direct access files on disc. Customer records would be accessed using either the customer number or name to find the record and the address would be used to confirm that the correct record has been located. The telephone operator would also have particular hardware needs if a large volume of enquiries is anticipated. A headset and microphone to replace the standard telephone might be useful. This would free the hands to enable the keyboard to be used more easily.

DATA SECURITY

Choice of data security arrangements

Arrangements for data security should also be carefully thought out. The *ancestral* file system for file backup will be used and the times and frequency of backups should be stated. Arrangements for the physical security of files should be made. Each generation of backup should be kept in a different place. Fireproof safes, etc. may need to be purchased. Storage facilities at remote sites may be necessary in some cases.

PROGRAM SPECIFICATION

Systems analysis and design is a searching, in-depth look at the proposed system. It results in an exact statement of the input, processing and output needed and the hardware, software and data required to meet these needs. The system design details what will be done, how it will be done, the purpose in doing it and the cost. This will be described using system flowcharts, tables, diagrams, screen layouts, etc.

The processing will be divided into programs to do specific tasks. The system may be designed as one or more inter-related programs. A **program specification** will be written for each computer program. This specifies in detail the input, processing and output to be done, the file structure, and any other details needed. The program specification gives sufficient detail to allow the programmer to write the program.

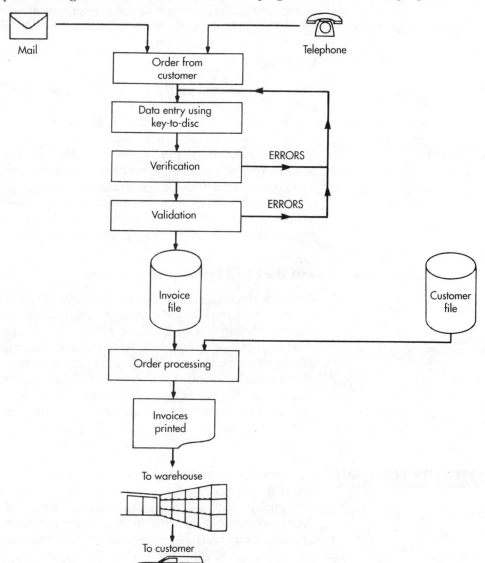

Fig. 13.8 An orders processing system

PROGRAM DEVELOPMENT

The design, coding, testing and documentation of a program

The program specification written during the analysis and design of the system is handed over to a *computer programmer*. It contains enough information about the program to enable the programmer to design a program to do the required processing. The structure of any data input or output will be specified and also the type of file access used. The program to be written may be part of a large system involving many programs. It should not be necessary for the programmer to know how the whole system, or any other program in the system, functions in order to design the program. The programmer will read the specification carefully, then design the program.

PROGRAM DESIGN

The **program design** can be illustrated in various ways. Often a flowchart is drawn, or alternatively a top-down design may be written in pseudo-code. There are a variety of design methodologies that can be used. The design is often **dry run** to test if it works. In a dry run the programmer uses examples of the input data and processes it according to the program design to see if the expected output results.

CODING

When the program has been designed, it is **coded**, i.e. written in a computer language. There are a variety of computer languages and the programmer may be free to choose which one to use. However, it is more likely that all programs in the system will be written in the same language. An appropriate language to use for the order processing system would be COBOL. COBOL is a very good language for file handling as it is easy to define and manipulate records and fields. Commercial applications are often dominated by file handling making COBOL particularly appropriate. In the order processing system used as an example there are no complex calculations to be done, but there will be considerable file processing.

TESTING

Next, the program it **tested** to see if it works. The programmer tests the program using test input data to see if the program produces the expected output. Test data may be typical data likely to be generated when the system is running under normal conditions, but it should also include extreme or rare data unlikely to occur in practice. The aim is to write a robust program that can deal with any input data, either processing it or reporting errors and continuing running. If the test data causes unexpected output or crashes the program, i.e. stops it running, due to an inability to process the input data, then the programmer will have to amend the program and do another test run. The cycle of testing, amending and re-testing continues until the programmer is satisfied that the program works.

DOCUMENTATION

Program documentation is done throughout the design, coding and testing of a program. It is based on the original program specification and will cover the program design, including flowcharts. There will also be a listing of the source code of the final version of the program with details of test data and the resulting output. File structures for all input and output files and samples of printed output and screen displays will be included. The purpose of the documentation is to provide enough detail for a different programmer to understand what has been done in case the program unexpectedly crashes and the original programmer is not available to put it right.

IMPLEMENTATION

If the extra hardware needed to run the new system has not been bought at an earlier stage, it will have to be purchased and installed before proceeding further. Consumables, such as printer stationery and discs, will need to be purchased. Extra electric wiring must be installed in the user department for powering terminals, etc. and a room with special features, such as air conditioning, may be required. Additional specialist computer staff will need to be employed to run the computer equipment and maintain the system.

When the *individual programs* that make up the system have been tested separately then the *entire system* is tested as a whole. Test data is used and the output checked against that expected. If errors are found they must be corrected and the system re-tested.

When it appears that the system is working correctly, it is **implemented**, i.e. it is put to work. However, there will still be a possibility that the system does not work as intended. To avoid costly mistakes a **parallel run** takes place (see Fig. 13.9).

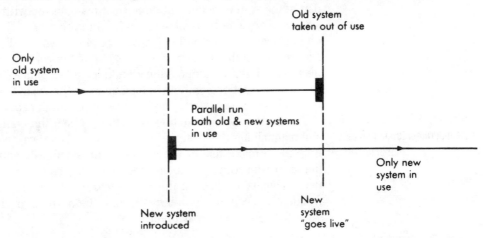

Fig. 13.9 A parallel run

Both the new system and the old system are run on real input data and the results from the manual and the computer based system are checked against each other. It is not unusual when looking for the reasons for differences in the output between the old and the new systems to discover that the new system is correct. Frequently, manual systems that have evolved piecemeal are found to be inferior to properly designed information systems.

When the new system can be relied on to work correctly it 'goes live' and the old system is no longer used. This does not usually happen overnight. It is a gradual process, as parts of the old system are discontinued and replaced by the new system. Eventually, the only system in use is the new system.

System implementation also involves training users in the new system. There may be changes in practice which staff in the user departments, e.g. the order processing department, have to understand and follow. If the change is from an entirely manual system to a computerised system, staff will need to gain confidence in using the new

technology.

System implementation involves the installation of both hardware and software and the employment and training of staff. It is extremely complex and requires adequate planning and finance if it is to be successful. Even so, mistakes *will* occur and it is important that these are seen simply as problems to be overcome rather than personal faults of particular employees. The implementation of a computer based system demands personal change and adjustment of all employees. This must be recognised in a considerate way if the new system is to be implemented smoothly.

SYSTEM DOCUMENTATION

System documentation is a written record of the analysis, design, testing and implementation of the system. It is written throughout the development of a system. It will include systems flowcharts for the implemented design and detailed file structures for the data files.

PROGRAM DOCUMENTATION

The **program documentation**, for all the programs in the system, forms part of the system documentation. There will be a listing of the final source code for the program in the program documentation. Samples of printed output and screen displays will also be included.

The purpose of the documentation is to provide all the detail needed to understand *what* the program does, and *how* it does it. This will be useful to those unfamiliar with the system, such as new employees. If the system goes wrong, the documentation will be helpful to the maintenance programmers who will attempt to make the system work again. Similarly, if there is a need to *extend* the system, so that it can do extra tasks, the program documentation will make it easier to build on additional processing capability.

USER MANUALS

User manuals or **user documentation** that explains how to run the system are also part of the system documentation. User manuals are written to help employees use the system. They can be read separately from the rest of the system documentation and do not have the same in-depth coverage of the system. They are needed when staff are trained to use the system and so that staff can refer to them for help in the future if necessary. User documentation should include a general review of the job done by the system, instructions on how to load and run the system and a description of the input required, the processing done and the output produced.

The differences between system documentation and user manuals

The system documentation is written to help the computer department in running and maintaining the system. The user manuals are written for the user departments to help them make use of the system. The system documentation will be stored in a library by the computer department, so that it can be referred to when necessary. The user manuals are kept in the user departments and are likely to be referred to fairly frequently. Technical problems beyond the scope of user departments will be passed on to the computer department.

12> EVALUATION

When the system was first thought of it was hoped that it would solve certain difficulties in running the business. In the case of the order processing department, the system was expected to ensure the processing and delivery of the correct order, within a stated period, and charging customers the right price. On implementation, the new system will achieve these objectives. However, in due course the same problems could arise again as the volume of orders increases once more.

Evaluation of the system aims to check that it is still effective in doing the job it was designed to do.

Anticipating the need for change

It is easier to deal with problems if they are anticipated. Instead of waiting for angry customers to draw the attention of management to the breakdown of the system as it becomes overloaded again, constant evaluation of its effectiveness will identify problems before they result in customer dissatisfaction and lost business. If problems are known to exist, they can be avoided by either increasing the effectiveness of the existing system or developing a new system.

At some point in their life cycle all systems become obsolete and are replaced by new systems. Even reliable, well designed, systems will become obsolete at some time, if only because the underlying hardware technology used is superseded.

13> MAINTENANCE

Any system, however well designed and tested, is likely to go wrong at some time. There may be an error in the logic of one of the programs, or a condition or circumstance may arise which was not anticipated. **Maintenance** of the system involves the correction of errors in existing programs, or the extension of the system to cope with different tasks. Maintenance of the system may involve changes to any of the components of the system. It may be necessary to re-program existing software, design and write new programs to extend the capability of the system, repair existing hardware or buy new. The system documentation and user manuals will need to be updated as the system changes.

Correcting errors and extending the system

14> JOBS IN IT AND IS

The organisation of an IT department in a large company is shown in Figure 13.10. It is not the case that *every* IT department is organised in this way, but many are organised in a very similar way.

Roles in the IT department

The IT department organises the highly skilled workers who develop and use information systems for the maximum benefit of the company that employs them. As companies vary in terms of size and organisation, so do IT departments. In some cases jobs done by individuals are broader, and in other instances narrower, than will be suggested, but the tasks to be done are the same whether they are done by one person in a small company or several in a larger company.

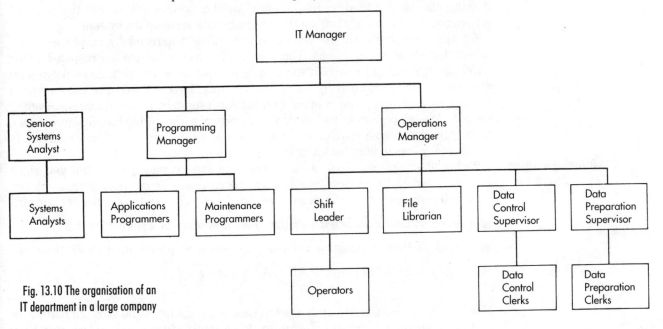

Fig. 13.10 The organisation of an IT department in a large company

THE IT MANAGER

The **IT Manager** is in charge of the IT department. Senior Systems Analysts, the Programming Manager and the Operations Manager all work under the supervision of the IT Manager.

THE SYSTEMS ANALYST

The **Systems Analyst** is directly responsible for the development of an information system through all the stages of the system life cycle (see Fig. 13.11). An analyst is usually given responsibility for a system and will see it through from its birth to system termination. The Systems Analyst responsible for a system often works on it alone, but frequently acts as a team leader, organising others in their work on the system.

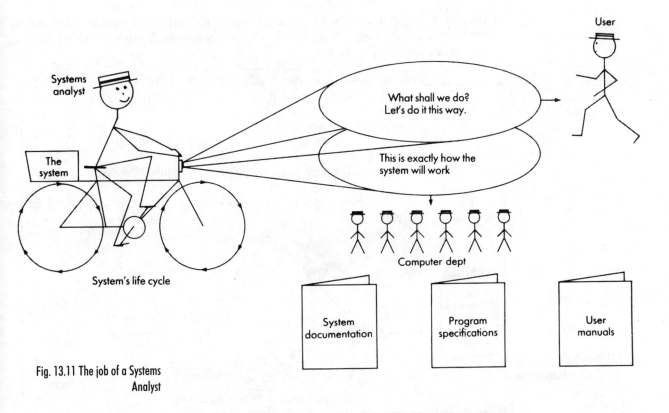

Fig. 13.11 The job of a Systems Analyst

Responsibilities of the Systems Analyst

For example, during the stage of systems analysis and design the analyst responsible will lead a team of analysts who will develop the system design as directed. Similarly, during the stage of program design, coding, testing and documentation the analyst responsible for the system will direct the team of programmers who are working on the programs that make up the system.

Computer systems are developed as a result of *teamwork* by employees with different skills and specialisms. The Systems Analyst is the person responsible for developing the computer system and leading the various teams working on the system at different times. A good Systems Analyst must have a thorough knowledge of computers, commerce and people. Systems Analysts must be good communicators, creative, logical, persistent and work well as part of a team. This knowledge can only be acquired through hard work, training and experience. Systems analysis is intellectually demanding, but interesting and varied.

Becoming a Systems Analyst

To become a Systems Analyst you will need to find a company to employ you, since *experience* and *ability* are worth more than qualifications. To convince a company you are a good prospect to take on as a trainee, useful qualifications to acquire are one of:

- a degree in Computer Science or Information Systems or a similar subject.

- an HND or HNC in Business Studies or Computer Studies or Information Systems.

- a degree in a related subject such as Accountancy or Law.

However, many Systems Analysts start as humbler employees and through hard work and perseverance work their way up. Frequently, firms encourage study for membership of professional organisations. The British Computer Society (BCS) entry exams are popular. They not only improve professional skills and knowledge, but also lead to membership of the BCS. System Analysts are important employees and a prudent company will pay them well and invest in their training.

Systems Analysts are employed wherever there are information systems in development or use. They are employed by large companies, software houses, local government, the Civil Service, universities, etc. Good Systems Analysts will get to know the companies they work for very well indeed. They will probably change jobs from time to time to gain yet further experience. This overall view of business organisation can be a useful stepping stone to higher management positions or consultancy work. Salaries tend to be high for those with proven ability and experience.

COMPUTER PROGRAMMER

Computer Programmers write programs in a computer language that tell a computer to do the tasks described in the program specification provided by the Systems Analyst (see Fig. 13.12).

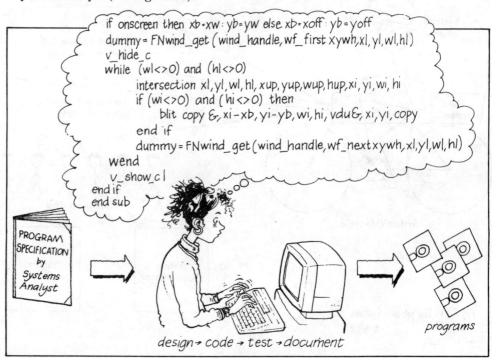

Fig. 13.12 The job of a Computer Programmer

●● Responsibilities of the Computer Programmer ●●

Programmers may specialise in the development of new programs or the maintenance of existing systems. Applications Programmers design, code, test and document new programs using the program specification given to them by the systems analyst. Maintenance Programmers put right programs in systems that are already in use, but have been identified as having errors in them. They rely on the program documentation written by the Applications Programmer to help find these errors.

The program specification describes the input, output and special processing required. File structure and access type is also given. The Applications Programmer designs the logic of the program, perhaps expressed in a flowchart. The program is then written or coded, using a suitable computer language. The program is tested using both typical and unusual test data. The program documentation written by the Applications Programmer contains the program specification, flowcharts and other details of the processing done. A listing of the program is included, as well as a report on the testing carried out. This detailed documentation is used to maintain the program in working order should errors be found in the future.

●● Becoming a Computer Programmer ●●

Programmers need to think logically and be good at solving problems. Programming is an interesting, high pressure job, not really suitable for those wanting a quiet life. Working hours can often be extended at short notice when an urgent job has to be done. Programmers must work well with others, as teamwork is usual. They need to be flexible and not too worried about having a routine life style. A measure of enthusiasm and an obsession with the job are also useful!

Programmers are valued for their skill and experience. However, qualifications are useful in finding a job. Most employers would expect A-levels, preferably including Maths and Computer Studies. GCSEs in Maths and English are almost essential.

Most companies would provide training in the computer language needed where a programmer was not fluent in that particular language.

As they gain experience, Programmers often specialise in an area of programming, such as Operating Systems. Another common alternative is to become a Systems Analyst.

Programmers are generally found in employment where Systems Analysts are also employed, i.e. companies, local government, etc. Skilled programmers are highly paid and there are opportunities for foreign travel. Programming skills are in short supply in most industrialised countries.

OPERATIONS MANAGER

The **Operations Manager** has overall responsibility for the organisation of the use of the computer, including the supervision of the Data Preparation department, the Data Control department, Computer Operators and the File Librarian. The Operations Manager reports directly to the DP Manager.

DATA PREPARATION CLERK

●● Responsibilities of the Data Preparation Clerk ●●

When data has been captured or collected for input, it may not be in a form the computer can read. For example, an order from a customer may be written on a piece of paper. The computer cannot read the writing on the paper so the information is transferred to magnetic disc or tape. Data preparation is the entering of data at the keyboard of a key-to-tape or key-to-disc machine. This is the job of a **Data Preparation Clerk** (see Fig. 13.13).

Fig. 13.13 The job of a Data Preparation Clerk

Data preparation is an essential part of any information system that does not use direct data capture, e.g. laser scanners, temperature sensors, etc. Data Preparation Clerks usually work in a department that deals with the data entry requirements of all the systems run by the company. All organisations that use large computer systems will have a Data Preparation department.

Good keyboard skills are important. A skilled Data Preparation Clerk can maintain speed and accuracy while doing repetitive work. Qualifications at GCSE level in English, Office Practice or Typing might be useful in getting a job, but again, it is the *ability to do the job* that is important. Touch typing skills and familiarity with wordprocessing are almost essential.

❝❝Becoming a Data Preparation Clerk❞❞

Payment is often related to the number of key depressions per hour when entering the data on the keyboard. Hours are regular, but shift work is normal. Often short shifts or limited hours can be worked. A fast keyboard operator can earn high wages in comparison to similar work, perhaps typing in an office, as the wage paid relates to the volume of work done rather than the time spent.

A skilled Data Preparation Clerk can progress to a supervisory position or move into computer operations. It is possible for a determined and capable employee to be promoted from data preparation, through operations, to programming and beyond.

DATA CONTROL CLERKS

When a system is in use, the input, processing and output are carefully controlled. **Data Control Clerks** monitor the flow of data through the system as it moves from data preparation, to verification, validation and processing on the computer (see Fig. 13.14). They collect any printed output and send it to the appropriate person. Data Control Clerks make sure that no data gets lost and that it is processed as required. The Data Preparation department receives most of its work through the Data Control department as data to be input to working systems will be sent to Data Control initially. Enquiries from other departments about the progress of their data being processed are dealt with by Data Control. Data Control Clerks need to be thorough and reliable, with a good understanding of the computer systems used by the company they work for.

❝❝Responsibilities of the Data Control Clerk❞❞

❝❝Becoming a Data Control Clerk❞❞

Working hours are normal office hours. A Data Control Clerk works in a modern office environment, at times using a network station to monitor the progress of the data being processed. Often a copy of the operator's console screen display is used. This can be quite complex. Data control is a good training for operations work and a period in data control is often part of the training schedule for newly employed operators.

Fig. 13.14 The job of a Data Control Clerk

COMPUTER OPERATORS

Computer Operators look after the computer while it is running (see Fig. 13.15). They start up the computer and close it down. Computer Operators also monitor the status of programs running on the computer and provide tapes and discs as requested. They change the paper in the printer and keep all other peripherals in the computer room supplied with media.

Operators are employed at all mainframe computer installations. Most have purpose-built computer rooms where the operator works. Mainframe computers need a carefully controlled environment in which to run. They need air-conditioning to disperse the heat generated by the computer and air filtering to keep the air clean so that discs, tapes and machinery are not damaged. A computer room will have a false floor and a suspended ceiling so that cables and wiring can easily be concealed when laid from one part of the computer room to another. A Computer Operator works in the computer room. These are possibly the best working conditions experienced in any job!

 Responsibilities of Computer Operators

Fig. 13.15 The job of a Computer Operator

Becoming a Computer Operator

Operators need to be alert and react calmly in a crisis. They will need to respond in a sensible way if problems such as machine failure do arise. Attention to detail and care in doing routine tasks are very important. They must work reliably on their own, without supervision. It is not unknown for one or two Computer Operators to be left in charge of a multimillion pound computer.

Most companies train their own operators. Operators need to know *what* the computer does, *who* uses it and *for what purpose*. This is best learnt through a combination of on-the-job training and day-release courses. However, GCSEs in Maths, English and Information Systems could well help in getting a job as an operator. Experience and ability rate more highly than qualifications once basic skills have been learnt.

Most operators will work shifts as large computers are kept running twenty-four hours a day. Operators are paid extra for working shifts and overtime is usually paid for extra hours worked. There will be a **Shift Leader** appointed for each shift to take responsibility for the team of operators working the shift.

Career opportunities are good. Operating is a skill that is transferable from one company to another. Operators may become Shift Leaders and go into Operations Management. Operating provides a good opening to higher level work with computers. A move into programming is not uncommon.

OTHER JOBS IN IT

Computer manufacturers employ sales staff to *sell* computers. They may also employ staff to provide *technical advice* to customers and *equipment maintenance* as part of their after-sales service. Research and development staff may be needed to develop new products, and there will be engineering jobs available in production and quality control.

There are also jobs available in teaching and training. These may be in training departments in large companies, or as part of customer services provided by computer manufacturers. Most schools, colleges and universities now offer courses in computing, Information Technology or Information Systems.

LOOKING FOR A JOB IN IT?

If you want to work with IT and you are looking for your first job, the best thing you can do is get some experience and qualifications. There are several possibilities:

■ Buy or borrow a personal desk-top computer and learn how to use it.

■ Talk to someone who works in IT and if you are lucky they may show you where they work and what they do.

■ Learn the basics of a programming language.

■ Learn to use a wordprocessor, Desk Top Publishing and graphics software, a spreadsheet, a database and communications software.

■ Take a general course in IT and study for a specialist qualification at as high a level as possible.

You may not be able to find the time to do *all* these, but make sure you have done enough so that an employer will recognise you as a sound prospect for employment and further training. Remember, employers want *value for money*. If you can show them that you have done as much as you possibly can, short of getting a job, then you will have a much better chance in the employment market.

The next step is getting a job. Don't expect to start at the top. Do look for a job that offers *training*. However, any job is better than none and you can always use the experience gained when looking for better employment.

■ Look in the local papers for jobs. Buy computer magazines. In particular, try and get hold of Computer Weekly and Computing. Most trade papers in computing are crammed with job adverts.

■ Write to companies and agencies advertising for IT staff and ask if there is any possibility of being taken on as a trainee.

■ Visit local agencies specialising in IT staff.

There is a national shortage of IT specialists but this varies from place to place. You would probably find a job more easily in a city such as London, Birmingham, Manchester or Leeds. Don't be put off because your first applications are unsuccessful. The next job could be yours. Good luck!

EXAMINATION QUESTIONS

Q1. When a cheque is paid into a bank, a magnetic ink encoder prints one of the following on the cheque.

(a) the payee's name   [   ]
(b) the payer's name   [   ]
(c) the value of the cheque   [   ]
(d) the date.   [   ]

(City and Guilds, 1993)

Q2. QUESTION DATA

> Sue Saddler buys a micro-computer from Vision Computing for £800 and pays for it by cheque.
>
> Sue has an account with Barston Bank and Vision Computing has an account with Llyndell's Bank.

Put the following statements into the correct order to show how Sue's cheque is processed.

(a) The Clearing Bank sorts the cheques into bank and branch order.   [   ]
(b) £800 is added to Vision Computing's account.   [   ]
(c) Llyndell's Bank sends the cheque to the Clearing Bank.   [   ]
(d) Vision Computing pay the cheque in to Llyndell's Bank.   [   ]

(City and Guilds, 1993)

Q3. (a) Write down **TWO** applications which must use on-line processing

(b) Write down **TWO** applications which must use computer control.

(MEG, 1993)

Q4.

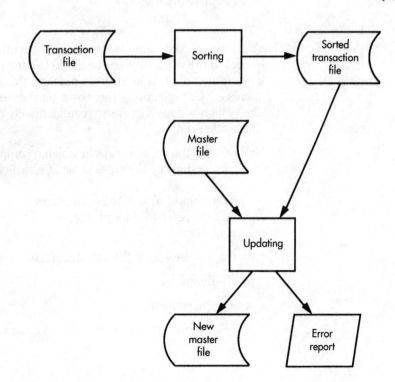

(a) Why is it necessary to sort the transaction file?

(b) There are three different processes that can be carried out during updating. What are these three processes?

(c) A transcription error made when entering data can be detected by a verification check. Explain how this check can be carried out.

(d) A date can be validated as well as verified. A date is to be input in the form 25 APR 1994 (a two digit day, followed by a three letter month, followed by a four digit year). Describe the validation checks that could be carried out on dates of this form.

(SEG, 1993)

Q5 Many supermarkets now use computerised systems to add up sales, produce till receipts and check stock levels.

State two effects that such systems have on:

(a) Shoppers

(b) Management

(c) Employees

(NEAB/WJEC, 1993)

Q6. A company wants all administration centralised. The consultant, therefore, recommends a mainframe computer is installed in the company headquarters, and networked to the other sites.

(a) Explain the main parts of the mainframe computer, and what they are used for.

The finance department first looks at transferring the payroll onto the mainframe, from all the sites.

(b) Explain what sort of information they would need to transfer to the mainframe.

(c) Explain what IT applications would be needed to store the information, and calculate the wages.

(NDTEF, 1993)

Q7. A group of estate agents have joined together to give the customer greater access to the properties on the market. They are considering having a computer system installed to help them manage this information transfer and also to manage more effectively their own businesses and work schedules. Obviously the system will need to ensure confidentiality of individual business activities but share other data.

(a) Discuss the various ways in which a computer system could be of use to the partnership and the types of facilities which would need to be included.

You should also discuss the hardware and software requirements. You should refer to data protection, data security and the input and output requirements.

(b) discuss the effects the introduction of the system might have on:

(i) the owners

(ii) the community

(iii) the manufacturing/installation companies

(NDTEF, 1993)

Q8. Describe the following stages involved in producing an information system:

(a) Designing

(b) Testing

(NEAB/WJEC, 1993)

Q9. Chris has had his office computer for 6 years. It has a 20Mb hard drive and two 5.25 floppy drives. He has a 9-pin dot matrix printer that does not produce good quality printouts but does enable him to use NCR paper for invoices. He has decided to upgrade the system.

(a) Chris understands that a Feasibility Study Report should be undertaken covering hardware and software, staffing, operating costs and expected benefits. Explain how such a study would help Chris to choose what he needs.

(b) Explain the steps he has to go through to produce a specification that could be sent to prospective suppliers of the new system. What information should the specification contain?

(c) What equipment, hardware, software and peripherals would you recommend that Chris purchase? Give reasons for your choice.

(d) Explain how Chris might go about choosing the correct supplier after he has received a number of quotations.

(e) Once Chris has chosen a system, how should he get it up and running in his firm?

(RSA, 1993)

Q10. A computer is being installed in a theatre to deal with bookings. It is to replace the manual system used for bookings.

(a) Give **THREE** activities which a systems analyst should carry out when analysing an existing system.

(b) When the system is installed parallel running takes place.

(i) What is parallel running?

(ii) When is it no longer necessary?

(MEG, 1993)

ANSWERS TO EXAMINATION QUESTIONS

A1. (c)

A2. The correct sequence is

(d), (c), (a), (b)

A3. (a) Two from:
Database interrogation
Viewdata
Electronic mail
Any suitable answer

(b) Two from:
Building cars
Building any product using robots
Flight simulators
Railway points control systems
Any suitable answer

(MEG, 1993)

A4. (a) So that it is in the same order as the Master File. This will speed up the Updating program.

(b) Records can be inserted, deleted and amended.

(c) When the data is being entered, it is entered by two different people. The data entered by one person is compared with that entered by the other. Any differences indicate input errors, such as transcription errors.

(d) You could do Type checks to ensure that the leftmost two characters are numbers, the next three characters are alphabetic and the last four characters are numbers.

You could do range checks to ensure that the leftmost two digits are more than 00 and less than 32 (for April), the next three characters are one of JAN, FEB, . . . NOV, DEC and the last four characters are within some sensible range for the application.

A5. (a) Shoppers:

■ receive itemised bills. This reassures them that they have been charged correctly.

■ cannot easily do price comparisons within the supermarket as the price of the product is marked on the shelves not on the product.

(b) Management:

■ receive up-to-date accurate information on sales.

■ can direct the computer system to order stock automatically. This relieves managers of unnecessary work.

(c) Employees:

■ The job of a checkout operator is simplified as the IS does the more complex tasks.

■ Management can use the IS to see which checkout operators handle the most sales. This puts the jobs of some operators at risk.

A6. (a) CPU: Central Processing Unit - this does all the processing.

Memory: stores programs and data that are in use.
Backing Storage: discs and tapes; used to store programs and data not in use.
Printer: for printed output.
Communications hardware: to handle communications with terminals via LANs and WANs.

(b) They would need an 'employee' file with a record for each employee containing fields, such as, name, address, rate of pay, tax code, etc. They may need other files with current information, such as, the number of hours each employee has worked in the current week. A file containing tax and national insurance details may also be needed.

(c) They would need either software specifically written for payroll or they could use a spreadsheet.

A7. (a) A networked system, possibly based on a mainframe computer, should be used. There will need to be separate terminals for customers and employees. Employees will use the computer system for payroll, accounts and other administrative tasks. They will also set up and maintain a database of all the houses being sold by the group. Only the information needed for the task will be collected and this will be organised so that only those who need access to it have access to it. For example, customers will not have access to the names and telephone numbers of vendors. Input will almost always be using a keyboard and output will usually be on screen with print facilities available when needed.

(b) (i) The system will allow sharing of information and access to it wherever and whenever it is needed. Customers can be given details of all houses for sale at all estate agents within the group.

(ii) The community benefits through improved access. Customers can find out details of houses in districts a long way from their homes. This is useful if they have to move.

(iii) The job of manufacturing/installation companies becomes more complex and must be organised over a wider area. However, they can expect increased sales of products used with networks, such as, modems, etc.

A8. (a) The design of an information system involves:

■ designing the data capture form (if any)

■ specifying the input needed

■ specifying the output needed

■ designing the format of the output

■ designing the file structures

■ specifying the backup and security features to be used.

(b) The testing of an Information System should involve:

■ Designing test data for extreme, standard and unusual input data.

■ Working out the results expected from the test data.

■ Comparing the output from the IS with the output expected using the test data.

A9. (a) A Feasibility Study would evaluate the possible options available to Chris. It should indicate the costs involved in acquiring additional hardware and software and the match between existing staff capabilities and the new skills needed. The type and extent of training needed would be identified and costed. All aspects of the development and operation of the system would be identified and costed. The expected benefits should be clarified and evaluated.

(b) Chris should decide exactly what the new system should do. The specification should clearly show prospective suppliers what is required and when it is required. A specification for the IS should contain:

■ An explanation of the need for the system placed in the context of the business.

■ The expected volume of data to be handled.

■ An exact statement of the performance requirements of the system that have been developed as a result of the feasibility study.

■ Timescales for development of the IS.

(c) Hardware and peripherals:

■ 486 processor

■ SVGA monitor

■ High density floppy discs (1.44 Mbyte)

■ 200 Mbyte hard disc

■ keyboard

- mouse

- laser printer

- a scanner

- CD-ROM

- MODEM

Software:

- A GUI, probably Microsoft Windows.

- Wordprocessor, Database, Spreadsheet, DTP, Graphics software.

- Applications software such as, accounting packages.

Some reasons for these choices are:

- The 486 processor will speed up the operation of Chris's software.

- The SVGA monitor is of a high resolution suitable for DTP, etc.

- High density floppy discs store more data than double density floppy discs (720 Kbytes) so fewer discs are required.

- A larger hard disc enables more or larger programs and data to be stored on it. The more powerful, easy to use, modern programs are also larger.

- The mouse is helpful with all software but especially graphics and DTP.

- A scanner can be used to scan photos, etc into the computer for use with DTP.

- A MODEM would allow Chris to communicate with on-line databases and acquire useful business information.

- A CD-ROM would allow Chris to access useful information, clip art, etc. stored on it.

(d) Chris will have to judge which proposal best suits his needs. The availability of after sales support could be important.

(e) Chris could pay the company supplying the system to set it up and test it. He will need to test it himself and ensure his staff are trained to use it.

A10. (a) Three from:
Study existing system and identify any shortcomings
Analyse the output requirements
Establish the information required by the system
Analyse the processing required
Analyse the constraints of the system
Analyse the cost
Analyse the time schedule
Analyse problems caused by volumes of data
Consider possible future changes

(b) (i) Running the old system at the same time as the new system

(ii) When the new system is producing the same results as the old system for a significant time

(MEG, 1993)

STUDENT'S ANSWER WITH EXAMINER'S COMMENTS

Question

A large store uses point-of-sale terminals.

(a) Write down two methods by which the code on the item can be input automatically.

(b) The record for each item on the computer file contains its price and the number left in stock. What change is made to the record each time an item is sold?

(c) Some of the steps required to be carried out at a terminal when an item is purchased are as follows:

Add price to total
Input money given
Input item code
Look up price
Set total cost to zero
Work out change

Put these processes in order, showing clearly which items need to be repeated by using suitable control systems.

(d) Explain the steps required automatically to re-order stock. (You may use a diagram if you wish).

(SEG, 1993)

Student's answer

(a) You could use a laser scanner or a light pen.

(b) The number left in stock has 1 taken off it and the price is added to the total.

(c) 1. Set total cost to zero
2. Input item code
3. Look up price
4. Add price to total
5. Ask customer for money
6. Input money given
7. Work out change

(d) You should tell the computer to re-order stock when there is not enough stock.

Examiner's comment

●● (a) This may be correct, it depends on the answer scheme being used! The question is not entirely clear. Laser scanners and light pens are different peripherals but they both read bar codes.

The mark scheme will probably give two marks for mentioning both laser scanners and light pens but it might not. If the examiner regards 'bar codes' as one method you will need to mention another, such as Kimball Tags. A good answer would cover both interpretations of the word 'method'.

(b) The answer is correct but the fact that 'the price is added to the total' is irrelevant. It is worth mentioning that the price is not changed in the record.

(c) There are two errors in this answer:

■ The student has put in another step not mentioned in the question. This is irrelevant.

■ The student has failed to mention that steps 2 to 4 should be repeated for each item sold.

(d) This answer is correct but lacks detail. You are expected to explain how the computer knows when there is not enough stock.

REVIEW SHEETS

1. Refer to the payroll information system.

Each employee in the warehouse is issued with a stripe card. The stripe card has the employee's number stored on it. When an employee arrives at work or leaves work, they must pass their stripe card through a stripe card reader.

(a) Will each worker still need a clock-card? If not, where will the clock-in time and clock-out time for every day worked be saved?

_____

_____

(b) How will stripe card input affect the jobs of the data preparation and control clerks?

_____

_____

(c) What arrangements will need to be made for data verification and validation?

_____

_____

(d) Draw a flowchart of this new information system for payroll processing.

(e) What additional arrangements would need to be made for file backup?

_____

_____

_____

2. A large theatre uses an information system to organise seat bookings. Tickets can be booked at the theatre or at ticket agents spread throughout the country.

(a) Draw a diagram of the hardware needed to operate this information system.

(b) What are the advantages to customers when this information system is used?

_____

_____

(c) What precautions should be taken to ensure the security of this information system?

_____

_____

(d) Would this information system need to be a real time system? Explain your answer.

_____

_____

3. Refer to the stock control information system.

(a) The computer system cannot be described as 'dedicated'. Why not? Explain your answer.

_____

_____

(b) Describe the information stored on a bar code.

_____

_____

(c) Where is the price and description of a product stored?

_____

_____

(d) After a bar code is read, the price of the product and its description are printed on the receipt. Describe the process that makes this possible.

_____

_____

_____

(e) The bar codes of products delivered and the quantity delivered are input in the warehouse. The bar codes of products sold are input at the checkout. How does the computer know what quantity of each product is in stock? Describe the algorithm in detail.

_____

_____

_____

_____

4. Describe how a Geographic Information System could be used by:

(a) a local authority planning department._____

_____

(b) a bus company._____

_____

(c) the gas board. _____

_____

(d) the army. _____

_____

(e) the National Health Service. _____

_____

SOCIAL IMPLICATIONS

GETTING STARTED

Information technology has had, and is still having, a great impact on our lives. As it is introduced into the work place, old skills are no longer needed, existing jobs are done in new ways and entirely new jobs are created. Workers must re-train in order to adapt to the new technology or be made redundant. Young people starting work will need some knowledge of how Information Systems and Information Technology work and know when to use them. Information Systems can store very large volumes of information and give fast access to it. Information about an individual can be stored on computer files, which is useful to doctors, hospitals, the DHSS, local authorities, schools, the police, the security services and others. Information Systems help keep down administration costs and improve services.

However, individual **privacy** - the right to control information about oneself - may suffer. Some organisations which keep information about individuals are more concerned with profit than individual welfare. The **1984 Data Protection Act** gives individuals some rights to know what information is kept on them and to control its use.

Lifestyle and **leisure** have been affected by new technology. Domestic work has been made easier. *Automatic* washing machines have replaced manual washers. TV, microcomputer and video technology has greatly affected leisure in the home. Remote control units, satellite TV, videotext and computer games have altered the way we spend our time at home. Home computers can be linked to other computers via the telephone network, using a modem, giving access to home banking, information services, electronic shopping, teleworking, etc.

Computers are used for **financial control** by the banks and other institutions. The use of cash cards may lead to the *cashless society* where cash in notes and coins is no longer used.

The pace of change is rapid and will continue. It is important to keep up-to-date with new developments in order to ensure that we use technology effectively.

INFORMATION TECHNOLOGY AT WORK

THE INFORMATION EXPLOSION

INDIVIDUAL PRIVACY

LIFESTYLE AND LEISURE

THE PACE OF CHANGE

ESSENTIAL PRINCIPLES

New technology has an effect on the lives of individuals and changes the way society is organised. These changes affect us at home, at school and at work. The way we do domestic chores and spend our leisure is affected. Technology has an immediate and lasting impact. It is important to understand what changes have taken place and to ensure that these changes are used to make the world a better place to live in. This chapter looks at some of the most important changes that have taken place as information technology has been introduced throughout society.

> **1** INFORMATION TECHNOLOGY AT WORK
>
> 66 New technology brings new skills 99

Many people have lost their jobs because of the introduction of information technology into the workplace. The development of new technology often results in older skills and occupations dying out as they are no longer needed. These changes cause unemployment, but also create employment. Different skills and knowledge are needed to use new technology. Older workers must re-train or face redundancy and young people must be prepared to use modern technology when they start work.

THE NEW TECHNOLOGIES

There are many examples of this process of change from old technologies to the use of microprocessor and computer technology. Mechanical Swiss watches were once highly prized for their accuracy and were consequently very expensive. In 1979, a cheap mechanical watch costing around £10 might be accurate to within five minutes per day. Modern digital watches (see Fig. 14.1) based on microprocessor technology cost less and are accurate to within one hundredth of a second per month. As a result, digital watches dominate the market. The skills of the mechanical watchmaker are much less in demand. Digital watches are manufactured and assembled in highly automated factories.

Fig. 14.1 A modern digital watch

Robots

Cars were once completely assembled by a team of mechanics. As production techniques changed, cars were built on assembly lines where each worker repeatedly performed one highly specialised task, such as welding. Now, microprocessor controlled robot welders (see Fig. 14.2) have taken over from these workers. The robot welder is programmed to do the required task by an expert human welder. This human expert does not do the repetitive welding but programs the robot to do the task. Once programmed, the robot can do the required task indefinitely.

> 66 Microprocessor-based technologies in car production 99

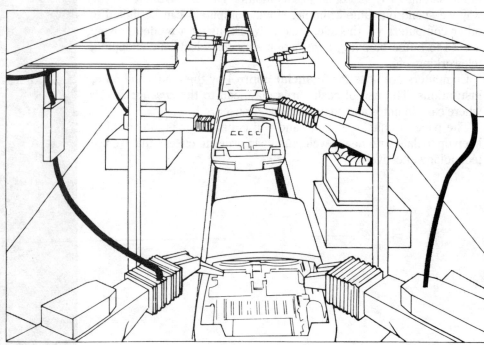

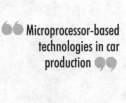
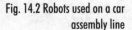
Fig. 14.2 Robots used on a car assembly line

Petrol pumps

Self service petrol pumps are now almost universally used at garages. These are controlled by one employee, who also collects the payment from the customer. Before the introduction of computer and microprocessor technology, several petrol pump attendants were needed to supervise the sale of petrol from mechanical pumps and collect the money. These attendants worked outside in all weathers. Their job is now done from the comfort of the garage reception area.

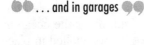

66 . . . and in garages 99

Telephones

Telephone exchanges were once staffed by large numbers of operators who connected callers to the line they required. Now, computer controlled exchanges (see Fig. 14.3) automatically switch callers, giving access to the national and international telephone systems.

Fig. 14.3 A modern automatic telephone exchange

Offices

In commerce, large numbers of clerks were once employed to do payroll, stock keeping, sales records, etc. These tasks involved careful written recording of all transactions. These tasks are now done using IT. The clerk's job has changed and now involves control of data as it passes through the information system.

Companies once employed large numbers of typists. It was not uncommon for fifty or more typists to work in the typing 'pool'. Much of the work was routine copy typing and standard business letters. This work is now done by a few wordprocessor operators. The skills required to operate a wordprocessor are quite different from those needed to use a mechanical typewriter.

66 Typists replaced by word processor operators 99

In the above examples, fewer workers were required, if any, when the new technology was introduced. Where there was a continuing need for workers, the skills involved were quite different from those used previously. However, the examples are all of changes to *established* industrial products and commercial practices. Information technology has significantly extended the way some jobs are done and created *entirely new* products and employment opportunities that did not exist previously.

JOBS IN IT AND IS

66 New employment opportunities 99

Information Technology obviously creates jobs in the industrial and commercial sectors concerned with its own design, manufacture, sales, maintenance and use. Many people now work in jobs in these areas. There are designers, assembly line workers, sales staff, installation and maintenance engineers, data control clerks, data preparation staff, operators, programmers, systems analysts, etc. There are journalists who write about Information Technology and technical authors who write manuals for computer software and hardware.

New jobs

The jobs created are not only replacements for old jobs, in the sense that exactly the same job is done in a different way. Information Technology may be originally used to do the same job more efficiently, but, once the potential is understood, it is then used to dramatically extend the scope of the job or for entirely new tasks that were impossible or impractical before. For example, stock control has always been an essential routine task for a shopkeeper, but many supermarkets have taken advantage of information technology to install POS terminals with laser scanners for on-line stock control. Most people now use some form of information technology at work.

New products

66 New products based on microprocessor technologies 99

Many new products have been designed and manufactured that are based on microprocessor technology and improvements have been made to old machines. Electronic calculators (see Fig. 14.4) are an entirely new product made possible only through the use of microprocessor technology. Washing machines have changed from mechanical, manual washers to single program machines to multiple program machines. These programs are stored in a microprocessor which controls the washer. The heating and lighting in buildings may now be monitored by a microprocessor programmed to maintain different temperatures in different rooms and to switch lights on and off at certain times. The work involved in the manufacture, installation and maintenance of such devices has created jobs.

Fig. 14.4 An electronic calculator

New technologies

There have been radical changes in telecommunications technology. Metal core lines are being replaced by optic fibre cables; long distance cables laid under the ocean or overland are replaced by satellites; automatic exchanges have been installed in place of manually operated ones. IT is used to control the operation of these systems. These changes have improved local, national and international communications. This process of improvement and innovation has created entirely new jobs.

2 THE INFORMATION EXPLOSION

The use of Information Technology has created *demand*. **Information** is more readily available, which has created the demand for more information. This is known as the information **explosion**. Cheaper, more reliable microprocessor based products have broadened the market, making these products available to more people. This has increased consumer demand. Increased demand for more information and more goods has led to new jobs in factories and offices.

Information Technology is increasingly used for creative work. Artists, cartoonists, graphic designers, authors, journalists, etc. are now making use of IT in their work. Computers can be used to control synthesisers playing music and for musical design. On television, computer graphics are now common. Information Technology has opened up many possibilities for the expression of human creativity.

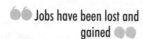

 Jobs have been lost and gained

It is not clear whether the introduction of computer and microprocessor technology has led to overall job losses or gains. Jobs have been lost, but jobs have also been created. There have been other effects of the increased use of computers at work which are also important.

Job skills

The skills required in many jobs, where Information Technology is now used, have changed. For example, a wordprocessor operator uses different skills than a typist. Many repetitive tasks have been automated so that fewer people now have boring, routine factory jobs. Some complex tasks have been made easier, for example, the use of CAD/CAM has speeded up the design to manufacturing cycle, allowing more flexibility in changing the design, so that better products are made sooner. Improved production control has also contributed towards a better quality product. Productivity per employee is high and the finished product is better designed and manufactured.

Working conditions in computer related jobs tend to be pleasant, perhaps because most computers require a clean, dust-free environment at about the same temperature that people find comfortable. Salaries tend to be above average, perhaps because of the general lack of understanding of Information Technology and the high demand for staff with these skills.

Working from home

It is increasingly common for employees who use Information Technology to work at home, using a computer to communicate with the central workplace via a modem and the telephone network. This is called **teleworking**. There have been a small number of disabled workers working with Information Technology for many years, particularly blind people. Teleworking has allowed more housebound or disabled workers to find jobs. Other employees often prefer teleworking, because there is no commuting and working hours are flexible. From the employer's perspective, teleworking reduces the need to provide expensive office accommodation. Teleworking is expected to increase. Some estimates have suggested that over half the working population will work from home within a few years.

Information Technology is now essential to most businesses and is widely used in most jobs. The introduction of computer and microprocessor technology has taken place at the same time as many other remarkable changes, such as the development of new synthetic materials for use in manufacture. These changes have not taken place in isolation, so their direct consequences are impossible to determine. It is certain that Information Technology had a dramatic effect on employment and it is here to stay.

INDIVIDUAL PRIVACY

Information about individuals is kept on computers (see Fig. 14.5). Because Information Systems can store large volumes of data and access it very quickly, they are a more useful way of storing data than in a filing cabinet. The information can be accessed from a large number of widely spread out locations so that it is available immediately where it is needed. Usually there will be a large, central mainframe computer system which is accessed using terminals. Access will often be via the telephone network using a modem and may be possible from a moving car or van. The DHSS, the police, the DVLC, the Inland Revenue, credit card companies, mail order firms and many other organisations keep information about individuals in this way.

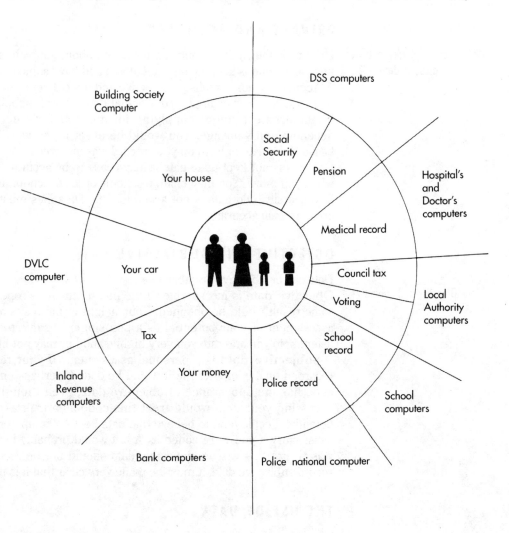

Fig. 14.5 The information about individuals kept on computers

PERSONAL DATA

❝❝ Uses of personal data ❞❞

Keeping **personal** data about individuals on information systems has advantages and disadvantages. For example, it is important that the police have access to information to help them arrest criminals and to enforce the law. If my car was stolen I would be very pleased if this information was available to police forces throughout the country, so that the car could be returned to me as soon as possible. I would be less enthusiastic if other organisations had access to the files linking my name, address and the type of car I own. This personal data could be useful to companies selling car insurance, new cars or specialising in spare parts for my car. These organisations might use this personal data to send me unwanted advertising literature by mail. The same information could be used for individual surveillance. This may or may not be acceptable, depending on the situation. It is reasonable to track a criminal or terrorist in a free society, but the same computer system could be used by dictators to enforce unreasonable levels of social control.

In any society there is conflict between the rights and freedoms of individual citizens and the need of national organisations to control and limit individual freedom in the interests of society as a whole. Similarly, businesses acting in their own interests may be in conflict with the needs of individuals. How these conflicts of interest are resolved is particularly important to you, because it may be possible in the future to hold all the data about you on one national information system. Your medical, school, employment and criminal records will all be fully integrated and any information about you will be available instantaneously. You should have no need to worry if this information is used reasonably. However, events in Europe during the second world war, for example, may suggest the need for some concern. Might not Hitler have eliminated the Jews much more efficiently with the use of computers? The major problems for individuals are concerned with privacy, accuracy, how the data is used and security.

PRIVACY AND ACCURACY

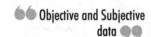 *Need for privacy and for accurate data*

Privacy is the right to control information about yourself. To do this you will need to know if anyone is keeping data about you and have some control over how they use it.

Accurate data is realistic, objective and up-to-date. Data is realistic if it describes a real situation. For example, your actual date of birth should be recorded. This could be important if you are applying for a car driver's licence, which is restricted depending on your age. You would be upset if you were not issued with a licence because the date of birth on your record was incorrect.

If data is not kept up-to-date it may cease to be accurate. Your address will change when you move. You may change schools or leave school to get a job or go to college, or university. Old data is not accurate data. Data files must be kept up-to-date if they are to remain accurate.

OBJECTIVE AND SUBJECTIVE DATA

Data can be objective or subjective.

Objective and Subjective data

Objective data is measurable. If the measurement is repeated by someone else, the same result would be obtained. Your height in metres is *objective* data. However, an assessment of your potential as a pop singer is *subjective*. One person may enjoy listening to you and rate you very highly, another may not like you at all.

Subjective data is a personal assessment. If your rating as a pop singer was recorded on a computer file it would be coded, perhaps on a scale from A to G. This code has the appearance of objective data, even though it is subjective. Anyone accessing your data would treat this code as a true assessment of your singing potential. People tend to believe that data kept on computers is accurate. This may be satisfactory if you were coded as A but would probably be unacceptable if your code was G! For this reason subjective data should not be recorded. If it is important to record subjective data, it must be made very clear that it is not objective data.

THE USE OF DATA

The **use of data** is an important aspect of privacy. This is where the needs of individuals, organisations and society may come into conflict. For example, suppose you have invested some money in a bank. The bank will pay you interest on the money. The bank will also tell the Inland Revenue, which collects taxes, that they have paid you interest. This may lead to a demand from the Inland Revenue for payment of extra taxes. As an individual, you may not want to pay extra tax and feel it is unfair for the bank to give information about your income to the Inland Revenue. This might lead to you withdrawing your money from the bank and investing it elsewhere. The bank does not want to lose your investment, but is legally obliged to tell the Inland Revenue about interest paid to you. The Inland Revenue wants to collect all the tax that is due. This tax is used to benefit the whole of society. In this case, individuals cannot be allowed complete control of their own personal data, as this would lead to social injustice. However, it is important that you know what is being done with this information. How personal data is used by the organisation that holds it could influence what you do.

DATA SECURITY

If personal information is to remain private and accurate, and is to be used only in ways agreed by the individual or controlled by the law, then the data must be kept secure. **Security** is the protection of data from corruption and misuse. Data is normally recorded on a backing storage medium such as disc. Data recorded on disc may be corrupted due to faulty hardware, faulty software, accidental or deliberate interference. If data is corrupted, it is important to be able to restore it to its original state as soon as possible. This is done by keeping backup copies of data files. If the current copy of the data file is corrupted, it is restored from the backup.

Network security precautions

Deliberate interference with data is always a possibility, especially where networks are in use. To prevent unauthorised access to data files several precautions should be taken. To prevent unauthorised copying of data files saved on backing storage, discs and tapes should be kept in a safe when not in use. Physical access to terminals on the network should be restricted using security guards or electronic locks that only open when identity cards are inserted. The network cable should be inaccessible and shielded to prevent intruders connecting themselves to it. If unauthorised users do connect to the network there should be a system of user identification with passwords at all levels to prevent access to the system and to data files. A log should be kept of all users so that illegal access can be identified and traced.

THE DATA PROTECTION ACT

The **1984 Data Protection Act** establishes the principles of data protection and gives individuals some right to control personal data. Anyone who holds personal data on computer files must register with the *Data Protection Registrar*. You have a right to know if personal data is kept on you and what that data is. Personal information must be obtained fairly and lawfully. You have a right of access to information kept about you and a right to have incorrect data changed. The data can only be used for specified purposes. Personal data must be accurate and up-to-date. It can only be kept as long as it is in use. Security measures against unauthorised access, corruption of data files, copying of files, and loss or destruction must be taken.

Although the Act protects individual privacy to a greater extent than was the case prior to 1984, it has been criticised for not dealing with some important issues. Manual files, that is, files kept on paper in filing cabinets, are not covered. Besides being a disincentive to use Information Technology, this allows any infringement of privacy in this area to continue. The police and security forces are exempted from all the provisions of the act. While this is understandable, it is unfortunate. For example, there are occasions when doctors may need to cooperate with the police. Doctors are covered by the Act but the police are not. This could affect liaison between doctors and the police for the good of individuals and the community. It is unfortunate that these issues are not covered in what is otherwise a comprehensive Act.

Another criticism of the Act is that misuse is an offence under civil law, rather than criminal law. This means that individuals must seek damages for misuse of personal data through the civil courts. Individuals are unlikely to do this because of the cost of taking court action.

LIFESTYLE AND LEISURE

Earlier in this chapter, the effects of the use of Information Technology at work was discussed. It was noted that this leads to better working conditions and higher productivity. This, in turn leads to higher wages and lower prices. Many people spend a large part of their life at work and depend on their wages to buy the goods and services they need. Better working conditions and greater purchasing power are important improvements in lifestyle. They are welcome in themselves and also because they open up other possibilities. A wider range of lifestyle and leisure options becomes available.

INFORMATION TECHNOLOGY AT HOME

In the *home*, domestic work has been made much easier. Programmable automatic washing machines and tumble driers allow clothes to be washed and dried with a minimum of effort. It is no longer necessary to spend a lot of time and effort on this necessary task. In the days of manual washing machines and clothes lines only, the family washing could take a day or even longer in bad weather! It is a pity the ironing has not been similarly automated!

Microprocessors are used in the manufacture of most domestic appliances, keeping prices down and quality up. Television viewing is more convenient because of remote control pads to alter the volume and contrast, change channels and switch the set on or off. Video recorders have similar facilities. TVs with a built-in teletext receiver can display pages from Ceefax or Oracle. The pages contain general information, including the times of TV programmes. These features make viewing more convenient, particularly for housebound or disabled viewers. Computer and microprocessor technology is an essential factor in providing these services.

Home computers

Home computers are often used for leisure pursuits. Many people play computer games or use the computer for personal amusement. Programs are available for Wordprocessing, databases, etc. that can be run on a home computer. Software packages are available for home and financial management.

Home finances

Many people have plastic cash cards or credit cards (see Fig. 14.6). These cards can be used to access a wide range of financial services:

■ Money can be withdrawn from automatic teller machines throughout Europe;

■ cheques can be guaranteed;

■ goods can be paid for in shops or by telephone;

■ wages can be paid directly into the account by an employer;

■ bills can be automatically paid at regular intervals by standing order.

Fig. 14.6 A cash card

It is easy to get a statement of payments made or received and find out how much money is left. This can be done in the bank or at an automatic teller machine. Some banks allow customers to access their accounts from home using a computer and a modem to connect to the bank's central computer. They can transfer money between different accounts, pay bills or do any other transaction while on-line. The banks and credit companies themselves rely heavily on Information Technology to operate these systems and keep accurate records of all financial dealings.

Electronic shopping

Electronic shopping using national or local viewdata systems is possible. The customer connects to the host computer via the telephone network using a computer and a modem. A selection of goods is offered for sale. These can be ordered and paid for by credit card. Companies operating national schemes often sell goods at a lower price than in the shops. The goods ordered are delivered by mail. Some local schemes allow groceries and other consumables to be ordered. This type of service is particularly useful to the housebound or disabled. The use of cash cards, credit cards and electronic shopping are features of the **cashless society**. Some people believe that these and other developments will eventually lead to money in notes and coins becoming obsolete. Money will then only exist as numbers recorded on the bank's computer system.

The cashless society

Improved transport and communications have helped families that live apart to keep in touch. They have also led to families becoming more widely dispersed. Cars are designed using Information Technology and are built to much higher standards using microprocessor controlled robots. Motorways are planned and designed using Computer Aided Design. The telephone network is also designed, built and controlled using microprocessor and Information Technology.

The institutions of society, that is, Local Authorities, Hospitals and doctors, schools, the police, libraries, the DSS, the DVLC, etc. all use Information Technology to keep administrative records and to help improve operating efficiency. This is also true in a European and International context.

<table>
<tr><td>**5**</td><td>**THE PACE OF CHANGE**</td></tr>
</table>

Most of the changes that are described in this chapter have taken place during the last thirty years and are mainly due to the widespread use of computer and microprocessor technology.

■ The range of *consumer products* has greatly increased. Their quality has improved and their price has dropped.

- Old skills have become redundant and knowledge of Information Technology is now essential for all workers.
- Employment patterns have changed; jobs have been created and lost.
- Concern for individual privacy is not new, but before the introduction of national information systems, it was not a widespread problem.
- The standard of living has improved greatly for those in employment.

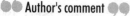 **Author's comment**

My experience of technology as a teenager was very different from that of teenagers today. The pace of change has obviously been extremely fast. I believe this will continue. What you are learning for GCSE will be a sound basis for the future. However, I am sure that some new event will soon occur in the rapidly changing world of Information Technology. It is important to learn about these new developments. Try to constantly update your knowledge by reading magazines, visiting exhibitions and local shops that stock computers. Don't be afraid to admit things are new to you too. It is important to learn to deal with rapid, unexpected change. Try to anticipate the effect of new technology on yourself and others. This will help you to use technology effectively for your benefit and for the benefit of society as a whole.

EXAMINATION QUESTIONS

Q1. Ring **TWO** developments which make it easier for people to work from home.

teletext	cheap personal computers	bank cashpoints
electronic mail	computerised supermarket checkouts	digital watches

(MEG, 1993)

Q2. A school stores dates of births of pupils. Give **TWO** ways in which it might sensibly use this information.

(MEG, 1993)

Q3. Banks store personal information about their customers on computer files.

(i) Suggest three items of personal information (other than name and address) which a bank might store on customers.

Members of the public are often concerned that personal information stored in computer files may be misused in some way.

(ii) How might these items of information be misused?

(NEAB/WJEC 1993)

Q4. Describe Electric Funds Transfer at Point of Sale together with its benefits and drawbacks.

(City and Guilds, 1993)

Q5. A librarian has access to personal data concerning borrowers which is stored electronically.

Explain how he could misuse this data in a way which is difficult with a manual ticket system.

(RSA, 1993)

Q6. It has been suggested that motorists might be charged for their use of roads by having a system which identifies each car and when a car passes over a sensor in the road a central computer will record that car's entry into a charge zone. One of the side-effects of this is that a record could be kept for every car's movements.

Discuss some of the social implications of such a system, giving reasons why certain groups of people may be for or against the system.

(SEG, 1993)

Q7. People are concerned about their personal information being held on a computer. Give three possible ways in which personal details held on computer could be misused.

(City and Guilds, 1993)

Q8. QUESTION DATA:

Suggest possible consequences of the exchange of information, identifying the advantages and disadvantages of these links.

The following organisations holding personal information have direct computer links:

The banks and the Inland Revenue
The Police National Computer and the DVLC.

(City and Guilds, 1993)

Q9. Credit card companies use computers to calculate the monthly bills for all of their customers. This means that there is a large amount of personal data being stored. This information is now protected but there are a number of ways that it could be used against cardholders even without them knowing.

(a) List two other organisations that might like to use this information.

(b) State how this could affect the customer.

(c) Describe the ways that, in the period of an average week, a person could give personal information to organisations which might keep it on a computer system.

(NDTEF, 1993)

Q10. (a) How would the installation of an 'electronic' office enable Chris to find information quickly? What equipment would you expect to find in this office?

(b) Explain why electronically stored personal data could be misused more easily than manually recorded data. Describe how you would prevent this misuse happening.

(c) In the future the business may be linked to customers and suppliers by computer/modem links. The warehouses may be automated and linked to the stock control and accounting packages.

List the possible effects of these developments on Chris, his employees, his suppliers and his customers.

(RSA, 1993)

ANSWERS TO EXAMINATION QUESTIONS

A1. Cheap personal computers

Electronic mail.

A2. Two from:

to make sure they are in correct year group/classes

to print out on school reports

Any suitable answer

A3. Any three, for example:

(i) The amount of money in their accounts.

Details of any loan they might have.

Their credit rating.

Their telephone numbers.

Their employer, etc.

(ii) Knowledge of the amount of money in a customer's account could be useful to people selling insurance, etc.

(iii) Knowledge of the details of existing loans and a customer's credit. Knowledge of the customer's credit rating could lead to the customer being refused credit.

A customer would be embarrassed if a credit agency knew their employer and informed the employer of their outstanding loans.

A4. EFTPOS terminals in shops are connected via the telephone system to the bank's computer. When a customer's magnetic stripe card is read, money can be transferred directly from the customer's account to the shop's account.

Benefits

To the shopkeeper:

■ No handling of cash or cheques.
■ Immediate payment.

To the bank:

■ No handling of cash or cheques.
■ Fewer staff needed, therefore lower costs.

To the customer:

■ No need to carry cash.

Drawbacks

To the shopkeeper and the bank:

■ Expensive to install and maintain.
■ Fraud using EFTPOS is difficult to detect.

To the customer:

■ Could slow down the payment process delaying the customer. Cash payment is faster.

A5. A library computer system stores borrowers' names, addresses and the books, videos, etc. they borrow. This information could be used to find out who is interested in what. The librarian could sell this information to bookclubs, video shops etc. so they can target their advertising.

A6. This system ensures that users of particular roads pay to do so. The roads charged for are likely to be in city centres or be motorways.

Charging for the use of roads in city centres encourages commuters to use public transport. Bus and railway operators would benefit as the number of passengers would increase. However, the number of people travelling into city centres might fall overall. This could result in reduced sales for city centre shops.

Charging for motorways would encourage road users not to use them. Traffic on roads other than motorways would increase. There would be more traffic passing through villages, towns, etc. Residents would not like the increased congestion, noise and pollution. The drivers who can afford motorway charges would benefit as there would be less traffic on them.

If the computer can record every car's movements, a car could be followed wherever it goes. The police could track criminals and terrorists. However, not all governments are democratic and respect individual freedoms. The ability to track the movements of a car could be used to control and restrain people for political or similar purposes. This deprives people of their human rights.

A7.
■ Information may be accessed by unauthorised people.
■ Information may be transferred or sold to organisations which mis-use it.
■ Information may be incorrect or out-of-date. This may lead to authorised users taking inappropriate actions.

A8. *Banks and the Inland Revenue:*

Advantages to IR:

■ Tax can be deducted directly from a taxpayer's account, e.g. tax on interest earned.

■ The Inland Revenue can check up on taxpayers' finances and fraud can easily be detected.

Advantages to the Inland Revenue could be considered disadvantages to taxpayers.

Police and the DVLC:

Advantages to police:

■ Car owners can be traced easily.

■ Criminals could be prevented from legally owning cars.

Advantages to the police are often disadvantages to criminals.

A9. (a) Inland Revenue, Mail Order companies, etc. That is, any organisation interested in how much money you have.

(b) Customers could be sent junk mail.

The Inland Revenue may suspect that a customer is spending more than their declared income and investigate them for tax fraud.

(c) You could register as a patient of a doctor, dentist, etc. You could join a library or buy a bus pass. You could open an account at a bank or building society.

A10. (a) An 'electronic' office uses paper less than a traditional office. You would expect to find computer systems, on a network, running IT software, such as, a wordprocessor, database, spreadsheet, DTP, etc. CD-ROM would give access to a wide range of information sources. You would also expect the computer systems to have access to WANs based on the telephone network. Computers use MODEMs to communicate across the telephone network. This allows the use of E-mail and gives access to extensive on-line databases, bulletin boards, etc.

(b) Electronically stored data is easier to manipulate than data stored on paper. You can search, sort and report on the data selected quickly and easily. You can make several copies of the data and transfer it across a network quickly and easily. These are reasons why we use IT, however, it also means that the impact of misusing information is increased. We can try to prevent misuse by:

- storing only the information needed.

- storing the information only while it is needed.

- check the information to make sure it is correct.

- restricting access to IT using security guards, coded locks, etc.

- preventing unauthorised access using user identification numbers and passwords.

- keeping a log of who uses the network.

(c) Chris and his employees will be relying on their information system. If the system does not function properly, the business could be affected. Chris and his employees will need IT skills more than before. The suppliers and customers of the business will need to have compatible information systems or they will not be able to do business with Chris's company.

STUDENT'S ANSWER WITH EXAMINER'S COMMENTS

Question

'ABC Books' is a company that sends out books by mail order. It keeps its customer list on a computer. 'Shark Loans Ltd' asks them for a copy of their customer list so that they can send out some literature advertising their loans. What response should ABC Books make to Shark Loans? Give reasons for your answer.

(SEG, 1993)

Student's answer

ABC Books can sell its customer list to Shark Loan Ltd. This would help ABC books make more money.

Examiner's comments

❝ This answer is correct but incomplete. It is expensive to collect and keep up-to-date large data files. Selling its customer list would certainly help ABC Books with these costs. However, not all the customers of ABC Books will want to receive advertising from Shark Loan through the mail. This is widely regarded as junk mail. Many customers will stop buying from ABC Books if they know their details will be given to Shark Loans.

More importantly, the Data Protection Act only allows data to be used for the purpose it is collected. ABC Books can only give it to Shark Loans if all their customers agree. ❞

REVIEW SHEET

1. Describe the impact the use of Information Technology at work has had on:

(a) the number of jobs available.

_____

(b) the skills needed to find a job.

_____

_____

(c) the exposure of employees to dirty and dangerous working conditions.

_____

_____

(d) the productivity of workers.

_____

_____

(e) the purchasing power of workers.

_____

_____

2. Complete these sentences using these words:

> confusion
> demand
> down sizing
> teleworking

(a) The instant availability of information has created _____ for more information.

(b) Working at home, using Information Technology to communicate with the central workplace, is called _____.

3. Your school keeps personal data about you on an information system. The 1984 Data Protection Act gives you a right to know if personal data is kept on you on a computer file and what that data is.

(a) Describe the personal data about you that is kept by your school.

_____

_____

(b) Are you certain this personal data is realistic, objective and up-to-date? How can you find out?

_____

_____

_____

(c) Describe three items of objective personal data that are kept by your school.

_____

_____

(d) Describe three items of subjective personal data that are kept by your school.

_____

_____

_____

(e) What can you do if there are errors in your personal data?

_____

_____

4. In 1980, fewer people had bank accounts and the use of stripe card technology in banking information systems was just being tried out in some areas. There were no national banking information systems that could be used by bank customers. To withdraw cash, you had to go inside the bank.

(a) Describe the facilities now available to the banks' customers that depend on Information Technology.

_____

_____

_____

(b) Describe the advantages and disadvantages to the banks' customers due to the use of national banking information systems.

_____

_____

_____

(c) Describe how the use of Information Technology at work has changed the job of a bank clerk.

_____

_____

_____

_____

(d) Describe how the banks' use of Information Technology has changed the job of a shop assistant.

_____

_____

_____

(e) Describe the advantages of the `cashless society' to a shop owner.

_____

_____

_____

5. These sentences all refer to the impact of the Information Technology at work.

Use these words to complete these sentences.

(a) The range of consumer products has _____.

| compulsory |
| essential |
| increased |
| optional |
| price |
| quality |

(b) The_____of microprocessor based products has increased and their _____ has dropped.

(c) Knowledge of Information Technology is _____ for all workers.

(d) The requirements of the Data Protection Act are _____ for all users of computer based information systems.

INDEX